Big Jim Thompson of Illinois

Big Jim Thompson of Illinois

by Robert E. Hartley

RAND McNALLY & COMPANY

Chicago   New York   San Francisco

For my children, Carolyn and Andy,

and my parents; people worth knowing

Copyright © 1979 by Robert E. Hartley
All rights reserved
Printed in the United States of America
by Rand McNally & Company

First printing, 1979

Library of Congress Cataloging in Publication Data
Hartley, Robert E.
   Big Jim Thompson of Illinois.
   Includes index.
   1. Thompson, James R., 1936–   2. Illinois—
Politics and government—1951–   3. Illinois—
Governors—Biography.   I. Title.
F546.4.T47H37   977.3'04'0924 [B]   79-19262
ISBN 0-528-81824-4

Contents

Preface

Quick and easy.

If there are words in common usage which characterize today's "modern politics" those come to mind. If there are names of individuals who qualify as practitioners they are Jimmy Carter, Jerry Brown, and Jim Thompson. There may be others—some will be mentioned later—but for purposes of this exploration Jimmy, Jerry, and Jim will do nicely.

There are differences among them which help explain why one is president of the United States and the others just want to be. They come to their work from vastly different backgrounds and parts of the nation. Carter is a decade older than Brown and Thompson. Yet, they seem less influenced by age and geography than a common approach to politics, and a common goal: The presidency. Their similarities are what make them prime examples of "modern" politicians.

In a narrow sense it might be enough to compare Brown and Thompson, for there are some interesting surface parallels. They are virtually the same age (Thompson was born in 1936; Brown in 1938); each graduated from law school. They had early religious involvements, although Brown's years as a Jesuit novice are more dramatic. Thompson's experiences were traditional and subtle. Both were bachelors for long periods (Brown still is) and have reputations for single-minded devotion to work. They exude charisma and attract young, energetic, and loyal followers. Both had short periods of involvement in public affairs before being elected governor.

However, adding Carter to the comparison gives it body, for in more than age Brown and Thompson are his followers. Also, because Carter moved along the path to the White House before the others, there is a track record to explore. Some assessments can be made as to whether background and experience as governor adequately prepare one for the presidency. In that context we may learn if "modern politics" has the meat and muscle to endure.

There is no time here for an exhaustive comparison of the three but some examples are helpful in drawing preliminary conclusions and preparing for the discoveries of Thompson and his personal run at the presidency which are contained in this book.

I will not attempt to define "modern politics" or its companion in

6

brevity "new politics." There is, in reality, nothing modern or new about any of it. "Old-style" politicians such as Hubert Humphrey, Lyndon Johnson, Richard Nixon, John F. Kennedy, and Gerald Ford all shared the common experience of slogging in the political trenches until opportunity knocked. Many are remembered as champions of causes, or are associated with programs of great change: Humphrey with social security and civil rights; Johnson with the social programs of the Great Society; Nixon, for all his liabilities, with grand gestures in foreign policy. As we put our memories in gear, these men all seemed to have ideas, or to have been associated with ideas. Furthermore, their records include momentous achievements. They never denied they sought power, but the cold eye of reality tempers that memory and makes us more conscious of time as the critical element. If we were looking at them as contemporary politicians, in their own time, they would have an uncanny similarity to the "modern" politicians of today. Issues aside, they all indulged in gimmickry, manipulated the media and projected their personalities as far as they would take them. The differences are there; the similarities are large as life.

Carter, Brown, and Thompson are master manipulators of media. Their successes are measured in those terms, thus making that a key element in understanding "modern politics." Remember, however, there was no greater manipulator of media than Franklin D. Roosevelt, whose distinctive style and voice romanced millions during his "fireside chats." Manipulation is not new; the techniques may be.

Techniques are what bind Carter, Brown, and Thompson in their political behavior, but the similarities are not restricted to those three. Politicians embraced by "modern politics"—several of whom were elected in 1978—are pragmatists who believe in expendable concepts and approaches and are willing to abandon them if something more advantageous comes along. They believe in partisan party loyalty as a necessary element of presidential, gubernatorial, or senatorial politics, but much of the time they appear to have no party affiliation or philosophy.

Lee Sherman Dreyfus, now governor of Wisconsin, epitomized this aspect of "modern politics" in 1978. A former chancellor of the University of Wisconsin at Stevens Point, he used personal appeal and wit to crush his opponent. Dreyfus started his campaign from outside the Republican party and only barely entered it for appearance's sake. John W. Warner, elected senator from Virginia in 1978—noted as much for his spouse Elizabeth Taylor as his record or promises—had never held public office and his party affiliation was undetermined. Forrest "Fob" James, now governor of Alabama, virtually had to take a loyalty test to get endorsement of the Democratic party in his state, for he had forsaken party loyalty long before his ambition peaked.

Regardless of those facts, some caution should be exercised. There are times when party affiliation helps and the "modern" politician stays outside only until the risks become too great. That explains why Dreyfus, Warner, and James played the party game eventually. That is why Brown maintains close contact with labor unions and Jewish contributors and Thompson has mastered reaching into the bottomless pockets of wealthy Republican donors.

It also is clear after listening to the "modern" politicians and watching them in office that they believe it is more honorable to be led by the public—as expressed in opinion surveys—than to lead. Their appeal is to "the people," not to party leaders, and they eschew traditional leadership methods and solutions. They deal in images: Carter's loving touch, Thompson's jeans and boots, Dreyfus's red vest, Warner's wife, Brown's rock star girl friend.

As opportunists—all successful politicians are—Carter, Brown, Thompson, and the others are constantly searching for what it takes to outdistance the field. If opportunity does not present itself in time, they create it.

During Carter's 1976 campaign the press, persistent though not always consistent, nudged Carter for details of his program to restructure government, reform the tax system, and bring morality to foreign policy. He hedged, preferring vague images to satisfying the media. Even now details of his theories are unclear, but they remain and constitute the backbone of Carter's lingering anti-Washington theme.

Brown, characterized by several biographers as long on style and short on substance, in 1979 became the unbridled champion of a constitutional amendment to control federal spending and taxation. Details? Brown dispatched questions with a wave of his hand. He dismissed skepticism in Congress by warning members of the grass-roots demand for ceilings on spending. Thirsty for results, the public listened to what it wanted to hear and Brown became the spokesman.

In 1978 Thompson was caught in Proposition 13 hysteria without a tax scheme. So he discovered the "Thompson Proposition" which gave the public a chance to vote on the principle of a ceiling on taxes and spending without binding the governor or the state. The press asked for Thompson's plan, but he stalled. When he made a proposal in 1979, specifics were lacking. Labeled "meaningless" by the media and political opponents, the "Thompson Proposition" nevertheless gave citizens an outlet for expression and kept Thompson's finger on the public pulse.

All "modern" politicians sense the citizenry is leery of old ideas and worn out answers, especially if offered by the tired faces of the past: i.e., Ronald Reagan, Jerry Ford, even Ted Kennedy. The "modern" politician pitches softly. In Brown's case that approach is called the "laid back" style. It lacks the harshness of political stump speakers such as John Connally and Reagan, who leave the impression they might tear the very fabric of government and maybe drive us to some unnecessary foreign conflict just to prove our national prowess. "Modern politics" means antigovernment sentiment, but doesn't espouse revolution. That goes down more easily.

Are they charlatans? If they are hoodwinking the public it is by raising expectations and not delivering. If that is a continuing characteristic of "modern politics," its practitioners are assured of brief tenures when the public grows weary of promises and finds some other political magic.

Can they govern? We may never find out unless they stay in one place long enough. None has shown an inclination to "earn" his way to the top by achievement in programs. Their political instincts say they have to operate on a fast track to reach Washington before their lights burn out. So they may not have time to govern, which means they will leave state and national business to others. The reality for the rest of us is living in the wake of "modern politics." Images don't reduce inflation, rebuild cities, find energy alternatives, feed the poor, or forge lasting foreign alliances.

"Modern" politicians share another, more alarming similarity. We have learned from watching Carter as president, and Brown and Thompson as governors, that the qualities of rising to the top of the political pile in these times are not necessarily the qualities of leadership. Having sought and attained power, they are reluctant to use it unless there is a survey of public opinion in support. The risks they take are with gimmickry, not programs. They deny the inherent strength and power of the executive, and defer to the legislative, thus demeaning their positions and shirking the mandate.

All who confront "modern" politicians will do well to heed Edmund Burke, who said: "Your representative owes you, not his industry alone, but his judgment; and betrays, instead of serving you, if he sacrifices it to your opinion."

ROBERT E. HARTLEY

May, 1979

Sources & Acknowledgments

Robert W. Sink, longtime editor of the *Courier* in Champaign-Urbana, Illinois, retired from active newspaper work in 1975 and in the course of cleaning out a half century of personal files shipped me an accumulation of folders full of tearsheets, clippings, and notations on James R. Thompson. Given as Sink was to admonishments, he said Thompson bore watching. The clippings Sink had assembled from Chicago newspapers from 1971 through 1975 formed a rich source of material about Thompson's days as a U.S. attorney in Chicago, and I have relied on these in outlining the idea for this book. Sink's personal observations were especially keen. He had "discovered" Thompson while covering the trial of Otto Kerner for Lindsay-Schaub Newspapers and gathered information from a number of Thompson's associates whom I later interviewed for the book. Several remembered encounters with Sink. Always watchful for talent, whether in the newsroom or the courtroom, Sink soaked up information on Thompson and predicted the prosecutor would make a prime book subject. I am thankful for Sink's foresight. My only regret is that he did not live to see the book completed. Bob Sink died on April 22, 1978.

During preparation of the manuscript, several persons provided badly needed sustenance and criticism. Hal Neitzel, who nurtured my book on Charles Percy, asked the right questions at the right time. One that never ceased to prod me: "What is the essence of Jim Thompson?" Journalism associates read and commented on portions of the manuscript. Foremost were Robert Reid, an expert on Illinois public affairs, and Thomas B. Littlewood, longtime *Chicago Sun-Times* Springfield and Washington correspondent, and now a journalism educator.

Thompson's U.S. attorney years provided major challenges in research and analysis and required an understanding of countless law enforcement cases that moved through the federal court system in the 1960s. Especially helpful with the threads that linked *Escobedo* and *Miranda* was *The Self-Inflicted Wound* by Fred P. Graham, now with CBS television news. Ramsey Clark's *Crime in America* is an excellent musing on the turbulent period. Richard Nixon's motives in questioning directions of the United States Supreme Court are explored in James F. Simon's *In His Own Image*. Interviews with William J. Bauer, Samuel Skinner, Marvin Aspen, Henry Petersen, and Joel Flaum filled in vital details of the 1969–75 period regarding important activities in Chicago and Washington.

Factual assistance was drawn from the definitive one-volume history of Illinois by Robert P. Howard, *Illinois: A History of the Prairie State*, and *The Illinois Fact Book and Historical Almanac, 1673–1968*, by John Clayton. The almanac is a gold mine of background on Illinois government. Chicago politics was more easily understood after reading *Clout* by Len O'Connor and *Don't Make No Waves—Don't Back No Losers*, the best biography of Richard J. Daley, by Milton Rakove. Chicago's traditions and relationship to the rest of Illinois are carefully documented in *Building for the Centuries: Illinois 1868–1898* by John H. Keiser; *Chicago* by Finis Farr; and *Horner of Illinois* by Thomas Littlewood. Press reports from Chicago newspapers were imperative for an understanding of the media in Thompson's public life. Jeanne Grinstead's research of *Sun-Times* and *Tribune* editorial pages from 1977 opened a door for insight.

Syndicated columnists Jack Germond and David Broder shared their wisdom about Thompson's political future, as did many participants in national politics and public affairs who asked not to be identified. Information on the presidential primary system, in all its frailty, came from *Presidential Primaries: Road to the White House* by James W. Davis, and two of Theodore H. White's presidential campaign books, *The Making of the President, 1968*, and *The Making of the President, 1972*. Jules Witcover's explanation of Jimmy Carter's 1976 conquest in *Marathon* gave life to assumptions about 1980's presidential race. The underlying issues of a presidential campaign and how they can influence the outcome have never been explained more thoroughly than by Richard H. Scammon and Ben J. Wattenberg in *The Real Majority*, from which background information was drawn. Research for the Percy book four years ago provided an understanding of moderate Republican politics and its quadrennial impotence.

Substantial information about Thompson's political career and attitudes came from interviews and conversations with him at various times beginning in the fall of 1975 and continuing through 1978, mostly as part of my work for Lindsay-Schaub Newspapers, Inc. As a result of habits developed from a newspaper career, I never threw away a note from those discussions. That formal interview record was supplemented in 1978 by interviews specifically related to his early years and the Chicago prosecutor periods. Thompson was accessible and responsive to questions.

The persons who influenced Thompson's life for the first thirty years or so gave unselfishly of their time, and I am grateful to Bob and Agnes Thompson and to Fred Inbau, whose enthusiasm for his former student led him to open his mind and files for the project.

One of the earliest workers on the book was Andy Hartley, who provided a continuous clipping service. His sister, Carolyn, proved to be right and left hands by typing the entire manuscript while home from college between semesters. While chaos swirled all around during those days, Mary Hartley, bless her, kept all eyes on the road ahead.

As this book was nearing completion, tragedy struck my Rand McNally editor of five years, Steve Sutton, and his family, all of whom died in the crash of a DC-10 jetliner near Chicago. I will remember Steve as a dedicated and understanding editor, and never forget the encouragement he gave a newcomer to the book writing business.

Relationships

When Jim Thompson's high school class held a reunion celebrating the 20th anniversary of its graduation everyone gathered at the home of William Seawall in suburban Chicago. That was in 1973.

Thompson was United States attorney in Chicago, single, and riding the crest of immense public attention. During the festivities, the prosecutor told his host, "Next time we'll have the reunion at my house."

So, when plans for the 25th anniversary reunion of North Park Academy were made, Seawall, a member of the committee, reminded Thompson of the 1973 pledge. True to his word, the governor invited the entire class to the mansion in Springfield for a gala reunion in August, 1978.

At the center of festivities were the Thompsons—Jim, Jayne, and Samantha Jayne—and the governor was at his sentimental best during a short talk. "We spent four very wonderful years together, and all of us have fond memories of the school," he said.

Seawall proposed a toast to the governor's family, and Nancy Haver Larson, another of the reunion organizers, presented a plaque to the Thompsons with the inscription:

"Next reunion—the White House, perhaps your destiny."

The people who knew Jim Thompson in high school are lucky. They have information that gives them an advantage over most persons in understanding Thompson's character and actions as prosecutor and governor. But it is a thin advantage at best, for the gap in time from North Park to the governor's mansion leaves a serious shortage of information on which to evaluate the man. In reality his school chums know only a little more about Thompson than can be learned from his press clippings which started to flow in 1971.

There is much more to know about Thompson before picking up the threads of his public life. His first thirty-five years are rich in detail for shedding light on the essence of the man.

As prosecutor and governor, Thompson is a reflection and amplification of his early years, and the product of relationships with those close to him and his career.

Jim Thompson had his share of heroes, just like many boys growing up in the 1940s and 1950s as children of parents who struggled through the Great Depression and World War II. Most of those whom Jim admired, including Governor Adlai E. Stevenson of Illinois, and U.S. Senator Robert Taft of Ohio, popped out of newspaper and magazine stories as the boy fed a curiosity about politics. Later in life, Jim idolized men in politics and law, which reflected his career direction. However, none of history's lights or contemporary mentors compared with his father, J. (James) Robert Thompson, whom Jim describes respectfully as "a good man," "kind," and "a hard worker" whom he admires for how "he has conducted himself" as a father, husband, and doctor.

There is much to admire about Bob Thompson, and his wife, Agnes, for they are survivors of a period in history when society rewarded those who persevered and practiced frugality. Bob Thompson's steps were taken surely and carefully, without the benefit of "breaks."

Bob and Agnes Thompson are rural, small-town Midwesterners. They spent their early years within about eight miles of each other, but did not become acquainted until after Bob left home for college. Agnes lived in DeKalb, about fifty miles west of Chicago, and Bob lived on a farm south of DeKalb near the town of Waterman (1970 population 990). Bob talks about the farm with reverence—"the homestead" he calls it—and was pleased some years ago when Jim, then U.S. attorney in Chicago, drove his secretary out to see the home place.

After graduation from high school Bob worked on the farm a year, then in the fall of 1929 enrolled in the University of Illinois at Urbana for studies in the dairy business. Agnes lived at home in DeKalb. Unable to manage the costs of college as the Depression deepened, Bob left Urbana and headed first for DeKalb, and then Chicago, where he took up pre-medical school studies at the Lewis Institute in the fall of 1932. After nine years of night school—he worked during the day as a medical technician—Bob completed the necessary three years of undergraduate work and was finally ready to apply for medical school.

Sharing the burden of those years with him was Agnes, whom Bob had met in DeKalb and married in 1934. They lived in an apartment complex near Garfield Park on Chicago's West Side—an area of the city where they were to live and work for most of their lives.

On May 8, 1936, the Thompson's first son was born at Lutheran Deaconess Hospital in Chicago. They named him James Robert and called him Jimmy, then Jim, but never "Junior." Four years later, they had a second son and named him Donald. Larry Thompson was born in 1949, and Karen in 1951.

In 1941 Bob Thompson entered the University of Illinois College of Medicine in Chicago to begin studies in pathology. He provided for his family by working as a morgue attendant; they got rid of their car, and as Bob recalls, "I had a wife who skimped and saved."

Young Jim Thompson remembers those days as "difficult," in contrast to days of later affluence. The Jim Thompson seen on television in the 1970s is a product of those times: the same boy who played with his family and friends in a West Side Chicago neighborhood, carried newspapers, worked in libraries, and tried a hand at door-to-door sales. ("White Clover salve," says his father.)

Bob Thompson graduated from medical school in 1944, in an accelerated program developed because of the need for doctors during the war. Young Jim, at age eight, looking on as his father received the degree, "enjoyed every minute of it," his father recalls. Bob trained as an intern at Cook County Hospital, then joined the Municipal Tuberculosis Sanitarium in Chicago, where he worked as a pathologist—with the exception of two years in the Army—until his retirement in 1970.

Unlike doctors in a more recent era, Bob Thompson did not find sudden wealth following his graduation from medical school. Already in his mid-30s, he continued the daily pattern developed in the Depression, of working all day in the TB lab and evenings at a general practice of medicine, making house calls and giving physical examinations for insurance companies. Frequently he did not return home until midnight.

While her husband was completing medical school and starting his life's work, Agnes Thompson raised her family in the Garfield Park apartment. She taught Jim to read before he attended Samuel F. B. Morse grade school; with this early training, he developed the habit of reading periodicals, especially for political news. Jim discovered politics on his own, not because of any push from his parents. There were no politicians in either family. "I told him if he wanted to get into politics, he should think about studying the law, because most politicians are lawyers," his mother says.

His father also remembers the early interest Jim had in politics and the specifics of its development. He tells a story of when Jim was ten or eleven years old and a WGN radio crew visited his Sunday school class at Central Presbyterian Church to ask the children what they wanted to be as adults. Jim told them, "a politician." From that story and other similar ones told by his parents and friends, the legend developed that Jim had wanted to be president "since age eleven."

Another story Bob tells was passed on by his brother-in-law, who lives on the family farm in Waterman. Jim visited the farm occasionally, and when he did, his uncle often "would find Jim standing up on the hay rack giving political speeches."

Many years later, in an interview with the *Christian Science Monitor*, Thompson explained in his own words this early fascination with politics:

> I grew up in the generation that told every American boy in 1947 it was not a crime to want to be president. That was part of

our culture. There was something wrong with you if you didn't. Once you decided you didn't want to be a fireman and fastened onto the presidency, you were all right.

Jim's parents encouraged his interest in politics, but they also exposed him to their value system, which included activity in the Presbyterian church. Bob served as elder and clerk of Faith Presbyterian Church in Oak Park and taught adult Sunday school classes. Jim was installed as a deacon of the church and during his college days taught a Sunday school class. He underplays the influence of the church on his sense of morality, ethics, and fairness—all of which are attributes cited by high school and college associates. But Marvin Aspen, a colleague of Thompson at Northwestern and in the Cook County state's attorney's office, believes the emphasis on religion in the Thompson home made an imprint on Jim. Nevertheless, as Thompson became engrossed in law school and full-time legal work, his involvement in church activities dwindled.

No one was surprised that Jim took cues from his father's interest in church work, for they were a pair in many ways. Jim did not acquire his full six-foot, six-inch height until late in his teenage years, but people could tell he would pass his father at six foot, one inch. As a child Jim was thin, blond, and green-eyed, with light complexion, just like his dad. They even shared a common lack of athletic ability, and they compensated for that by enjoying sports as spectators.

During the years Bob Thompson practiced medicine at night, he took along one or more of his children—often Jim—while making house calls and giving insurance examinations. It gave him a chance to talk with the children alone and minimized his absence from home. Jim, thinking back after he had become governor, spoke of being impressed with his father's hard work and compassion. Bob, his memory more vivid about what happened, says Jim often spent the time in the car "practice driving."

The father and son enjoyed a number of activities together, such as fishing and attendance at athletic contests. Both followed the Cubs and the Bears closely. The father encouraged his son's interest in animals—especially dogs—and helped him with photography by building him a darkroom. Reminiscing about her husband and oldest son, Agnes Thompson listed their similarities: "outgoing, friendly, kind, and generous."

There were early signs of precocious behavior, such as the ease with which Jim conquered school work. With reading skills learned from his mother, Jim found first-grade work no challenge, and he was quickly accelerated to the second-grade level. The same change occurred in the fifth grade, so that Jim graduated from high school at the age of seventeen, a year younger than most of his classmates.

While jumping ahead in school can cause social adjustment problems for some children, Jim's parents do not recall any such difficulty. His relationship with other children appeared normal, although like many young boys he is remembered as "girl shy." Dating was not one of his major high school activities. Jim spent a good deal of time playing with his brothers and sister, and he seemed to enjoy the role of "father." He was especially close to the boys, looking after them and protecting their interests in the neighborhood. Remembering some of the effects of Jim's affection for his brothers and sister, Agnes says, "He spoiled them."

The admiration Jim's youngest brother and sister had for him became evident in their choices of careers. Both became lawyers. Larry, thirteen years younger than Jim, tried a hand at being a prosecutor and then entered private practice in Chicago; Karen has worked as an assistant state's attorney and as a public defender in Cook County. Don, four years younger than Jim, is a professor of geology at California State College in California, Pennsylvania.

Jim seemed to have enough interests so that acquiring a lot of close friends was not necessary. Ray Cunningham, almost exactly the same age, lived in the Garfield Park apartment building; the two remained friends through high school and attended the University of Illinois at Navy Pier (forerunner to the Chicago Circle Campus). Other than Ray, there were not any persons from the neighborhood who became lasting friends of Jim.

After Jim completed the eighth grade at Morse school, the Thompsons enrolled him in North Park Academy, a private high school associated with North Park College in northwest Chicago. Many students at North Park were members of the Swedish-founded Evangelical Covenant Church, the financial supporter of the school. Although a direct religious affiliation with the Evangelical Covenant Church was not necessary for attendance, some financial means was. The high tuition cost meant that most students were from upper-middle-class and wealthy families. By the time Jim was ready for high school, his father was beginning to realize the financial benefits of being a physician, and the cost was not a burden for the family. In 1950, for instance, the Thompsons were able to buy their first home, which was located in the Galewood section of Chicago's West Side. (In 1956 they bought their second home in nearby Oak Park, where they live today.)

The Thompsons were concerned about Jim attending high school in the changing social atmosphere of the West Side. "We didn't send him for scholarship," Bob says by way of explaining the decision for a private school. By the early 1950s schools in the Thompson's neighborhood were filling up with black students, and stories told by parents of public high school students bothered the Thompsons. While Jim got along with students in grade school, "he wasn't the rough and ready kind," his parents thought, and his mild-mannered nature made him vulnerable.

The TB sanitarium where Bob Thompson worked was not far from North Park, so Jim often rode to school with his father. Approximately six miles from his home, the private school took Jim out of contact with his neighborhood chums and threw him together with children from all over the Chicago area, most of whom were there to escape the public school system. One of the boys he met in 1949, his first year, was Bill Seawall, a gregarious youngster who became one of the school's star athletes. Another of Jim's acquaintances during the high school years was Barbara Leske (now Mrs. Edward Roob). Barbara and Bill remember Jim as a serious student who did not run with the "in" crowd but had plenty of friends. Jim was handy when Seawall needed help with his studies, too. "He was a regular guy, good friend, someone who helped me with my work when I needed it." The issues of life for North Park students did not differ greatly from those concerning teenagers in countless towns and cities across the nation during the 1950s. Remembering some of them later in life, Thompson said: "I was the original (Mike) Royko of the North Park campus. The burning issues of 1953 were compulsory chapel and should juniors be allowed to go across the street for lunch."

A good student—but not among the top scholars of his class—Jim participated in several school activities. The yearbook for the graduation class of 1953 listed his activities and personality traits: "Magic Club, Press Club, Science Club, current events, President—politician ... up on the latest happenings ... likable." The reference to "president" and "politician" indicated that Thompson's ambition was known widely among students at North Park. One of Seawall's prized possessions from those days is a page in his senior yearbook, where Thompson wrote near his class picture, "Good luck to North Park's best athlete." The message was signed, "Jim Thompson, Pres. of U.S. 1984–1992."

Seawall, an influential and successful commercial real estate broker in Chicago—he served a term as president of the Chicago Real Estate Board—became one of Thompson's major links to campaign contributors. Over the two-year period from 1976 to 1978, Seawall served as vice-chairman of a half-dozen major fund-raising dinners in the Chicago area. For each affair he sold tickets for tables of ten persons at $1,500 a table to friends and associates. The Roobs were less involved, but their children campaigned actively for Thompson.

After graduation from North Park, Jim looked toward college. His desire to study law became evident as he enrolled in a general course of study, with emphasis on history and politics, at the University of Illinois at Navy Pier in Chicago. He considered the University's Urbana campus but the size frightened him, and he stayed in Chicago and lived at home for two years. Later he regretted not attending a larger school away from home. His grades were acceptable, but he did not make the honor roll, and one of the reasons may have been his habit of cutting classes to attend sessions of the Chicago City Council.

Bob Thompson uprooted his family—the youngest child, Karen, was three years old—in 1954 for Army duty in St. Louis. They knew it was temporary and planned to return to Chicago when the service ended. Jim went along, enrolling for his junior year at Washington University and growing increasingly anxious to complete his undergraduate work and begin law school. In those days, an undergraduate degree was not required for admission to law school; Thompson, therefore, finished his third year of college and took the national law school entrance tests. He qualified for admission to several law schools and chose Northwestern.

Law professors are always on the lookout for bright prospects, because they often are in a position to recommend the best students to prestigious law firms or head them in destiny's direction. Most of the faculty at the Northwestern law school pegged Thompson as one of a kind. He showed up in Evanston as a tall, skinny, somewhat shy twenty-year-old in the fall of 1956 (commuting from his parents' home) and blossomed quickly, creating a stir in his wake. Professor Fred E. Inbau quickly recognized his potential: "Jim was one of those students who from the beginning showed the makings of an outstanding lawyer."

Of all the professors and classmates Thompson met in three years at Northwestern, none made such an impression on him as Fred Inbau. Jim saw many of his father's best characteristics in the veteran professor—an admiration of integrity above all else—and he admired him accordingly. The professor's achievements were many, especially in the field of police relations, and his reputation impressed Thompson. Inbau was a celebrity among law enforcement people—"Freddy the cop" one student named him—and those people helped shape the legal attitudes and career of Jim.

In contrast to his reputation as a hard-nosed defender of policemen's rights and their interrogation techniques, Inbau was a mild-mannered man who is remembered by most students as uncommonly fair and balanced in his classroom presentations, but given to firm convictions outside the classroom. Thompson told an audience years later, "He taught future defense lawyers with the same vigor that he taught future prosecutors... and with the same horrible jokes."

Inbau maintained a variety of outlets for his pronouncements and kept in constant contact with prosecutors and policemen. He was an academic spokesman for the men in blue. His activities included being supervisor of the *Journal of Criminal Law, Criminology, and Police Science,* and author of a controversial manual for policemen entitled "Criminal Interrogation and Confessions." He started an annual workshop for prosecuting attorneys and produced a constant stream of books and articles. Thompson, with a flare for public speaking, a knack for writing, and an intense interest in the law quickly fit into Inbau's interest and activity patterns.

Although neither of them realized it then, they stood together on the threshold of one of the most exciting and traumatic eras in United States legal history. Before it passed the two men shared dozens of victories and defeats; finding comfort even in the losses.

Thompson also began making acquaintances of persons who would be companions and colleagues in the years just ahead. One was Marvin E. Aspen, a year ahead of Thompson in law school and also one of Inbau's protégés who served as editor-in-chief on the *Journal*. They met and got to know each other through *Journal* work, and a couple of years later made marks together in their work as prosecutors. Otherwise there were few close associations begun at Northwestern. Thompson kept his distance with contemporaries, preferring for close company older persons such as Inbau.

Thompson mixed studies and extra curricular activities much as he had in high school, shunning slavishness to the academic side, and choosing opportunities for self-expression. He maintained an interest in politics but neither Inbau nor Aspen recall overt political activity by Thompson in those years.

From his law books Thompson developed new heroes: Supreme Court justices Hugo L. Black and William O. Douglas, stalwart liberals with roots deep in the New Deal. Thompson's idealism, which led him to consider a career as defense attorney, clashed with Inbau's conservatism but did not alter their mutual admiration and respect. Thompson found Inbau fair and open-minded in their relationship.

In one instance, Inbau made a highly unusual gesture toward the young student: he added him to the list of speakers for his annual prosecutors' workshop. No other Inbau student had been granted that privilege. Inbau believed Thompson had something to say to the prosecutors and that the exposure on both sides would be healthy. Thompson loved the opportunity to speak publicly, and addressed the workshop each year until 1976, when he became governor of Illinois.

By his third year at the Northwestern University School of Law Jim Thompson had established a reputation as self-starter, hard-worker and developer of ideas. "He didn't have to be told what to do," according to Inbau. Thompson wrote extensively and eventually became student editor-in-chief of the *Journal of Criminal Law, Criminology, and Police Science*. As well, the young Chicago native demonstrated an idealism not uncommon to law students of the 1950s and early 1960s.

So, it didn't surprise Inbau or other associates when Thompson penned an editorial entitled "New Act for the Indigent," which appeared in a 1959 issue of the *Journal*:

> Everyday in this country, through poverty or ignorance, Americans by the thousands stand before courts empowered to deprive them of their liberty without the aid of counsel.

If the current programs of governmental agencies and the organized bar are inadequate in the trial, appeal and post-conviction areas—and they plainly are—what steps can be taken to provide relief? One such step, it is submitted, should be to provide indigent persons in these cases with the aid of student counsel—second and third year law students, working under the supervison of faculty advisers and representatives of the bar associations, who would be empowered, by statute or rule of court to represent indigent misdemeanants at the trial level. Such students could also lend effective aid in drawing, and in some instances prosecuting, appellate and post-conviction petitions.

Inbau says that was the first he had heard of the idea. He notes that nearly twenty years later a program utilizing students to help indigents was instituted in Illinois.

As time approached in 1959 for Thompson to determine his direction after graduation—he faced no military service because of 4-F status due to asthma and a hernia—Inbau began suggesting that he turn from the defense attorney path. "All students want to be another Clarence Darrow," he declared. He wanted Thompson to think of spending a few years as a prosecutor to sample the other side of the business. He said the best defense attorneys know all the moves of prosecutors and inferred Thompson's choice was naive. As Inbau explained to this author years later, "I'm not the kind to convert, but I wanted him to see it and experience it." Thompson decided to heed Inbau's advice and made contact through a friend—the godson of State's Attorney Benjamin Adamowski—for an assistant state's attorney job in Cook County.

It is ironic that Jim Thompson began his legal career under a Republican prosecutor in Cook County who built a reputation as a fighter and bucked the political tides. Ben Adamowski was the boy wonder of Chicago politics in the early 1930s, having first been elected to the Illinois General Assembly as a protégé of Democrat Anton Cermak. In the late 1930s, Adamowski broke with the Democratic organization of Edward J. Kelly and began a career of waging battles with the party establishment.

Unable to gain public office with the Democrats in the mid-1950s, Adamowski turned Republican and became the party's nominee for state's attorney in 1956—one year after Richard Daley's election as mayor. He won election, becoming the first Republican state's attorney in twenty-four years. During his term, which ended in 1960, Adamowski and a band of energetic assistants poked at corruption, criminal activity, and the closed political and judicial process in Chicago and Cook County. They often failed, but they never failed to be colorful.

Thompson went to work for Adamowski—although he came with no political sponsorship—after graduation in 1959. He began in the appellate division—not considered one of the glamor offices—where he did research, wrote briefs, and quickly gained a reputation as an indefatigable worker. That first summer, even before he had been admitted to the bar with others of his class, Thompson became involved in a case that was to be argued before the state supreme court. However, Thompson could not give the oral presentation because he was in between graduation and admission to the bar. Adamowski called Walter V. Schaefer, a state supreme court justice and graduate of Northwestern law school, and asked that Thompson be admitted to the bar a month early so he could argue the case. Schaefer granted the request, and Thompson made the first of dozens of appearances before the state high court.

The energy and devotion to work in his first year out of law school ranked high on the list of legendary Thompson stories. He claims to have worked most nights and every weekend but one in the first twelve months, occasionally stopping on Friday nights for a few drinks. Colleagues from that period, including Marvin E. Aspen (his associate at Northwestern) and Alan Ganz (a young lawyer from Indiana) who joined Adamowski about the same time as Thompson, agree. "He had the advantage of being single without a family," Ganz says. They all agree working for Adamowski was a highlight of their careers. "It was probably the most rewarding and hardest work I put into my professional life," Thompson says. His devotion to work seemed an appropriate response to Joseph Story's famous quotation from "The Value and Importance of Legal Studies" (1826): "...I will say that it [the law] is a jealous mistress and requires a long and constant courtship. It is not to be won by trifling favors, but by lavish homage."

Adamowski knew better than most persons in Chicago where the machine bodies were buried, but he refrained from personal vendettas. Years ahead of the state legislature, Adamowski filed suits to end the practice in Cook County of allowing public officials to hold a second government job—such as a ward committeeman also being employed by the park district. He also filed suits to permit open proceedings in the City Council. One of Adamowski's most publicized cleanup drives occurred in Calumet City where gambling rings were smashed and lengthy legal battles begun. Many of the cases ended up in Thompson's appellate division. Adamowski raised hell with the Cook County political system, and the young assistants joined in along with him, but they steered clear of making it a Republican-versus-Democrat contest. Adamowski gave his assistants free rein, under the guidance of older professionals such as Francis X. Riley. In the first eighteen months of Thompson's work, Adamowski became his model, and new hero.

As might have been expected, Adamowski got too close to many powerful Democrats; he incurred the wrath of Daley and became a major target in the county election of 1960. The Republican party in Cook County existed little more than on paper, and the state's attorney depended on Democratic friends and Independents for support. Daley triumphed and Daniel Ward, former dean of DePaul law school, took over as state's attorney in 1961. Normally, such a change means a massive turnover of assistants, as the incoming prosecutor makes as much patronage use of the office as possible. Given the intensity of feeling toward Adamowski, there were some special incentives for the Democrats to clean house.

Although appointed by a Republican state's attorney, Thompson had no partisan political affiliation, and his reputation as an attorney transcended politics. Because of his work for Adamowski, Judge Richard B. Austin had chosen Thompson to serve on a committee that was to spend four years revising the state criminal code. (Another committee member was William J. Bauer of DuPage County, who later would play a major role in Thompson's career.) Based on his observations of the young man, Austin, a longtime Democratic politician, persuaded Ward to retain Thompson.

Although most of the assistants in the offices of Adamowski and Ward had their work in common and became more than casual acquaintances, two men developed lasting friendships with Thompson. One was Ganz, who worked in the state's attorney's office two years. The other was Aspen, who joined the office in 1960 and stayed until 1963; he later became a judge, first at the local, then at the federal level. Aspen, Ganz, and Thompson were thrown together in the appellate division of the office, and they spent long hours working and talking. During those years, all criminal case appeals had to be argued before the state supreme court in Springfield; Thompson and Aspen frequently traveled there for several days at a time to argue cases. Aspen, a Democrat, believes no two attorneys appeared more before the state supreme court in those years than he and Thompson. The cases were scheduled so that each attorney might argue as many as four or five in a day. It required ability just to keep the details of cases straight. Nevertheless, there was some time on the trips for the assistant prosecutors to make acquaintances in Springfield; one such acquaintance was Michael Howlett, auditor of public accounts and a longtime chum of Thompson's boss, Riley. The jolly Irish Chicagoan and the tall young attorney began a lengthy personal relationship.

By the time Aspen and Thompson became associates, Thompson had emerged as an effusive person. Given assignments to appear before community organizations on behalf of the state's attorney, Thompson continued to take advantage of his ability to deal with an audience that Inbau had noticed earlier. Aspen noticed this ability, too; he remembers Thompson as "ambitious in the good sense of the word" and able to ingratiate himself to persons who could help his career. The strengths of his character, which were evident in high school and college, continued to impress associates. Aspen found him forgiving, industrious, independent, and never hypocritical. Thompson had few intense friendships and almost never dated; as Aspen says, "the law devoured him."

Ganz, who later entered private practice in Chicago and became Thompson's personal lawyer, was a contrast to the cool and efficient Aspen and the increasingly outgoing Thompson. ("You never saw Ganz on Rush Street," Thompson says.) A serious, often called "tough," young lawyer out of East Gary, Indiana, and Harvard law school, Ganz recalls Thompson as a classy professional who kept his distance personally. Ganz respected Thompson's devotion to work and his desire to stay out of the personal lives of those he knew. A sign of their friendship was Thompson's attendance at Ganz's wedding.

Having put in long hours at the office, assistants often had dinner and drinks together before heading for home. Thompson frequented these social activities after the first year, and that is when conversation turned to law and politics, obviously Thompson's passions. Still, neither Ganz nor Aspen got any indications from these encounters that Thompson harbored thoughts about a political career.

Given increasing freedom to pursue cases on his own and to stray outside the appeals division, Thompson was able to gain greater visibility in the years under Ward. Examples of Thompson's sense of public needs and his ability to respond to those needs began to surface.

There was rising community feeling against pornography in the early 1960s and, after being contacted by several prominent newspaper persons and politicians, Thompson began working with policemen to crack down on book stores and movie houses. He became known as the "porno prosecutor" and was pictured riding in the back of a truck atop a pile of confiscated pornographic material and literature.

Obscenity law changed rapidly in those days, with the U.S. Supreme Court playing a major role, and Thompson's conviction rate in the pornography cases was not much to brag about. One person whom Thompson pursued was the comedian Lenny Bruce, a frequent performer in the Chicago area. After Bruce's conviction for obscenity, Thompson took the matter on appeal. He lost, remarking that "they changed the law on me between the trial and the appeal." Thompson later acknowledged that Bruce's language and nightclub act wouldn't excite today's prosecutors, but "I'm not ashamed of what I did. We acted properly under the law as it was at the time. The law has moved on, social custom has moved on and I've moved." He denied the cases had overtones of First Amendment encroachment. Inbau, in defense of Thompson's actions, says: "His feelings were hard to control. He wanted to see that children were protected."

Of all the cases Thompson handled as an assistant state's attorney, none compared with *Escobedo* v. *Illinois*, which Thompson argued for the state before the United States Supreme Court in 1964. The case of Danny Escobedo, convicted murderer, and the techniques used to gain a confession from him, provided the basis for a series of Supreme Court decisions in the 1960s that swept away decades of law and police procedure and replaced them with a broadened concept of the rights of suspects and defendants in criminal actions.

Danny Escobedo was a suspect in the murder of his brother-in-law. He obtained a lawyer before going to the police station for questioning, but the lawyer was not with him in the interrogation room. In fact, it was not the practice for a suspect's attorney to be present during an interrogation. In the course of questioning Escobedo, police used an old trick by telling him that an accomplice had confessed, naming Escobedo as the murderer. Under pressure, and ultimately confronted by the accuser, Escobedo named the accomplice as the person who fired the gun. By naming the accomplice, Escobedo implicated himself in the murder.

In those days such an admission was considered a voluntary confession, and the process was recognized by the court system as legitimate. However, Escobedo's lawyer appealed the conviction of his client and asked that the confession be declared inadmissible. Arguing against Escobedo's lawyer was Thompson. In what Inbau called Thompson's finest hour—"his finest oral argument"—the twenty-eight-year-old prosecutor defended the validity of the confession. But the Supreme Court disagreed, and in a 5–4 decision against Thompson and in behalf of Escobedo, fired the first shot in a revolution that altered all practices in questioning suspects and obtaining confessions.

Arthur Goldberg, writing the majority opinion for the Warren Court, said if a defendant had a right to an attorney at arraignment and in a preliminary hearing, the right should be extended to the police station where the process begins. He wrote that use of sophisticated interrogation techniques without a lawyer on hand mocked the safeguards of hearings and trials. In the process, the Court in effect abandoned the theory of voluntary confessions. Escobedo's confession was declared invalid because he had been denied his right to have an attorney present during questioning.

Lawyers declared the decision heresy for discarding previous law and procedure, and as Thompson recalls, "It shook up the police and prosecution world." As a chief defendant of the previous police interrogation system, Thompson became an instant hero and in demand on the banquet circuit across the nation. He rose to the challenge and predicted further Supreme Court encroachments. In fact, Escobedo did lead to more Court decisions, capped in 1966 by Miranda v. Arizona, in which the Court laid down the specific practice of warning suspects they have a right to counsel, and a right to remain silent, and that anything a suspect says may be used against him.

Coming off the Escobedo case in 1964 and seeing the end of Ward's term, Thompson grew anxious to leave the state's attorney's office. Inbau had begun to think in the same terms; he had a Ford Foundation program under way in criminal justice and opportunities on the Northwestern campus to bring the experienced prosecutor in touch with students who were thinking about legal careers. Inbau's timing was perfect; he felt that "five years in that field is enough for anybody."

Northwestern University, one of the nation's most prestigious private schools, is more than a picturesque campus nestled among the trees along the shore of Lake Michigan. Its proximity to the metropolitan area of Chicago gives students and faculty access both to one of the nation's largest urban centers and to influential persons in commerce, industry, and politics.

In 1964, when Jim Thompson accepted Inbau's offer to return to Northwestern as an assistant professor in the law school, he was not retiring to the ivy covered walls of academe, never to be heard from again. There was one statistic with which he was quite familiar—three governors of Illinois had graduated from Northwestern and had practiced law or worked in the metropolitan area. They were Frank O. Lowden, governor from 1917 to 1921, a Republican; Adlai E. Stevenson II, governor from 1949 to 1953, a Democrat; and Otto Kerner, governor from 1961 to 1968, also a Democrat. Furthermore, Lowden was nearly nominated as the Republican candidate for president in 1920, and Stevenson was nominated twice by his party for president, in 1952 and 1956.

Through law school and his first job as assistant state's attorney, Jim Thompson's life and work took form; patterns began to emerge that would continue to be a part of his story. Foremost among these patterns was the development of an eye for opportunity, and the boldness to seize it, especially if it meant being singled out from the crowd. That is why law books did not hold him down, and why he sought outlets in writing and public speaking. In the offices of Adamowski and Ward he discovered opportunity in the appellate division, which most assistants avoided. He jumped at the chance to pursue obscenity cases, inspired by public demand. And sometimes lightning struck, as with the *Escobedo* case. There was no way Thompson could tell in advance that it would become a landmark decision; and when a new opportunity presented itself after *Escobedo*, Thompson grabbed it.

In several ways, Thompson's change to Northwestern was a part of a continuum. He was reunited with his mentor, Inbau, and had the opportunity to work with him; and Inbau gave Thompson opportunities to jump into a growing national battle on the side of law and order. The pro-defendant field was crowded, and Thompson saw opportunity in being on the side of policemen and prosecutors.

If Inbau had attempted to lure Thompson to campus with a soft job in the classroom, he would have failed. Thompson had experienced the "real world" and had tempered his opinions about law school. "I went out of law school with stars in my eyes. I found that law school is an artificial place—not the real world—just words, philosophy." Inbau, therefore, gave Thompson an opportunity to share his experiences from the real world with law students.

Knowing of Thompson's involvement in prosecuting obscenity cases, Inbau asked his new staff member to lecture to law students on the subject. Thompson showed up at Inbau's classes with props: specific examples of pornographic materials and literature. Inbau applauded the stunt, as it dramatically illustrated the vile nature of the material, and he ignored suggestions that pornographic materials shouldn't be displayed in the classroom. "We were dealing with older persons pursuing a profession, not freshmen," he recalls. For Thompson, performing in a classroom at the center of attention was merely an extension of the public speaking he had done with Inbau's prosecutors' workshop, with the state's attorney's office, and as an appellate advocate. "He was good in the classroom," Inbau says. "He had charisma with the students; they loved him."

A major attraction for Thompson at Northwestern was a Ford Foundation program, administered by Inbau, in graduate legal studies for prosecutors. The program took Thompson to most of the nation's major cities and brought him into contact with the problems and concerns of the post-*Escobedo* legal world. Thompson also traveled as part of a program begun at Northwestern through which policemen were provided personal legal advice and assistance.

As an assistant professor in the law school, and later as an associate, Thompson enjoyed a good life. He lectured to undergraduates, kept a finger in professional work by taking some indigent and legal defense cases, and traveled with Inbau's police legal adviser program. He also returned to writing, and over the four years at Northwestern he participated with Inbau in writing three criminal law casebooks. In an understatement, Thompson refers to it today as "a very statisfying period."

Thompson expanded his social life a bit, but he still dated infrequently, according to his associates at the time. Marvin Aspen, who until 1966 lived a couple of blocks from Thompson on Chicago's Near North Side, did not see much change in Thompson's work and leisure patterns from the state's attorney days. Aspen describes him as "one-dimensional . . . he was interested in sports and law and I think he was probably asexual in those days—it was just not part of his life—he wasn't interested." Aspen saw less and less of Thompson as they pursued different career choices, but they still remained friends.

Thompson met one law student who interested him. She was Jayne Carr, from Oak Park, a tall (five feet, eleven inches) dark-haired, striking woman with a quick smile. They met when she was a student in one of his seminars, and it became obvious to him that she was determined to have a law career. At the end of her second year of law school, she applied for one of twenty summer fellowships in a federal program run by Thompson, in which law students were placed in police and defense agency work. He turned her down for the fellowship, but "to make up for it," as he says now, he got her a job in the state's attorney's office as a clerk. They saw each other occasionally, but nothing blossomed.

Thompson infrequently socialized with students. In later years, when media reporters attempted to build his image as a swinging bachelor, he commented, "I haven't been to a singles bar since I was at the law school and went to The Store, where some of my students worked—I went maybe twice."

The contemporary relationship which grew most during the Northwestern period was with Joel Flaum, a 1963 graduate of the law school, and a noticeable contrast in personality to the increasingly ebullient Thompson. Flaum—shorter, quieter, studious, and serious—became a sidekick of Thompson and eventually joined the Northwestern faculty as a lecturer in 1967. He also worked with the police legal adviser program. For a period of eight years, until Flaum was appointed a U.S. district court judge, the two were hardly out of sight of each other professionally.

There were minor distractions, but the law still pervaded Thompson's life, and Inbau provided the outlets and challenges to devour his energies. They watched in horror as defendants in criminal cases walked free because police officials and prosecutors were unable to interpret Supreme Court rulings, and they were anxious to do something about it. Inbau expressed his chagrin openly: "It annoyed the hell out of me that guilty people were set free." Thompson says Inbau took every setback as a personal blow. They needed an outlet for their concerns. As a result, they met with O. W. Wilson, a former Chicago police superintendent, to consider forming an organization outside the law school that would be a recognized force in criminal justice circles.

In 1966 the three men organized Americans for Effective Law Enforcement, with offices in Evanston. Inbau was president and Thompson was vice-president. Immediately, the media branded AELE as an attempt to suppress civil liberties and individual rights. The organizers denied any such intent, but acknowledged an interest in providing competition for the American Civil Liberties Union.

The visionary of AELE was Inbau, because his feelings ran deepest. He remembers the frustration of appearing before a congressional committee considering law enforcement legislation in the early 1960s: "The committee room was filled with people from the ACLU and many other groups. The only persons testifying for the police were the chief of police of Washington, D.C., a few others, and I." AELE organizers sensed a need for balance, especially in court cases where the ACLU often appeared as amicus curiae, or friend of the court. The prosecution side needed to be represented in those forums, Thompson thought, just to keep things even. In discussing the AELE today, he leaves the listener with the impression that Inbau and Wilson—and not he—provided the missionary work needed to get AELE moving. "I could comfortably have been a member of ACLU," he says now.

From the beginning, AELE attracted some of the nation's most strident conservative voices in law enforcement and public affairs. Three men active in recent years are Peter Coors and Joseph Coors, both members of the family that operates the Coors Brewery in Golden, Colorado, and both sponsors of conservative programs and politicians; and M. Stanton Evans, conservative writer and lecturer. Those of a more moderate nature who have been involved with AELE are former governor Richard B. Ogilvie and Thompson's colleague, Alan Ganz. Regardless of the ideological standing of some supporters, few legal experts doubted the impact of AELE on the American legal system.

Thompson played a principal role in one of AELE's earliest successes. Shortly after AELE was organized, the Supreme Court ruled on *Miranda* v. *Arizona*, prescribing procedures to be used by police in interrogating witnesses. Also in the court system at the time was *Terry* v. *Ohio*, a case involving a policeman's search of a suspect on the street without apparent cause or a warrant. It became known as the "stop and frisk" case and eventually inspired many legislatures to adopt "stop and frisk" laws. Indiscriminate searching of suspects by police was a common occurrence in many cities, and often the suspects were black, poor, or both.

AELE entered *Terry* v. *Ohio* as a friend of the court with a brief written by Thompson which argued for preserving the right of police searches. Thompson said it seemed a reasonable approach to life in the city, where policemen's lives are threatened by those who walk the streets.

Suspicions were that the Court would follow *Miranda* with another ruling limiting the access of police to suspects. The Court had set the trend in the 1960s of favoring the rights of individuals, sometimes at the expense of the rights of society, and it seemed disinclined to alter this trend. However, those predicting more of *Miranda* were stunned by the *Terry* v. *Ohio* decision.

Chief Justice Warren, writing for the majority, said the police could search persons "on suspicion" without probable cause if necessary to discover weapons and protect police. Inbau, Thompson, and others who had suffered legal reverses since the early 1960s rejoiced at the 8–1 decision. Only William O. Douglas, one of Thompson's earliest legal heroes, dissented. Writing in the *Journal of Criminal Law*, Thompson and Inbau admonished police that victory in *Terry* did not mean they could take indiscriminate action against suspects.

Thompson had not intended to teach, travel, lecture, and make an occasional appearance in court for the rest of his working life; by 1968 he was actively looking for opportunities to move back into active prosecution work, law enforcement, or politics. Decisions of the Warren Court, civil unrest in the cities, growing discontent with Vietnam involvement, and the discordant notes of a society in turmoil had prepared the nation for Richard Nixon's comeback and created a demand for persons in high office who would work to strengthen the nation's "peace forces," as Nixon called them.

James R. Thompson's emergence in Illinois and in the nation as an important member of these "peace forces" was about to begin.

The Prosecutor

It is an exaggeration to say Jim Thompson owned Chicago from 1971 to 1975. He did not, of course, because Richard J. Daley was the owner and proprietor. The fact is, however, that in Chicago Thompson was No. 2 in popularity behind Daley, and from that vantage point produced an enviable record as U.S. attorney for the Northern District of Illinois. That record became an escalator to the governor's mansion.

Thompson's rise from an unknown assistant attorney general in 1969 to a place of esteem in the minds of Chicagoans is an extraordinary tale, as complicated as it is heroic. It combines the ingredients common to stories of sudden professional and political stardom: friends in high places, boldness and daring, flawless timing, energetic associates, luck, and a warm public response. All of these sound trite, but in Thompson's case each played a decisive role.

In another city he might have been portrayed as a white knight astride a stallion, slashing with a sword at the wicked and corrupt. In Chicago, however, analogies have other origins. One that was appropriate appeared in a Chicago newspaper report: "He's the toughest gun we've had around here since Al Capone."

With an infusion of federal money, the enthusiasm of a young and determined staff, and the force of his personality, Thompson transformed the U.S. attorney's office in Chicago from just another legal extension of the federal government to a center of investigation and prosecution in the nation's "second" city. Adding to the drama of this transformation, Thompson proclaimed the work to be part of a "crusade to clean up Chicago."

Tough words flowed from Thompson through the media on the mission of the office. After a series of convictions in police extortion cases, he said: "This should serve to put Chicago on notice that we are fed up with corruption in this town and we're going to end it." On another occasion Thompson told U.S. Attorney General Richard Kleindienst: "I'm going to kick ass until I get rid of the crooks."

In a 1974 article, The Nation magazine quoted Thompson on his crusade.

I know Chicago and I think I know where the bodies are buried.

I vowed as a young prosecutor that if I ever had the opportunity to determine law enforcement priorities in this community and had the resources to do it, I would try to get rid of corruption in government.

Now I have it. I have eight grand juries sitting, the help of the Internal Revenue Service and the FBI, a large staff of top professional lawyers and a kind of unofficial mandate from the community to keep it up.

Frequently during his four years as U.S. attorney Thompson made similar statements. These statements inspired his staff to long hours of work, and encouraged ordinary citizens to come forward with information that could be used in prosecuting corrupt public officials. His success in fulfilling his promises built up a folk hero image around Thompson, not unlike that which surrounded Theodore Roosevelt, charismatic Rough Rider and U.S. president. One of Roosevelt's quotations is inscribed on a plaque in Thompson's possession. It reads: "Aggressive fighting for the right is the noblest sport the world affords."

In politics, not much is left to chance. Good timing is more than a coincidence; folk heroes are made, not born. When Thompson rose to the governor's mansion in 1976, he had more than ability, ambition, and a good press: he had an army of supporters, financial contributors, friends, and well-wishers. The same was true of Thompson's rise from law school professor to U.S. attorney. He had help—the right kind of help at the right time.

The list of those who promoted Thompson's interests includes familiar Republican names in Chicago and across Illinois. Most of them were lawyers, and more important, Chicago lawyers. They were members of prestigious firms whose roots sank deep into city and state politics. They worked in a familiar breeding ground for governors, state and federal judges, and wealthy lawyers, and had connections with influential businessmen and industrialists. Of the eight governors of Illinois since 1940, six had Chicago legal backgrounds. (William G. Stratton and Samuel H. Shapiro were from communities outside Chicago.)

The prominent Illinois Republicans who helped Thompson's ascension first to the state attorney general's office in 1969, then to the U.S. attorney's office in 1970, included: Richard B. Ogilvie, former assistant U.S. attorney, sheriff of Cook County, and president of the Cook County board, who was elected governor in 1968; William J. Scott, former assistant U.S. attorney and state treasurer, who was elected attorney general of Illinois in 1968; U.S. Senator Charles H. Percy, who, by virtue of Everett Dirksen's death in 1969, became the person responsible for nominating the state's federal prosecutors and judges to the president and Senate; and William J. Bauer, former state's attorney of DuPage County and state circuit judge, who was named U.S. attorney for the Northern District of Illinois in 1970, and then U.S. district judge in 1971.

Other individuals who were less directly involved in Thompson's rise to prominence included: Don H. Reuben, a Chicago attorney with the firm of Kirkland, Ellis, Hodson, and Chaffetz, a political activist, and counsel to the *Chicago Tribune*; and Fred Inbau, professor of law at Northwestern and founder of Americans for Effective Law Enforcement. They sponsored him and gave Thompson the opportunity to perform under fire. He responded by taking charge and seldom disappointing his mentors.

Thompson's Republican support and his reputation as a criminal lawyer with strong feelings about supporting law enforcement agencies meshed beautifully with the arrival of Richard Nixon, John Mitchell, and associates at the federal level in 1969. The president and the young prosecutor—who professed no strong political principles—had been on the same side of law enforcement issues through the turbulent 1960s, as the feeling grew that a sense of lawlessness was engulfing the nation.

A favorite target of Nixon during the 1968 campaign and after he became president was the Supreme Court under direction of Chief Justice Earl Warren. Nixon sounded the charge: "The *Miranda* and *Escobedo* decisions of the High Court have had the effect of seriously hamstringing the peace forces in our society and strengthening the criminal forces. From the point of view of the criminal forces the cumulative impact of these decisions has been to set free patently guilty individuals on the basis of legal technicalities...."

Thompson had argued against the *Escobedo* decision before the Supreme Court; he predicted it would lead to *Miranda* and further expansion of a criminal suspect's rights in the police station. Furthermore, Thompson had supported federal stop-and-frisk legislation and court decisions that gave policemen a right to search a suspect without obtaining a warrant. Thompson and Nixon shared feelings that court decisions in the 1950s and 1960s had strengthened the hands of criminals at the expense of law enforcement.

Nixon in 1969 and 1970 began to place constructionist justices on the U.S. Supreme Court and push through legislation, such as the 1970 Omnibus Crime Bill, that toughened criminal laws and placed more tools in the hands of law enforcement officials. At the same time, antiwar demonstrations and continuing civil disorder created a demand for federal prosecutors who could carry on the law-and-order fight outside Washington.

For all his involvement with Republican politicians, and his announced ambition to seek public office, Thompson considered himself nonpolitical. Friends and colleagues agreed that while he leaned toward Republican politics, Thompson seldom involved himself in partisan activities or campaigns for individuals. Critics claimed the political connectons with Nixon were strong from the beginning and ultimately influenced the selection of targets for prosecution. "I considered myself one of the law enforcement professionals," Thompson said. "By that time I had been in law enforcement for 11 years and served both Republican and Democratic administrations." But with Nixon as president, and Mitchell, a political creature, as U.S. attorney general, there was no way professional and political matters could be kept separate.

After four years on the Northwestern faculty, where he had served as associate professor, co-authored criminal law textbooks, and actively participated in Inbau's Americans for Effective Law Enforcement, Thompson concentrated his main interest on politics. The prospect of Republicans returning to Springfield and Washington meant opportunity, and there was not much else to accomplish at Northwestern unless he intended to make a career of teaching.

A first indication of Thompson's interest in seeking political office occurred well before the 1968 election, when Cook County Republicans began interviewing candidates for the party ticket. Thompson, supported by his sidekick Joel Flaum, as much in jest as anything decided to seek the party's nod for state's attorney of Cook County.

Thompson secured an invitation from Tim Sheehan, a county Republican activist and nemesis of Ogilvie, to appear before the slating committee. Obviously, Sheehan wanted to stir the waters, as everyone expected Robert O'Rourke, the choice of Ogilvie, to be chosen by the party and nominated in the primary.

Thompson and Flaum prepared carefully. "We rehearsed all the answers to questions we knew we'd get on patronage and about whether we would have money to campaign. We went down there and made this speech before the Republican Central Committee." Thompson stepped outside the slating meeting after his appearance and repeated some of what he had said for the TV cameras. "Then Joel and I went off to Fritzel's to celebrate and sat in booth number one, and called Kup [Irv Kupcinet, newspaper gossip columnist] just like the big guys did, and the committee voted unanimously to support O'Rourke."

Thompson's escapade was a lark, without question, but it illustrated a willingness to take chances and his interest in public life. As it turned out, Thompson had enough name recognition among influential Republicans that he did not need to use gimmicks for attention.

Thompson and Reuben, for example, had crossed paths several times during the 1960s, while Thompson served on the state's attorney's staff and later as a professor, and Reuben showed up frequently at legal conferences. Both remember a free press–fair trial debate on television in which Reuben defended the position of newspapers and Thompson took the antipress side. Each argued his position vehemently, and as Reuben remarked later, "I have always been impressed with Jim Thompson's presence, acumen, intelligence, and appearance in those early years."

Reuben also was an associate of William J. Scott. As Scott began to assemble a staff for the attorney general's office in 1968, he asked Reuben for names of prospective departmental leaders. Reuben suggested Thompson and brought Thompson and Scott together for the first time at a meeting in Chicago. Thompson thought he was being interviewed for the position of first assistant, but Scott had filled that and was looking for someone to head a new criminal division. A couple of days after the meeting, Scott offered the job to Thompson and he accepted.

Thompson served as chief of the criminal division during 1969. In 1970 he became chief of the Department of Law Enforcement and Public Protection. Meanwhile, as he worked for Scott, other events occurred that would shape Thompson's future.

The change of parties in Washington meant a change in U.S. attorney for the Northern District of Illinois, and that prerogative fell to Everett Dirksen, a U.S. Senator from Illinois since 1950. His task was to recommend a candidate for U.S. attorney to the Department of Justice and to Nixon, and subsequently to the Senate for approval. Thomas Foran, an appointee of Lyndon Johnson, announced his intention to leave the U.S. attorney post, but two events delayed his departure. First, the Chicago Seven conspiracy trial tied up the prosecutor in 1969, and the Department of Justice wanted Foran to remain and finish that task, regardless of his political affiliation. The second delaying factor was an argument between Dirksen and Percy over Foran's replacement.

Dirksen wanted to nominate John Bickley, a former assistant U.S. attorney (he served on the staff of Robert Tieken with Ogilvie and Scott) and once a candidate for Cook County state's attorney. Percy wanted William J. Bauer, then a circuit judge in DuPage County. Dirksen accused Percy and Ogilvie of agreeing on Bauer as part of a plan to strengthen their hands with the Cook County Republican party. Bauer had been an Ogilvie agent in DuPage County during the gubernatorial campaign of 1968. Dirksen opposed Bauer's selection because he suspected Bauer had worked for Ogilvie and not for the rest of the Republican ticket in 1968, an action that cost Dirksen votes in the suburban Republican stronghold. Harold Rainville, Dirksen's aide in Chicago, said, "We don't believe in that kind of politics."

A showdown between Dirksen and Percy never occurred, because on September 7, 1969, Dirksen died and the prerogative to nominate a U.S. attorney shifted to Percy. Percy moved toward Bauer immediately. The judge had his eye on a federal court appointment rather than the U.S. attorney's position, and he sought assurances from Percy that eventually he would be considered for a federal judgeship. Percy agreed.

Justice officials said they wanted continuity in the U.S. attorney's position and suggested that a first assistant be chosen who could slide into the top job when Bauer moved on. The choice of a first assistant normally was left to the U.S. attorney; but knowing this situation was different, Bauer counseled with several friends. He had Jim Thompson in mind from the beginning.

Meanwhile, during the fall of 1969 Thompson grew anxious to move beyond the state attorney general's office. He contacted Joe Woods, former sheriff of Cook County and brother of Rosemary Woods, Nixon's personal secretary, about the U.S. attorney position. Woods said he had no influence with Nixon or Attorney General Mitchell. Thompson looked elsewhere and settled on the Cook County sheriff's job. As he recounted later on:

"One day I picked up the phone and called the governor and asked if I could come down and expect to see him and he said sure. I drove down in a rainstorm and walked into his office. He said, 'I know why you're here,' and I said, 'Well, that's pretty good. I hadn't told anybody.' " Thompson said Ogilvie replied, "Yeah, it's about Bill Bauer's offer to you to be the first assistant U.S. attorney." Thompson told Ogilvie he hadn't talked with Bauer, and he wouldn't be interested anyway. He wanted to run for sheriff.

Thompson remembers the next exchange this way: Ogilvie asked, "Well, why would you want to be that?" I replied, "Well, I want to be governor."

Having taken the route to Springfield from Cook County sheriff, Ogilvie hardly could turn away the young attorney at that point. Ogilvie said he would support Thompson for sheriff, but Ogilvie thought Thompson should wait for Bauer's call.

Bauer and Thompson had an acquaintanceship that stretched back to Thompson's days as a Cook County assistant state's attorney. They served together on bar association committees and worked on revision and reform of the state's criminal laws. Thompson's name came to Bauer's mind immediately. He talked with Ogilvie and the governor agreed with the choice. Only at that point did Bauer agree to take the U.S. attorney offer from Percy.

Bauer called Thompson and the two visited at the DuPage County courthouse. The judge said he was about to become U.S. attorney and needed a first assistant. Bauer said later the subject of Thompson being heir apparent was on the table from that first meeting. Thompson's recollection is that Bauer hinted of the progression to U.S. attorney. Thompson hesitated and took the matter under advisement.

A second conversation, involving Bauer, Ogilvie, Thompson, and two Ogilvie aides, John Dailey and Jerry Marsh, occurred at the Chicago Club later in the fall of 1969. Afterward Thompson and Bauer had a drink and talked further. Bauer said Thompson fretted because a first assistant U.S. attorney could not participate in political activities and the job didn't have a high profile. He wanted assurances of promotion to U.S. attorney when Bauer became a judge, and Bauer gave them. Thompson accepted. Scott knew nothing of Thompson's negotiations with Bauer. When Thompson told him of the decision to leave the attorney general's office, Scott was miffed because Thompson had been in the office barely more than a year.

An interview with Percy followed, lasting about three hours. Later, Percy said: "By the end of the meeting I had a feeling here was a guy with a fresh, open mind, unquestioned integrity, who had guts and energy and would be an aggressive U.S. attorney." Thompson recalled this about the interview: "I told Senator Percy that I was a liberal on civil rights. I told him I favored giving young defendants the benefit of the doubt. I told him I approved of counseling before sentencing and liberal use of probation."

Thompson emphasized points that were not normally associated with the advocacy of a prosecutor but were not totally incompatible either. In an interview with a nonlawyer such as Percy, they may have been persuasive. Percy should have known that Thompson came from an environment that stressed convictions above all, and a relationship with Inbau that emphasized teaching policemen how to get confessions from suspects. Neither Thompson nor Inbau had a reputation for speaking in behalf of defendants.

The U.S. attorney arrangement for Thompson was greased from the outset, and only a classic blunder by the young prosecutor could have denied him the position. Thompson saw the opportunity clearly. "It was strongly implied that if I was a good first assistant, I would succeed him." Bauer had incentive to put a strong man in the first assistant job. "If I had picked a clunk, I'd never have gotten out of the job," he said.

As he took office in July, 1970, a path stretched before Thompson to the governorship, although not one he had considered before. Only two former U.S. attorneys in Illinois had taken that course to Springfield. Dwight Green, who was governor from 1941–49, held the U.S. attorney position from 1931–35, during which time he prosecuted Al Capone. Otto Kerner, U.S. attorney from 1947–54, served as governor from 1961–68 and then went on to the federal appeals bench. Green's prosecutions of gangsters gave him the momentum he needed to run for governor; but Kerner's years as U.S. attorney were uneventful, and he earned his political reputation as a Cook County judge from 1954–60. There he learned the Democratic political system and was available when Mayor Daley wanted a loyal candidate for governor in 1960.

If Thompson had any doubts about being prepared for U.S. attorney, they vanished soon after he began work with Bauer. Thompson ran the office, did the hiring, supervised assignment of the major cases to other assistants, and conducted much of the U.S. attorney's business. When they had disagreements, Bauer put their respective positions to a vote. On one occasion they disagreed on whether to use a statute for the first time to prosecute a purchasing agent who had taken bribes from suppliers. The indictment committee supported Thompson on a vote of 3–2, and Bauer let the decision stand. "He was pretty democratic about that," Thompson said.

On November 29, 1971, at age thirty-five, Thompson became the new U.S. attorney for the Northern District of Illinois. In a simultaneous ceremony, Bauer became a U.S. district judge. Both men had achieved their goals: Bauer's offered long-term security; Thompson's fulfilled short-term ambition.

Having served an apprenticeship of eighteen months, during which he gradually took over most of the critical responsibilities, Thompson noticed the only difference that day was that Bauer was no longer in the office. Otherwise, it was business as usual. There were newspaper announcements with shallow treatment of his background and minimal commentary on his vision of the task before him. He did mention that his career model was William Howard Taft. "He first became president, and then he became chief justice of the United States. I'd like to follow after him." Hardly an interview occurred in the next four years that did not mention Thompson's presidential designs.

What of this young prosecutor? Those who knew Jim Thompson and Bauer anticipated the change that occurred when Bauer moved to the federal bench. While the two worked well together, there were marked contrasts in their personality and style. Bauer was a cautious man in pursuit of job security; gruff and taciturn to those meeting him for a first time, and occasionally profane, he was the personification of judicial seriousness and decorum. While U.S. attorney, he made no attempt to become a media creature. Bauer was exactly what Percy wanted in his first U.S. attorney appointment: a respected legal person with a businesslike approach, and a preference for a low profile.

Then there was Thompson, who already had a charismatic effect on those who worked for and with him. Tall, a striking figure of a man, single, footloose and conscious of his image, Thompson drove a tobacco brown Mercedes and revealed an inclination to wear flashy clothing. The *Chicago Tribune* concluded an early interview: "Whatever Thompson chooses as his style, it promises to be swinging."

In the eighteen months Thompson and Bauer worked together, the office received a substantial boost in funds from the Nixon administration, and the staff of assistants was doubled to fifty-three. Within a few months after taking over, Thompson tripled the original staff, providing resources and opportunities never available to a U.S. attorney in Chicago. The Nixon administration had begun a nationwide increase of federal funds to implement the promises of Nixon's presidential campaign and take advantage of legislative initiatives, such as the Omnibus Crime Bill of 1970.

Thompson chose assistants with attributes he admired: youth, commitment to the law, willingness to try anything, and energy to work long hours. Their loyalty to Thompson was of immediate importance, inspiring Bauer to comment: "Jim develops the loyalty of the people who work with him. Without that he wouldn't be worth a tinker's dam. Everybody who works in that office wears the badge of the U.S. attorney on his sleeve. Assistants can destroy a guy, can make him look like a nincompoop. They have to have a guy they can look up to."

No sooner had Bauer moved on than a familiar face showed up as Thompson's first assistant. Joel Flaum, thirty-three, became the No. 2 person in the office; he was essentially in charge of administration and keeping the work flowing while Thompson charted directions. Flaum came from Scott's office, where he had been the attorney general's first assistant. He brought experience and long-standing friendship with Thompson, both of which Thompson needed. Flaum became Thompson's alter ego, offering unswerving loyalty and counsel. Their relationship extended beyond the office, too. Thompson was a frequent guest for dinner at Flaum's home and became good friends with members of the family. Thompson helped his friend Flaum in 1975 by recommending him for nomination as a federal judge. Because Flaum lacked some specific qualifications—he was just below the minimum age required by the American Bar Association—Thompson sought waivers and provided references. Flaum received the appointment. Since that time Flaum has maintained silence about the years with Thompson, declaring any personal comments to be inappropriate.

Another key person was Samuel K. Skinner, who was hired as an assistant by Thomas Foran in 1968. The same age as Flaum, the intense, extroverted Skinner had every reason to resent the quiet Flaum who moved into the No. 2 position. If he did, no one detected it. Skinner's value was as a detail man, an investigator, and a trial lawyer who took meticulous care in preparing cases. An accounting graduate from the University of Illinois, Skinner joined International Business Machines in Chicago. While working as a salesman during the day, Skinner attended DePaul law school at night and received his law degree in 1967.

With Flaum as chief administrator, Thompson gave Skinner increased responsibilities by placing him in charge of the special investigations division. The division's work provided much of the evidence for Thompson's prosecution of political figures. It also moved Skinner into position to succeed Thompson as U.S. attorney in 1975.

There were some assistants older than Thompson. Senior man on the staff was D. Arthur Connolly, who headed the criminal division. A graduate of the DePaul law school in 1952, he joined the office in 1957.

Another key person brought by Thompson from Northwestern was Gary L. Starkman. Devoted to the U.S. attorney, Starkman headed the appellate division, an area of the law that had attracted Thompson as a young Cook County assistant prosecutor. Starkman also displayed a literary streak and co-authored articles and book reviews with Thompson. He worked with other assistants to produce one of the Thompson-Inbau criminal law casebooks.

Thompson inherited several Democrats, and some of them remained. He claimed he never made a patronage appointment. One assistant, Gordon Nash of the criminal division, claimed roots "from a 100-year Democratic family." Several assistants had prominent fathers who were lawyers and judges, including Tom Mulroy, Jr., and James Murry. John Simon, at twenty-eight, the youngest division chief in the office's history, was hired by Foran. His father, Seymour Simon, was an independent Democratic alderman in Chicago.

Working in Thompson's office meant more than just having a boss-employee relationship, as assistants soon learned. Thompson wanted friendship as well as respect. Married assistants often invited him to dinner. He got along especially well with children of his employees, and his adopted families were those of Flaum and Skinner. Most of the assistants enjoyed being around Thompson, and if some did not, they kept their distance without being obvious. If an assistant shied from collegial spirit, he soon moved elsewhere.

The subject matter at work—which consumed the office personnel—also was a source of emotional involvement for Thompson. When circumstances brought achievement to one of his assistants, Thompson more than once shed tears of joy. One notable episode involved a young assistant and a civil rights case in which an eighteen-year-old black man had been beaten by a Chicago policeman.

Until this particular case, the Northern District of Illinois did not have a single civil rights case victory. Prosecutors had achieved guilty verdicts in cases against policemen in southern states long before Chicago counted its first. Thompson made the point: "Chicago is a tough, police-oriented town."

The specific case arose from an incident in which the black youth argued with a policeman over whether he or a white woman was entitled to a parking space on the street. The policeman administered a beating to the youth. Thompson gave the case to a young assistant, who won it. The judge sentenced the policeman to a year in the penitentiary.

Thompson recognized the achievement of his assistant as worthy of special recognition. Thompson led him from office to office to tell each colleague of what had been achieved. "When it was over I was crying and couldn't finish the explanation," Thompson recalled.

With a crew of assistants that included a mixture of talent and experience, enthusiasm and dedication, Thompson faced the agenda for his office in late 1971. At the top was a case against Otto Kerner.

As long as Thompson maintains a position in public life and ambition for others, his involvement with the Kerner prosecution will provide conversation. His enemies believe he persecuted an honorable man; his friends consider the case one of Thompson's finest hours. Thompson contends the case does not stand out as a personal accomplishment, and co-prosecutor Skinner has said, "I wish the Kerner thing would go away." But their careers and lives are forever intertwined with the case.

When Bauer and Thompson took over the U.S. attorney's office in 1970, Otto Kerner, Jr., sat as a judge on the Seventh Circuit Court of Appeals. Few public servants in Illinois history could rival his credentials as army officer, federal prosecutor, county judge, governor, and federal judge. A more unlikely target for a federal prosecution did not exist. Kerner had remained clean in a world of scandal and corruption that had touched governors and lesser state officials, past and present.

An investigation of Kerner by the Internal Revenue Service grew out of probes undertaken in the late 1960s as part of Operation CRIMP, an acronym for Crime, Racketeering, Influence, Money, and Politics. Some career IRS agents thought those elements existed in Chicago and authorized an investigation which began before Nixon was elected in 1968. A major part of the investigation included racetrack activities in Illinois, personalities involved with the business, and the relationship to politics.

The first recorded racing meeting in Illinois occurred in Chicago in 1845, and from that point the sport became one of the most popular in the state. By 1900 there were annual trotting and pacing events held in 80 county seats (102 counties in Illinois), and 95 other towns and cities. There was a direct link between racing and society in Chicago, and a chief promoter was General Philip Sheridan, the Civil War general who became a resident of the city in the late 1800s.

A major change in racing in Illinois occurred in 1927 when pari-mutuel betting at the tracks was made legal by the legislature. A racing commission was established for control purposes. (In 1965 it changed to the Illinois Racing Board.) Through the 1930s and the mid-1940s, racing languished, but after World War II and into the 1950s the sport grew rapidly. The entrepreneurs of racing in those years quickly recognized the importance of political connections, as legislation often was needed to protect and expand pari-mutuel betting and racing. As new tracks were opened, and old ones renovated, legislators and elected public officials were offered investment opportunities, usually stock in the enterprises.

Lawmakers and officials were in an ideal position to enhance their investments, as statistics from the growth years indicate. The key item was the number of racing days at tracks where pari-mutuel betting was permitted. The racing commission distributed the meeting days to the individual tracks. The number of pari-mutuel days totaled 222 in 1941 (when only thoroughbred racing had pari-mutuel betting) and increased to 628 days in 1966 (harness racing wagering began in 1946). The total pari-mutuel "handle"—gross amount of money collected from wagering—in the same period increased from \$60,078,214 to \$491,301,900.

An incentive for state government existed in those figures, too. The state receipts increased from \$1,657,469 in 1942 to \$33,897,037 in 1966. In that period annual attendance at the tracks increased from 2,075,405 to 7,299,314, at tracks in the Chicago area, with a lesser percentage at tracks in the vicinity of East St. Louis.

Because the commission administered the racing and pari-mutuel laws and established its own operating policies, the opportunity for manipulation and payoffs grew as the stake of investors grew. Commission members, appointed by the governor, had one vital task: establishing the meeting dates for tracks. With a proliferation of tracks the competition for good dates—those in the prime attendance season and when good mounts were available—sharpened. Bad dates could seriously reduce revenues; good dates could be a bonanza. Inducements from racing interests to members of the commission and those responsible for appointments were not unusual. The politics of horse racing permeated state government and at the peak of growth involved the legislature, the governor's office, major elected officials, the racing commission, and track people with connections to state government.

The most successful owner and developer during the period of greatest racetrack activity and growth was millionaire Ben Lindheimer. He had built a virtual monopoly in thoroughbred and harness racing in the 1950s. When he died in 1960, the racing empire was inherited by his daughter Marjorie, who by the late 1960s went by her married name, Marjorie Lindheimer Everett—Marje to those who knew her and of her.

Through Chicago Thoroughbred Enterprises, Inc., she controlled Arlington Park and Washington Park racetracks in the Chicago area, those developed by her father. CTE also owned controlling interest in Balmoral Jockey Club. By all accounts Marje worked hard at protecting her interests from the encroachments of politicians and competitors, and that is how she became involved with William Miller, Kerner, and Theodore Isaacs, a close associate of Kerner.

During the IRS investigation of racing and politics in Chicago, Marje told agents of a stock arrangement with Kerner, implicating Miller and Isaacs. Marje resented Miller for taking advantage of her in a series of actions regarding ownership of racetracks, and she told her story in detail and with enthusiasm. The investigation of Kerner, his indictment, and his conviction grew from these early conversations with the IRS. At the time, there was no knowledge of Kerner's involvement at the Department of Justice in Washington or the U.S. attorney's office in Chicago, where Foran was the prosecutor.

The IRS continued its investigation into 1970, a year after Richard Nixon became president. By midyear the agency had turned its information over to Henry E. Petersen, a Democrat and career bureaucrat in the Department of Justice who was assistant attorney general in charge of the criminal division. Petersen was not satisfied with the IRS investigation—given the seriousness of the accusation against Kerner—and turned it over to the tax division of Justice for further work. Petersen recalls the additional investigation took about four months, into late 1970. Petersen said later one of the benefits of the second investigation was discovery of evidence supporting an accusation that Kerner made a false statement about a meeting at which an offer of racetrack stock was made.

Bauer became U.S. attorney in July of 1970 and was informed of the Kerner investigation that fall. Petersen called Bauer to Washington because there was a "problem we want to explain." Bauer then learned of the IRS investigations that had occurred in Chicago, none of which had been logged with the U.S. attorney's office. When told of Kerner's involvement in the case, Bauer could not believe it. He returned to Chicago and said nothing about the matter. Later Bauer made a second trip to Washington and took persons from the office, but not Thompson, the first assistant. Thompson first learned of the investigation of Kerner early in 1971.

As Justice became more deeply involved in the investigation, Petersen and other officials kept Mitchell informed. Critics of Thompson have alleged the Kerner investigation was politically motivated and engineered from Washington through Nixon and Mitchell. Petersen refutes that assessment, while acknowledging that Mitchell knew of the investigation, and Nixon undoubtedly had been informed. There is no evidence that Nixon or Mitchell pressed the Kerner investigation.

In a letter to the author in January, 1979, Mitchell, then serving a sentence in the Maxwell Air Force Base prison camp at Montgomery, Alabama, denied discussing the Kerner case with Nixon. "As attorney general, I did not discuss prospective prosecutions with the president," Mitchell wrote. In the same letter he said, "To the best of my recollection I never discussed the prosecution of Gov. Kerner with anyone outside of the Justice Dept."

Mitchell concluded his letter: "If there was any political influence in the prosecution of Gov. Kerner I would not know where it might have come from. Such influence was not present in any of the discussions or decisions made while I was in the Department."

Nevertheless, the theory has persisted that Nixon wanted revenge for having lost Illinois to John F. Kennedy in 1960 by 8,000 questionable votes, and he saw a chance to get it by prosecuting Mayor Daley's friend and loyalist, Otto Kerner. Former Nixon aide Charles Colson has alluded to Nixon's bitter memories of the 1960 loss and the president's determination to even the old political score with Daley. Colson's comments have received extensive publication by Thompson's critics.

If scrutinized closely, the theory falls apart on two counts. First, while

Kerner had served Daley well through the years and had been repaid with a lifetime judicial appointment, they were not cronies and the public did not link the two as inseparable parts of the Chicago political organization. There is a question whether the prosecution of Kerner reflected badly on Daley. Some Nixon associates undoubtedly thought the conviction of Kerner would embarrass the Democrats, but their assumption was not based on an understanding of Illinois politics.

Second, although Nixon never forgot his losses, he and Daley had effected a working relationship during the early years of the presidency that recognized their respective political strengths. Thompson said: "The prospect always struck me as absurd that Nixon was sitting in the White House worrying about getting revenge on the Chicago Democratic machine by prosecuting Otto Kerner. It is a known fact that Nixon and Daley held each other in high regard and spoke well of each other."

In his January letter, Mitchell wrote: "To my knowledge the contacts between Pres. Nixon and Mayor Daley were very limited and related primarily to the mayor's support of the President's position on the Vietnam War and the war resisters."

Percy, who served in Congress during the transition from Johnson and the Democrats to Nixon and the Republicans, also discounted the vendetta theory. "Why would they want to get Kerner? I'd never heard a harsh word against Kerner (in Washington) and there was a hell of a lot of respect for Daley. I know Nixon had a lot of respect for him."

There was another important consideration: prosecuting a sitting federal judge was not the accepted means of gaining political revenge. It was contrary to all the rules politicians live by. If anything, politicians had sympathy for Kerner and his circumstances. Petersen said Mitchell's reaction was "sadness," reflecting the awesome nature of the charges. "Mitchell was enough of a politician to empathize with people in the public eye. He knew if Kerner had been acquitted his reputation would have been damaged irreparably," Petersen said.

In February, 1971, a federal grand jury in Chicago began deliberations on the Kerner case and related matters. In all more than 100 persons appeared. During the many months of proceedings all the principals testified, including Kerner, who appeared on June 10. Few doubted that indictments would be returned. New developments in the investigation of Kerner soon became the worst-kept secrets in Chicago, despite laws prohibiting discussion of grand jury proceedings by jurors and participants.

A major media release came on July 29, after Marje Everett had appeared before the grand jury. Chicago newspapers reported that Kerner made a quick profit of $150,000 on a racetrack stock transaction while serving as governor. The papers attributed details to "federal authorities." Kerner refused to comment. The reports lacked specifics and were inaccurate on some points, but they caught the flavor of the transaction as related by Marje.

Bauer also received that summer a memorandum from the Justice Department outlining proposed indictments, and he went to Washington for a conference with Mitchell. "Mitchell knew of the investigation but not the particulars," Bauer later recalled. Thompson did not accompany Bauer on this trip either. Around September 1, 1971, he brought Thompson fully up to date, and Skinner also learned of details. By that time Bauer's move to the U.S. district court and Thompson's promotion to U.S. attorney were only a couple of months away.

Matters rapidly fell into place that fall. Skinner, until then chief of the criminal division of the office, was appointed head of a new operation: Special Investigation Division. The major responsibility of SID was political corruption and in time Skinner was devoting all energies to the Kerner case.

Thompson and Skinner went to Washington for a separate briefing and to read the IRS report. Petersen told Thompson everyone in Justice agreed with a decision to indict Kerner, but a final judgment had to be made by Thompson. Petersen said: "If you think you've got a good case go ahead, if you don't think you have a good case, you don't have to go ahead. It will be on your head so you better be sure."

To check the validity of the testimony against Kerner, Thompson and Skinner flew to Palm Springs, California, where they conferred with the star witness, Marje Everett. She had left Illinois and was about to expand interests in California racing circles. Also attending that conference were her attorneys and representatives of the Justice Department. The two prosecutors returned to Chicago convinced of the case against Kerner.

Until then Thompson intended for Skinner to prosecute Kerner and others who were to be indicted with him. However, Petersen objected. It had become Justice's position that Thompson should sit at the prosecutor's table as co-counsel for the government. Petersen pointed out that Kerner would be only the second sitting federal judge to be tried and for the sake of appearances Thompson should be present. "That probably was the best decision Petersen ever made," Skinner said in reflection years later. "I wasn't so sure at the time—frankly, I was disappointed, being slightly arrogant—but thank God wiser heads prevailed."

All that remained to be considered was timing. Thompson decided to delay the indictments until Bauer had left the office for the federal bench. The consideration was for Bauer's professional relationship with Kerner, if the former governor were indicted and acquitted. Kerner and Bauer might have served together for another twenty years. Thompson did not want Bauer's name on the indictment. The gesture was symbolic but did not conceal Bauer's involvement from Kerner.

Three weeks before the indictments were made public on December 15, 1971, the Chicago Tribune declared Kerner knew what was coming. Chicago newspapers, publishing countless stories in November and December, left nothing to be reported except the details of the indictments.

On December 14 about 4 p.m., Thompson and Skinner paid a courtesy call on Kerner in the judge's office. It was Thompson's first major contact with the judge, although he had watched Kerner from a distance when Kerner made the June grand jury appearance. "I felt that I owed it to him to go up there and tell him before it happened," Thompson said. "The propriety of the relationship demanded that I do it."

Thompson told Kerner the grand judy had returned a nineteen-count indictment against the judge, alleging extortion, mail fraud, perjury, conspiracy, and bribery. Although Kerner knew the subject of the visit, Thompson and Skinner recalled the judge appeared stunned. "I think knowing the nature of Otto Kerner and his personality throughout the trial, he probably convinced himself that, since he was innocent, he never in the world would be indicted."

Kerner made only one comment before the two young prosecutors (thirty years Kerner's junior) left. "This is a very nice Christmas present."

The indictments named four persons in addition to Kerner. They were Theodore Isaacs, onetime director of revenue in the Kerner administration and an associate of the judge since the 1940s; William S. Miller, former chairman of the Illinois Racing Board and deeply involved in racetrack politics; Miss Faith McInturf, Miller's secretary and business associate; and Joseph E. Knight, director of financial institutions during the Kerner administration.

Kerner vowed to obtain an attorney and fight. Although authorities had kept Daley informed of the investigation, news of the indictment stunned the mayor. Kerner had not been a Daley ward heeler, but the association stretched over many years. It would not be the last time Daley felt the sting of Thompson's work.

Kerner led an almost storybook life in public affairs and earned the reputation of a man of "impeccable personal honesty and integrity," as Charles Percy once said. He was born on August 15, 1908, and attended the best schools in suburban River Forest. His father, an active Democratic politician, led Chicago's Czech community and eventually became a judge on the Seventh Circuit Court of Appeals, a position Otto Junior would someday hold, too.

Young Kerner graduated from Brown University in 1930 and then studied a year at Trinity College, Cambridge. He returned to the U.S. and attended Northwestern University School of Law, where he graduated in 1934. He practiced corporate law in Chicago and at the same time entered the Black Horse troop of the Illinois National Guard as a private. He retired in 1954 as a major general.

Also in 1934 he married Mrs. Helena Cermak Kenlay, daughter of Anton Cermak, the Chicago mayor who was killed in 1933 during an assassination attempt on Franklin D. Roosevelt. A daughter by Mrs. Kerner's previous marriage was killed in an automobile accident in 1954 and the Kerners, childless, adopted her two grandchildren, Tony and Helena.

After serving from 1947 to 1954 as U.S. attorney, Kerner was elected a county judge, bringing him directly in Cook County elective politics. He was re-elected in 1958. He ran for governor and defeated William Stratton, who sought a third term in 1960, and then defeated Charles Percy by 180,000 votes for re-election in 1964. During the gubernatorial years, the public identified Kerner as a cool, detached individual with a warm smile and military bearing. He seldom gave interviews and shielded his private life as much as possible from public gaze. Len O'Connor, a Chicago TV commentator, later described Kerner as "suave, slightly overbearing; [his] speech is slightly nasal and eastern."

Although Kerner looked after the interests of Chicago during his gubernatorial years, he earned a reputation as an efficient steward of the office who appeared not to play favorites. When, in 1968, only a few months before the end of his second administration, he was appointed a judge on the Seventh Circuit Court of Appeals, the public nodded generously—as if to say he deserved the honor and seemed suited to judicial robes.

One of Kerner's finest moments in the eyes of the public and the media occurred in 1967 when President Lyndon Johnson appointed him chairman of the National Advisory Commission on Civil Disorders, quickly called the Kerner Commission. It studied the causes and potential remedies of riots that tore the hearts out of several major U.S. cities in the early and mid-1960s.

The voluminous report identified racism as the underlying cause of the riots and confronted many issues that public officials had avoided. For that, the Kerner Commission was cited for courage by the media and President Johnson, although not many measures were introduced in Congress to solve the problems. One of the shortcomings of the report was the lack of attention paid to political causes of the riots. The few persons who criticized the report noted that one of the riots studied occurred in Chicago in 1966, and the persons responsible for restoring and keeping the peace were Daley and Kerner. The same persons knew that Daley's attitude toward racial matters and the political system's unwillingness to tackle the problems of housing were factors in the Chicago upheavals. They received little attention in the Kerner Report.

Of the other four persons indicted—the charges required sixty-four pages and outlined more than sixty overt acts—only Isaacs came to trial. Knight's case was separated from the rest because of his serious illness and never was pursued. Miller and Miss McInturf turned state's evidence and were granted immunity from prosecution in return for their testimony.

The indictments accused Kerner and Isaacs of conspiracy, bribery, mail fraud, and tax evasion. Kerner also was accused of perjury before a federal grand jury. The main count alleged that stock held by Kerner and Isaacs, and the profits from the stock, constituted a bribe by which Marje Everett's racing interests received favorable state treatment. Marje, once called the "queen of Illinois racing," was not indicted, although she was an acknowledged party to the bribery scheme.

If anyone doubted the influence of the persons charged by the indictments, the array of legal stars hired to defend them soon put that to rest. Thompson and Skinner were to face several of the nation's most respected and feared defense attorneys. Kerner, for instance, engaged the Washington law firm of Edward Bennett Williams, considered one of the most expensive and powerful law firms in the capital. Paul Connolly, a partner of Williams, took the case. One other familiar legal name appeared on the record, although he did not appear at the Kerner trial. F. Lee Bailey, flamboyant defense attorney, was hired by Miss McInturf to negotiate her immunity.

Isaacs originally hired Thomas P. Sullivan of the politically active Jenner and Block firm in Chicago, but he soon switched to Warren Wolfson, another Chicago lawyer. Sullivan became U.S. attorney in 1977 and Wolfson became a circuit court judge.

Kerner overshadowed Isaacs throughout preliminaries and during the seven-week trial, but the slender, soft-featured Isaacs played important roles in Kerner's political career. He served as Kerner's campaign manager in 1960 and 1964, although he resigned during the second contest after newspapers reported him to be a stockholder and attorney for an envelope company organized after the 1960 election and doing business with the state. He was indicted for collusion and fraud, but the charges were dropped. Isaacs was without question the most influential man in the Kerner administration; he was able to speak in behalf of Kerner and give him advice.

As attorneys and defendants prepared for the pretrial skirmishes, Justice Department officials became alarmed at matters transpiring in California. Marje had applied for a racing license in order to take a seat on the board of directors of the Hollywood Park Racetrack. A hearing before the California racing board was necessary. Knowing Marje would be asked about her involvement in the Kerner matter, and that her testimony would be public, Petersen sent Thompson and Skinner to California early in January, 1972, to talk with Evelle Younger, then state attorney general.

The two prosecutors explained they could not control Marje's testimony and she might say something that would damage the prosecution case in Chicago. Legally, Marje could not discuss her federal grand jury testimony, and Thompson refused to release a transcript of it for consideration by the California board. They asked Younger to postpone the hearing.

Differing versions of what was said at the meeting with Younger have been told over the years and these resurfaced during Thompson's 1976 gubernatorial campaign against Howlett. At least two books critical of Thompson's handling of the Kerner case have inferred that Thompson and Skinner went to California to help Marje get her license in payment for her testimony, which had not yet been given at a trial. Howlett, among others, accused Marje of "blackmailing" Thompson with her testimony and he charged that Thompson soft-pedaled her involvement with the Kerner case when meeting with officials.

Compounding the confusion, Thompson told a Chicago television reporter after the meeting that he had called Marje a briber when talking with Younger. He later corrected that statement, and others who were at the meeting or heard reports of it have declared that Thompson did not refer to Marje as a briber. Skinner said: "We didn't say she was a briber. It didn't matter to us, we had charged that she was part of a bribery scheme, and they knew that." Skinner said they told Younger that Marje was a participant in an extortionlike scheme and that Kerner and Isaacs had accepted a bribe.

The semantics remain unclear, but the result is on the record. The California board granted Marje a temporary license later in January, 1972. A year afterward Marje was Thompson's key witness against Kerner, and in April, 1973, while Kerner's appeals still prevented complete access to the records, the California board made the license permanent.

With Miller and Everett the two most important witnesses for the prosecution—and testimony of both necessary to complete the bribery case—negotiations led to immunity from prosecution for Miller. Thompson took Miller as "his witness" and Marje became Skinner's. They met with the principals and coached them in preparation for the trial. As the case dragged on in 1972 and took increasing amounts of Thompson's time, he turned the U.S. attorney's office over to Flaum.

In the Thompson-Skinner partnership Thompson had the flair and quickness, but Skinner provided a bulldog tenacity and penchant for detail that made him indispensable. Skinner's work during the trial moved one reporter to write: "His questioning of witnesses at the Kerner trial seemed spontaneous and extemporaneous. But each question had been written out in advance, to insure the evidence was presented in the proper order to prove the counts in the indictment."

Thompson and Skinner had few major differences of opinion regarding how to try the case, or who would take what chores. Their disagreements, sometimes at the witness table during the trial, resulted more from Skinner's excitable manner and Thompson's stubbornness. Skinner prevailed at one critical moment, Thompson remembers. "He made me tape my opening statement and listen to it two or three times before he was satisfied with it."

The performances of Thompson and Skinner—and defense attorneys Connolly and Wolfson—were recorded carefully during the trial; but the seeds of controversy that would follow Thompson during his prosecutor years and afterward were sewn outside the courtroom, in the year it took from the time of indictment to the actual start of the trial. Before any of the courtroom drama began, the Kerner case became the model for techniques Thompson used countless times: shotgun indictments, immunity to bribers, frequent media appearances to announce progress of a case, and use of statutes that were decades old (i.e., mail fraud).

One example—shotgun indictments—illustrates how the minds of the public can be influenced. In the Kerner case, nineteen indictments were issued listing sixty alleged illegal acts; the media frequently referred to the detailed, sixty-four-page list of indictments. Numbers create impressions, and in this case and others, legal experts feared Thompson influenced public attitudes toward the guilt of Kerner and subsequent defendants. A lack of sophistication among citizens about the legal process, especially in the pretrial stages, has been documented. It is not at all unusual for a casual viewer of television or reader of newspapers to watch a prosecutor, or read his remarks, and conclude that an announcement of guilt is being made. A normal reaction is: "Why would they list so many if he weren't guilty?"

Use of shotgun indictments is also one means of manipulating the public through the media. There are countless points of view on the technique, including that of Marvin Aspen. Believing that "a lawyer's place is in the courtroom," Aspen is critical of Thompson's use of media. "A prosecutor ought to keep a low profile," Aspen said in reviewing Thompson's career. "I don't like the way he manipulated the media. Press coverage is not the role of a prosecutor. But that's Jim. If the case warranted publicity he would get the maximum out of it."

Did Thompson, standing before television cameras reading a list of accusations against a noted public figure, create a sense of guilt? Never fully answered in Thompson's time, the question engulfs all prosecutors who have used the technique. It is interesting to note that in 1979 the Department of Justice issued a guideline prohibiting U.S. attorneys from using press conferences to announce indictments; this guideline of course does not govern the actions of local prosecutors.

At the time of the Kerner trial, few persons questioned the techniques. The granting of immunity to Miller and Miss McInturf got serious consideration in retrospect, as use of immunity became widespread in the prosecution of political personages.

On January 3, 1973, the Kerner trial began in Chicago with U.S. District Judge Robert Taylor of Knoxville, Tennessee, presiding. He was assigned the trial so that none of Kerner's judicial colleagues would be involved. Excitement, anxiety, curiosity, fear—a full range of human emotions—overflowed as the trial began. The media clamored to report events; each day hundreds of persons waited to get a first-person glimpse of the action. There was the unmistakable scent of history in the air.

Spectators discovered an entertainment element to the trial as it unfolded, concealing the complex nature of the charges and evidence. The dominant personalities were the prosecutors and defense attorneys, while the defendants sat emotionless. Reviews of performances after the trial gave Thompson good marks in the personal contest with Connolly and Wolfson. *The Nation* magazine gushed: "Thompson's hard-driving, almost evangelistic prosecution of the highly technical, complex case . . . was a clear demonstration not only of legal skill but of courtroom theater."

The technical nature of some evidence—in some ways more important than the dramatic appearances of Miller, Marje Everett, and Kerner—placed a premium on attorney theatrics, for there was always the question of how much the jury understood about the intricate matters of bookkeeping, financial intrigues and details, and endless discussions and interpretations of documents. Before the trial settled into the mundane details of guilt or innocence, the two central legal characters—Connolly and Thompson—traded swipes and jibes in opening statements. They set a tone of personal combat.

Connolly, exhibiting a slashing attack style, called Thompson's granting of immunity to Miller "one of the most cynical deals I have ever heard of in the history of American jurisprudence." Connolly labeled Miller as "the culprit . . . the most sinister man" who involved Kerner in the transactions and "who corrupted Illinois racing . . . ."

Thompson countered with his own sweeping condemnations. "At the heart of the matter this is a case of bribery and fraud, and lies and evasions to conceal this bribery and fraud." Drawing himself close to the jury, Thompson said, "Years from now you will recall the next few weeks as the most important weeks of your lives as citizens of this country." They remembered the days as difficult, too, for Judge Taylor sequestered the jury to prevent influence from press coverage and conversations with relatives and friends.

The lawyers were only two of the antagonists in the trial, and at times observers needed a scorecard to keep accounts on who hated whom. Sometimes the main contestants were Kerner and Thompson, with the defense drawing a picture of the political opportunist persecuting the honorable man. Other times Connolly focused on the motives and personality of Miller, whose testimony could ruin Kerner. Although Miller depended on Thompson for immunity, he disliked the prosecutor and resented Everett being untouched; and for her part, Everett said Miller betrayed her in business dealings.

Between the testimony of Everett and Miller, the prosecution outlined the circumstances of the stock arrangements with Kerner and Isaacs, then tied them subtly to the payoffs: favored treatment for Everett's interests. Other elements of the case related to accusations in the indictment received attention, too, but the bribery count was central and gained the most notoriety.

Everett took the stand first for the prosecution and carefully placed heavy blame on Miller, as she had been coached by Skinner. She said that under the influence of Miller, these events occurred:

- After her father's death, she formed Chicago Thoroughbred Enterprises as a holding company for her Arlington Park and Washington Park tracks and racing associations (jockey clubs). This, she said, was done at Miller's suggestion.
- Following Miller's advice, she contributed $45,000 to Kerner's 1960 campaign.
- Following Miller's advice in 1962, she executed a memo making twenty-five shares each of CTE stock, worth $1,000 each, available to Kerner and Isaacs. Everett said Miller told her Isaacs would be an important man in the Kerner administration.
- On two occasions men she felt would be detrimental to racing were proposed for membership on the Illinois Racing Board. She conveyed her objections to Miller. The appointments were not made.
- On at least two occasions bills were introduced in the Illinois legislature to increase the state's share of racing revenues. On the first occasion the bill died after testimony by Miller. On the second, a graduated scale increasing the state's take, proposed by Miller, was adopted.
- In 1966, in deals triggered by Miller, Kerner and Isaacs exercised their options to buy the twenty-five shares each of CTE. They backdated a promissory note to 1962 and paid interest on it. After a short time, she said, the stock was traded for 10,000 shares of Balmoral Jockey Club, worth $30 a share, permitting Kerner and Isaacs to realize approximately $150,000 profits each.

Connolly attempted to take the sting from Everett's testimony by admitting the stock transaction, but not the intent behind it. "There was nothing wrong with the governor of Illinois owning racetrack stock," he said. "There was nothing wrong with the governor of Illinois having an investment program."

Miller's testimony was to provide the links to payoffs for the stock. Without that testimony, bribery was just an accusation and suspicion, and at most Everett might have a claim to being extorted. Miller was not an especially sympathetic figure on the stand. A millionaire, suave, and steady as a witness, he was the person in the Kerner bribery scenario who made everything happen. His position on the state racing board was portrayed by the prosecution as giving Kerner direct access to decisions that would help some tracks and hurt others. In turn Miller had opportunities to ask Kerner and Isaacs for favors. The defense characterized Miller as a liar, cheat, and a thoroughly disreputable figure who damaged the reputation of everyone with whom he came in contact.

Miller said he visited Kerner at his Springfield office on November 8, 1962, where he told the governor that Mrs. Everett had agreed to make stock available for Kerner and Isaacs and that Kerner replied, "That's very nice of Marje." Connolly tried to discredit Miller's recollection of details of the meeting by pointing out the witness could not recall details of other meetings with Kerner. Miller said his memory was assisted by referring to extensive personal files he kept on such meetings.

The prosecution implied guilt in the stock transactions and the intricate means used by Miller and Isaacs to conceal ownership. Thompson and Skinner inferred the worst motives of Kerner and Isaacs regarding state racetrack dealings during Kerner's gubernatorial years. The defense said Kerner was interested only in increasing the state's take from horseracing to help pay for state programs, and that is why racing flourished and grew during his years as governor.

At no time during the trial did anyone provide specific proof that Kerner, Isaacs, or Miller took action themselves or with legislators or the racing board to protect Everett's interests, but that was the implication throughout the testimony. No evidence was presented that proved an absolute link among the principals and a bribe. The jury was left to weigh evidence and determine intent. Therefore, Otto Kerner wanted his turn on the stand to defend his honor and deny the charges. He thought a determined personal statement about his innocence would overshadow the questionable testimony of Miller and Everett.

Kerner left Connolly no choice but to call him as a witness. On the day, courtroom spectators felt uneasy with Kerner in the witness chair. It was an unlikely place for a former governor and a judge of the federal appeals court. He spoke clearly, so all could hear, and his military training and natural bearing made him a resolute witness. During two-and-one-half days of direct testimony, Kerner denied any wrongdoing. This exchange with Connally was typical of his determination:

CONNOLLY: Did you accept a bribe from William S. Miller or Marje Everett?

KERNER: Absolutely not.

CONNOLLY: Did you deprive the people of Illinois of good government?

KERNER: I did not.

CONNOLLY: Did you tell any falsehood to the grand jury?

KERNER: Never.

For pure theater and electricity, Kerner's testimony was eclipsed only by the contest with Thompson on cross-examination. Under Thompson's precise questioning, Kerner admitted several discrepancies in previous testimony and statements. The two men tested wills, and Kerner became sarcastic and emotional toward the end of Thompson's questioning. At one point Thompson persisted in trying to establish that Kerner had held a Sunday meeting in the governor's mansion to discuss racing laws with legislators. Kerner said he always tried to save Sunday to spend with his family. "No one in the room knows the sacrifices I made," he explained. "In all the years I was there I never scheduled a meeting in the mansion on a Sunday." For emphasis, he rapped the witness table.

Speculation has never ceased about the effect of Kerner's testimony. Most members of the prosecution team believe Kerner hurt his own case. Skinner believes Kerner's conduct was fatal. "Kerner killed himself as a witness. He turned the jury against him; I've never seen a more arrogant witness. He lied about little things and the jury didn't like that. He was convinced things happened a certain way and they didn't."

Closing arguments started on February 14. Connolly continued his slashing attack, accusing Thompson's office of Hitler-like tactics and saying again that Thompson was trying to advance his own political career at the expense of Kerner.

In an hour-long summary of the case, often hailed as one of Thompson's brightest moments in the courtroom, the prosecutor responded to Connolly's attacks. "That's me," he said, "a hard-charging, vigorous, ambitious prosecutor, but it won't lead to political longevity. Because an ambitious prosecutor doesn't indict a federal judge, particularly in Chicago. He just goes after the poor, the weak, the friendless, the powerless and ends up with a 95 percent conviction rate."

The Wall Street Journal later reported, "His argument left several of the jurors visibly moved."

Thompson and Skinner stayed at a private club near the courthouse on the night of February 18. The longer the jury took in deliberation, the more confident the prosecutors became. In their minds acquittal would have come quickly, if at all. Nervous and unsettled, the two wandered around the club, shot some pool, and then retired. Late the next morning, February 19, they received word that the jury had reached a verdict. All parties gathered in the courtroom. Because a court reporter had to drive some distance, nearly an hour passed before the jury came in.

As everyone waited for the jury, Kerner spoke softly to Isaacs at the defense table. Wolfson drew attention because of a bright red sport coat he wore. One reporter wrote that Thompson looked as if he were going to have a "bad day"; the defense team exuded confidence.

After the jury was seated the verdicts were read. Isaacs was first: guilty. Then Kerner: guilty. Kerner listened without expression and hardly blinked his eyes. He stared as the judge polled the jury.

Instinctively, as the ordeal ended, Connolly moved from the defense table to Thompson's side and shook hands, offering congratulations. Thompson recalls a look of anger on Kerner's face at the gesture. Thompson believes Kerner never doubted his innocence, and the verdict was truly a shock. "I'm sure he died thinking he was innocent. He had himself talked into that notion. He didn't want to believe otherwise."

Looking back on the verdict, Thompson says he felt sympathy for Kerner. "I felt sympathy when the verdict was in but I never felt sorry before that." The prosecutors celebrated, leaving the impression with some observers that they displayed too much joy at the verdict. "We spent a couple of years investigating, put months of our lives in the case, and six or seven weeks at the trial, so it was a natural sense of relief when it was over," Thompson said.

Some observers in the courtroom, especially those close to Kerner, detected a lack of sympathy among the prosecutors for the defendants. Later quoted in a book critical of Thompson's handling of the trial, Kerner's son Tony said, "There was no caring...no compassion... no consideration about what the verdict might have meant. I know they regarded Dad as a trophy. It was a big game hunt. Let's go after Kerner. A wild game hunt in the jungle, and a chance for them to bring something home to hang over the fireplace."

For more than a year, the case bounced through the appeal process, with the verdict upheld. Kerner resigned as a federal judge on July 24, 1971, and entered prison on July 29. On March 6, 1975, a parole board ordered his release. On May 9, 1976, suffering from cancer, Kerner died and was buried at Arlington National Cemetery in Virginia.

Time has shaped the conviction as a highlight of Thompson's prosecutor career because of Kerner's position and record of public service, especially work on the Kerner Commission. In spite of at least two books painting Thompson as a politically motivated opportunist who connived to convict Kerner, general public feeling has exonerated Thompson and concluded that Kerner took some wrong turns and was caught. The public, and public officials, are able to credit Kerner's memory with accomplishments while accepting the unhappy note on which his career ended.

There was a greater significance to the conviction, which helps explain the bitterness among longtime Chicago ward politicians and persons close to Daley. They reacted, not because one of their kind had fallen, but because Thompson had prosecuted and convicted Kerner without the political system stopping him at some point. Kerner, Daley, Nixon, Mitchell, and dozens like them were brethren in an unofficial understanding and use of the political system to protect each other. Whether at the national or state level, it existed as a shield to prevent the kind of episode such as occurred in Kerner's case.

None of the normal weak links in the political chain had snapped. Once the case left the Department of Justice and final decisions on prosecution were left to the U.S. attorney, there was no way to throw the cloak of political protection around Kerner. Nixon's preoccupation with the beginnings of Watergate distracted him and occupied the Justice Department.

The bitterness felt in Chicago political circles was frustration, not deep concern for Kerner. It was concern for themselves, for if the protective shield could be bypassed once, it might happen again. The extraordinary feat accomplished by Thompson, besides the legal work required to gain convictions, was that the prosecution of Kerner ran contrary to the rules of the game that had protected high-ranking political figures in Chicago and Illinois for years.

The Kerner conviction and other corruption cases in 1972 and 1973 encouraged citizens and officials to come forward with information and evidence to keep the shield weakened.

The adopted children of Kerner deeply resented Thompson for their father's conviction. They have on occasion made public statements accusing Thompson of bribery and conspiracy in dealings with Marje Everett. Tony Kerner raised the subject in the final days of the 1976 gubernatorial campaign, and cooperated with authors who wrote books and articles critical of Thompson's legal activities. Thompson met the Kerner children for the first time after the trial in May of 1977, during his first year as governor of Illinois. Regents of the Lincoln Academy—of which the sitting governor automatically is president—voted a posthumous award to Kerner in recognition of his service as governor. Normally the governor would have presented medals to Kerner's children, but the chancellor of the academy and former governor Dan Walker both suggested it might be embarrassing if Thompson made the presentation. They offered to work out another arrangement. Thompson said the decision should be left to the Kerner children. They did not object to a presentation by Thompson, and he left the Kentucky Derby early to fly back for the ceremony.

While the Otto Kerner trial occupied a handful of assistants and Thompson through all of 1972, the U.S. attorney's office dealt with two pieces of the Chicago fabric: police corruption and fraud. Thompson knew that many persons instinctively thought of both when describing Chicago's worst problems. He had been in the state's attorney's office in the early 1960s when the city suffered the trauma of yet another major police scandal, and he knew the main difficulty in prosecuting policemen—getting witnesses to testify against them.

The Austin police district in Chicago had been suspected as a haven for police corruption for several years. Articles had appeared in newspapers—notably those by Bob Weidrich in the *Chicago Tribune*—regarding police harassment and extortion of tavern owners. Policemen were accused of threatening to arrest tavern owners—often on trumped up charges—or otherwise cause the owners economic harm if they didn't provide cash payments. An investigation by Police Superintendent James B. Conlisk failed to result in criminal action against the policemen, but he demoted a district commander and transferred some detectives and a sergeant out of the district in 1970. The U.S. attorney entered investigations when violation of the Hobbs Act was suspected. The Hobbs Act makes it a federal crime to interfere with interstate movement of liquor.

After a lengthy federal investigation, tavern owners agreed to testify against policemen—for protection from prosecution by immunity—and in March the first grand jury indictments were issued, starting a process that continued for two years and resulted in indictment of more than sixty persons. Before the first indictments were made public, however, Thompson and first assistant Flaum paid a call on the man most likely to feel the impact: Richard J. Daley.

The meeting was the first and only face-to-face conversation between Thompson and Daley; for much the same reason that he had visited Kerner before his indictment, Thompson considered the visit a courtesy to Daley, since the indictments would occur on sensitive turf. The two young prosecutors talked with Daley for about thirty minutes, explaining the investigations and details of the indictments. They agreed it was a sad day when policemen were found involved in corrupt activity. As Thompson and Flaum prepared to leave, the mayor wished them good luck "in whatever it is that you are doing over there."

Thompson seemed subdued by the police investigations, especially with his background as a pro-cop lawyer and prosecutor. He told the *Chicago Daily News*: "I get no joy from investigating and indicting policemen, since they are members of the law enforcement establishment as I am. But we are going to find corruption and root it out wherever it is and whoever is involved."

The investigation of police extortion led Thompson's office into a labyrinth of negotiations with attorneys for bartenders and shopkeepers who wanted immunity from prosecution in payment for their testimony. Thompson insisted they were talking about extortion cases and the bartenders had been victims, not partners in a bribe, so they could testify against policemen without fear of implication or self-incrimination.

Consideration for the city's political system motivated the bartenders. They were afraid of being denied city liquor licenses if they testified against policemen, and they wanted politicians to blame the prosecutors— and not them—for dragging policemen into court. Otherwise, the bartenders threatened to "take the fifth"—refuse to testify against themselves under provisions of the Fifth Amendment—which would have spoiled Thompson's cases.

"There wasn't any way in the world that we could force them to testify without immunity, even though legally they were not entitled to it,"

Thompson said. He granted immunity rather than dismiss the cases and undertake another investigation for witnesses who would testify willingly.

The highest ranking officer convicted during the investigations was Captain Clarence Braasch, who led an extensive shakedown ring involving taverns and businesses on Chicago's Near North Side. Until Braasch, no officer of captain's rank or higher had ever been tried in Chicago.

The more aggressive Thompson's office became, the more threats of harm he received. At various times U.S. marshals provided body guard service, usually depending on the seriousness of the threats. Thompson appeared unconcerned. "About 70 to 80 percent of them were from drunks. You know, they are in a bar, start drinking, then stagger out to a telephone and call and say, 'Thompson, you son of a bitch . . . .'"

Feeling toward Thompson ran high at the police department during the 1972 and 1973 trials, inspiring one police investigator to suggest that associates be alert for opportunity to place Thompson in a compromising situation and blackmail him. Thompson told newspapers that his use of U.S. marshals was to prevent being "set up."

Still, Thompson had satisfying responses from policemen. During the trials for extortion Thompson often was stopped on Chicago streets at night by young officers in police cars wanting to whisper words of encouragement.

During the same period of time as the police investigation, Thompson's office participated in a vote fraud investigation with the *Chicago Tribune* and Better Government Association, focusing on the 1972 March primary election of candidates for local, state, and federal offices. The BGA and *Tribune* staked out precinct polling places where they observed illegal and unethical actions and recorded them for publication, while Thompson's assistants toured polling places across the city gathering evidence for prosecution. About the same time, *Tribune* investigative reporter William Mullen wrote of his undercover experiences with voter registration, explaining how officials had voted the dead, the ill, and the nonexistent. He won a Pulitzer Prize for his efforts.

The information was taken to a grand jury and eighty-one persons were indicted, with some pleading guilty; others were tried and convicted. A few were acquitted. Most jail terms were six months or less and were handed down by judges with no ties to the Democratic organization. Two federal judges gave light sentences and probation in most cases. They were Abraham L. Marovitz, who had close ties to the Democratic organization, and William Lynch, Daley's former law partner.

Most of the cases were processed before the November election in hopes they would have a deterrent effect on precinct workers and election officials. "I think that was a legitimate thing to do," Thompson said. "One of the purposes of criminal law is to deter others from committing crimes, not simply to punish wrongdoers." Poll watchers in November reported a dramatic reduction in election day illegalities.

Further evidence of Thompson's direction toward highly visible political cases arose during 1972 and 1973. In one series of cases, he brought charges against employees in the county assessor's office, and then brushed even closer to the mayor's office with prosecution of Cook County Clerk Edward J. Barrett, a longtime friend and associate of Daley. Although most people recognized the name of Otto Kerner, those in the political organization of Chicago suffered much more with the fall of Barrett, one of their kind.

Barrett had served in state and county government since 1931, beginning with the office of state treasurer. From 1933 to 1941 he was state auditor and from 1945 to 1953 secretary of state. With the election of Daley as mayor in 1955, Barrett succeeded the mayor as Cook County clerk. Barrett was elected to the position in 1956 and re-elected until the time of confrontation with Jim Thompson.

Barrett's importance to the city, Daley, and the organization was in his dealing with hundreds of contractors who wanted to do city business and in his dispensing patronage through the clerk's office. Contractors had been a source of campaign funds to minor and major officials through the years. Daley needed a trusted and loyal friend in the sensitive position.

On September 28, 1972, the U.S. attorney's office indicted Barrett on charges of bribery, mail fraud—both to become familiar charges against public officials—and perjury. The indictment accused Barrett of soliciting and receiving $180,000 in bribes from the president of a Pennsylvania voting machine company who wished to place the firm's machines in Cook County. The prosecution case hinged on testimony of the former president of the company to whom Thompson granted immunity in exchange for information about the Barrett deal.

The trial in 1973 stunned Barrett's associates, who had assumed that someone of his background could never be tried in the friendly environment of Cook County. At the trial Barrett seemed dazed and disoriented. Barrett's conviction came about three weeks after the Kerner decision, giving Thompson's office a second major political corruption victory. Barrett unleashed a public broadside at Thompson, saying: "[He's] an opportunist trying to get something for himself. Every day of the trial he was sure to be in the courtroom, parading around and letting the public see him."

With a conviction won, Thompson spoke in condescending tones. "I assume Mr. Barrett's outburst is the product of the very deep wound he feels over the verdict. I can understand it.... The conviction of Mr. Barrett is not a source of glory. It is not a stepping stone to any other office for me.... I wasn't present when the verdict was returned and when

I did attend the trial I sat in the audience, sometimes in the last row."

In a final irony for Barrett, Judge Richard B. Austin, a longtime Democrat, ordered the sentence of three years in prison and a $15,000 fine. Barrett never served the jail time. Because of poor health he was permitted to serve the sentence at home. He died in 1977.

Not all of Thompson's prosecutions in the early years resulted from cases initiated by his investigators and assistants. Some were carried over from the administrations of Edward V. Hanrahan and Thomas Foran. One such case involved the Chicago Seven—alleged conspirators in riots at the 1968 Democratic National Convention in Chicago. When Thompson became prosecutor, two separate cases arising from the original trial were in the appeals process. With more than a casual interest in these cases, because they involved law-and-order issues and the behavior of defendants and lawyers in the courtroom, Thompson worked closely with his assistant, Gary Starkman.

The bizarre trial began with eight defendants—Bobby Seale's case was separated from the other seven—in 1969. Foran prosecuted, U.S. District Judge Julius J. Hoffman presided, and the chief attorney for the defense was William Kunstler, an advocate of the protest that ignited riots at the convention. The trial dragged on interminably with the judge, defendants, prosecutor, and defense attorneys constantly at each other's throats and participating in antics seldom before or since seen in a courtroom. Disruptions surprised, then confused, then angered the judge, spectators, and the public.

At the trial's end, five of the defendants were convicted and two were acquitted. Judge Hoffman, as much an issue in the trial as the defendants, issued a number of citations for contempt of court. The contempt citations constituted one appeals case, and the convictions constituted another. Foran left the prosecutor's office, and Bauer and Thompson moved in. On appeal, the defendants—including the still-familiar names of David T. Dellinger, Jerry Rubin, and Abbie Hoffman—won both cases. The government and Thompson had to decide whether to retry the cases and reopen the wounds, the issues, personalities, and publicity. By that time, almost five years had passed since the 1968 convention.

The Department of Justice wanted to drop both matters. The Nixon administration had problems with the growing publicity and investigations of Watergate, which preoccupied Justice, too. Thompson agreed to drop the conspiracy cases because, as he said later, "It was time to bury that part of our history." But he fought to retry the contempt charges.

Thompson's sense of propriety and courtroom decorum had been offended by Kunstler and his associates. Thompson said: "I felt strongly about disorder in the courts and lawyers going beyond the bounds. We didn't stop to calculate any political advantages or disadvantages."

Still, Justice did not want to get involved. Thompson went to Washington for an audience with acting U.S. Attorney General Robert H. Bork. The meeting occurred shortly after the celebrated "Saturday Night Massacre" of late October, 1973, when Nixon fired special prosecutor Archibald Cox, Attorney General Elliot C. Richardson, and Deputy Attorney General William D. Ruckelshaus for not following orders on the investigation of Watergate-related matters. With those three removed, Bork accepted the temporary responsibility.

When Thompson met with Bork and his assistants in Washington, they expressed sentiment for dropping the contempt cases as a gesture to counteract bad publicity of the massacre. In an interview a year after the Washington meeting, Thompson told the *Wall Street Journal:* ". . . Bork was anxious to drop the case as a gesture of good will to the *New York Times.* But I objected, telling him that we'd be letting down every judge in America if we didn't enforce proper rules of conduct in the court." Thompson and Bork adjourned for cheeseburgers "and a couple of martinis," and Bork told Thompson to proceed if he wanted.

The retrial was calm, and Thompson won a victory only in principle. Contempt citations were upheld for Dellinger, Hoffman, Rubin, and Kunstler, but the judge imposed no sentence, saying that would be vindictive. Thompson felt the case set boundaries of deportment for lawyers while still protecting the freedom of lawyers to defend with zeal.

In 1974, during Thompson's third year as U.S. attorney, public speculation about his ambitions increased, inspired by criticism of his techniques by politicians and legal experts, and by a steady flow of media feature stories favorable to his image. In the last year before the mayoral election of April, 1975, with an unceasing stream of cases being tried by Thompson against political figures, it was inevitable that Thompson would be talked about as a challenger to Daley. Heightening the expectation was Thompson's publicly expressed interest in the race and Daley's health. The mayor suffered a stroke in 1974 and spent four months away from Chicago in recuperation. Rumors arose that Daley never would return and probably would not stand for re-election if he did.

Each case in 1974 took Thompson and his prosecutors one step closer to Daley. Four more Daley associates fell, all of whom qualified as friends and political allies of the mayor.

The first of 1974's prosecutions of political figures occurred in February. Earl Bush, Daley's former speech writer and personal press representative, was indicted on twelve counts of mail fraud and one count of extortion. The case involved Bush's secret ownership of a firm that had an exclusive contract with the city for all advertising and display promotion at O'Hare International Airport. Allegedly Bush received more than $200,000 of profit from the arrangement, about which Daley knew nothing.

On April 5 Alderman Paul T. Wigoda, a favorite among ward politicians, and a law and business partner of Daley's pal Thomas E. Keane, was indicted for tax evasion arising from a $50,000 rezoning payoff. On April 10 a grand jury indicted Matt Danaher, Cook County clerk, on charges of conspiracy and income tax evasion resulting from a real estate deal in which Danaher and his brother-in-law allegedly made a profit of $400,000.

Daley grew testy as Thompson took aim at many of his friends. After the Danaher indictment, the mayor said: "It's a sad day for him and his family. An indictment is not a conviction." On other occasions, Daley criticized Thompson in more personal terms. Prodded too often, Thompson offered rebuttal. "I agree with the mayor that an indictment is not a conviction. My regret is that the mayor quickly comments after an indictment, but never after a conviction. If Daley's associates had worked with the same fidelity as the citizens serving on federal grand juries, we wouldn't have this problem we have today. He ought to reflect on that."

The bombshell came in May, four days before Daley was stricken. Thomas E. Keane, the mayor's confidant and personal representative in the City Council, who had helped slate Daley for mayor in 1955, was indicted on seventeen counts of mail fraud and one count of conspiracy. The indictments alleged Keane used his connections to purchase tax delinquent real estate, which he then sold at profits to city agencies. During the trial, IRS agents claimed Keane made a profit of $135,000 on sale of seventeen parcels of land to the Department of Urban Renewal, the Chicago Housing Authority, the Chicago Dwelling Association, the Metropolitan Sanitary District, and the Chicago Park District.

Rubbing salt in the wound, Thompson granted immunity to Keane's business partner, John A. Hennessey, Sr., for testimony that eventually sent the alderman to prison. Circumstances of the Keane and Wigoda cases would be used many times afterward as evidence of Thompson's alleged political vendetta. Critics said Thompson gave immunity and freedom to nonpolitical parties who were as guilty as the indicted politicians.

One former Thompson ally, Ben Adamowski, was embittered by what he considered slipshod techniques used to build cases against political figures. The former state's attorney said many people will lie to keep from being prosecuted and, if tempted by immunity, will say anything a prosecutor wants. "Thompson forgot that he was supposed to protect rights of the accused, too, and not accept the word and possible lies of anyone who comes along."

Much of the 1974 workload for Thompson's office involved the trials of Bush, Wigoda, and Keane. Danaher's case was delayed until early 1975. That trial never took place, however, because on December 15, 1974, Danaher's body was found in a Chicago apartment, where he had died of a heart attack.

It was a busy fall for Thompson in a political sense, too. Speculation about his candidacy for mayor in September was exceeded only by the news that Daley, appearing rested and robust, had returned to work.

Reports continued that Thompson would seek the mayoralty, but later in September he declined to run. If Thompson had become a candidate or even remained a suspected candidate, the three trials in November would have created a media blitz on which to campaign. As it turned out, Thompson got plenty of media attention, but not with overtones of mayoral politics. The convictions came in a matter of days in November, inspiring the *Chicago Sun-Times* to call it the "most incredible week in Chicago judicial history." The tally read:

Keane: Guilty on seventeen counts of mail fraud, one count of conspiracy.

Wigoda: Guilty of failure to report a payoff on his income tax return.

Bush: Guilty on eleven counts of mail fraud.

All three men eventually served time in prison, although several of the cases were appealed and dragged on for months. Bush, for example, went through two trials before finally going to jail. In sentencing Keane, U.S. District Judge Bernard Decker spoke words that applied to each: "The frailty exhibited by Thomas Keane was simple greed and I do not consider that a defense...." Thompson added: "The sentence I think should serve as a deterrent to anyone in public service who wants to use his public office for personal gain."

Information from federal investigations that is not used in an indictment usually remains secret, and Thompson refrained from talking about probes that did not develop into prosecutions. As a result, the extent to which his office investigated the activities of Daley cannot be fully explored. Thompson did publicly acknowledge one investigation of Daley, undertaken in 1974, regarding disclosure that the mayor had formed a real estate holding company, Elard Realty, to keep secret his land holdings in the city. Thompson acknowledged the investigation because newspaper accounts made details a matter of public record. No violations of the law were found.

Thompson had comments about public officials, sometimes in a context that had no relation to his activities as U.S. attorney in Chicago. Such an episode occurred in the fall 1973, after Vice-President Spiro T. Agnew had pleaded no contest to a felony and resigned. Thompson, in Washington for consultation with Justice officials about the case, called Agnew "a common crook and the country is better rid of him." Thompson later said a television newsman goaded him into making the statement, but that took none of the sting out of reactions.

Thompson's statement infuriated many Agnew fans and some who were not but considered Thompson's comments unnecessary and improper, especially as they came from a public official. One who expressed that sentiment was Ramsey Clark, former U.S. attorney general, who called for Thompson's disbarment. Thompson, incredulous, said: "I'm astonished because not only is Mr. Clark incorrect in his assessment of my conduct, but it is totally out of character for one who has held the lofty position of attorney general to make a statement like that." The incident passed, and Thompson shrugged it off as "silly."

As Thompson neared the time he would enter the race for governor in the summer of 1975, questions of his effectiveness surfaced, accompanied by discussions of his use of legal tools. One measure of a prosecutor's record is the conviction rate, although statistics do not reveal all the considerations that influence the outcome of cases. It is a helpful barometer only when tempered with the understanding that federal prosecutors have great latitude about the cases they take to federal grand juries and considerable freedom to drop cases with weak evidence.

Various figures purporting to represent Thompson's "conviction rate" while U.S. attorney have been published, some without benefit of qualification and attribution. One report that appeared in the Chicago Tribune in 1975 has been declared accurate by Thompson, and his critics. The work was done by Robert Enstad, a reporter, who searched federal court files in Chicago for the years of 1973 and 1974. Enstad wrote that if all victories were considered—bench and jury trials and guilty pleas—Thompson had a conviction rate of about 94 percent. However, the writer added, "the great bulk of those convictions was based on guilty pleas by criminal defendants."

In contested cases that went to trial before a judge or jury, Thompson's rates were 66.6 in 1973 and 73.4 in 1974. Enstad compared those percentages with records of earlier prosecutors; Bauer, Foran, and Hanrahan. In 1967 and 1968, Hanrahan averaged 88 percent in contested cases. Using the same comparison, Foran had an 85.7 rate in 1969 and 78.6 in 1970. Bauer in his one year—1971—scored an 81.4 percent conviction rate. Thompson said he concentrated on having a "law-enforcement impact" by his prosecutions, not in creating favorable statistics for himself.

Thompson came under occasional harsh criticism from fellow lawyers and judges for use of obscure statutes to indict and convict the "big fish" politicians. The mail fraud statute frequently used by Thompson was almost fifty years old. Thompson conceded the application of the law by his assistants may have been different than intended when Congress passed the law.

No criticism became louder or more pointed than over Thompson's use of immunity and the inference that he let guilty persons go free just to convict a handful of politicians. However, immunity has been used widely by other prosecutors since expansion of its application by the 1970 Omnibus Crime Bill. Also, during the 1960s and early 1970s a series of federal decisions by the Supreme Court widened the latitude for granting immunity to obtain testimony that otherwise might not be offered by witnesses.

As a pragmatic prosecutor, Thompson followed the premise that one conviction is better than none. In his judgment, most of the convictions of politicians and policemen would not have occurred if he had refused to use immunity extensively. Thompson believes bribery is a secret crime, often involving only two persons and usually learned of only after it happens. Then a prosecutor must obtain the testimony of one of the parties involved to have a case. "I would like to prosecute both parties, but I can't always reach that ideal," he says.

Thompson's office operated with some specific guidelines on the granting of immunity, although Thompson admitted they were sometimes ignored because of the peculiarity of a case. First, immunity was to be given only as a last resort, when other means of obtaining evidence had been exhausted. In the instance of granting immunity to cement contractors who bribed legislators, a case that evoked cries of abuse, Thompson's office pursued other means of gathering testimony for a year without success. "It was either grant immunity or wash our hands of it," he says in defense. "We didn't think those people should be sitting in the legislature."

The second rule was never to give immunity to big-name politicians or businessmen to get "little fish." Thompson concluded that such usage of immunity would be repugnant to a jury and "our own sense of what was important." The rules provided some safety, but little is on the public record about how individual decision were made or the negotiations that took place.

One internal procedure supported by prosecutors to minimize the potential for lying by witnesses anxious to get immunity from prosecution is insistence on a polygraph test. Information from a "lie-detector" test is not admissible in a trial nor is it conclusive as to truth or falsehood, prosecutors say, but it can be used to affirm testimony. Also, some prosecutors note, witnesses that have altered truth often will correct their statements when confronted with a demand for a polygraph test. Thompson did not administer polygraph tests, but if he had in the Kerner case, for example, accusations about use of perjured testimony to convict Kerner might not rest so heavily on the record.

One federal judge who openly criticized Thompson's judgment in using immunity was Abraham L. Marovitz, a longtime Democrat and associate of aldermen and ward committeemen. He presided at the trial of Wigoda, an acknowledged friend. Wigoda was given a one-year sentence for failing to report a payoff on his income tax. Marovitz said afterward: "Almost every single person involved in the zoning payoff was granted immunity with the sole exception of Paul Wigoda. It is not obvious to me how one decides who shall be the target and who shall be the protected informer." Thompson replied with a snap, "Prosecutors take testimony where they find it. . . ."

But the answer was not sufficient, even if Marovitz's point of view was slanted by personal and political involvements. Prosecutors have great latitude in choosing who gets immunity, and in the wrong hands, used cynically and without care, the potential for an erosion of justice is present.

A short time after Marovitz's criticism Thompson named an assistant, Gary Starkman, to review a number of cases and circumstances in which immunity had been granted. Just before that announced study, the *Chicago Sun-Times* had called for the American Bar Association to look into the broad application of immunity. Starkman wrote in 1978 to this author's inquiries about the study: "Due to a variety of intervening factors, I was unable to complete the immunity study . . . prior to my departure from the United States Attorney's office in September, 1975. . . . I do not believe that the study was ever completed or the research made public . . . ."

Thompson argues, also, that safeguards exist in the courtroom process. He says all parties know whether a witness has been given immunity, so there is no attempted deceit; the jury can weigh that fact with evidence; defense lawyers can be expected to grill a prosecution witness who has been given immunity; and judges can give the jury instructions to view the testimony of the witness with greater care and concern than they might otherwise.

The weakness of those safeguards is that they apply to protection of the defendant against whom the immunized witness is testifying, but they have nothing to do with the decision about granting immunity. Suggestions for improving surveillance on the use of immunity have included urging a greater role for the state and national bar associations, and tighter restrictions on use through the Department of Justice. Protection against abuse of immunity may require involvement of professional organizations because prosecutors are not the only culprits. Defense attorneys—many of whom publicly decry the use of immunity—are among the first to seek immunity for their clients, if it means keeping them from becoming defendants. The two-edged sword reveals the sometimes peculiar nature of legal warfare, with lawyers working both sides of the street, in full and approving compliance with the theory of advocacy as a cornerstone to equal justice.

In a single dimension, Thompson's career as a prosecutor is a reference point for evaluating his past performance and speculating about his future. It is a benchmark for understanding how the man might treat challenges and confrontations as governor. But his achievements must be tempered against the environment which provided the opportunity and in which he operated. An exploration of that environment reveals the peculiarity of Chicago politics and the demonic nature of one-party domination.

Why Jim Thompson, anyway? Why wasn't Thompson just a part of a concerted and continuing effort by prosecutors and law enforcement officers—Democrats and Republicans—to root out corruption in Chicago?

Answers, elusive at best, begin with an understanding of the one-party political system in Chicago. So powerful and pervasive is this system that even though a number of Republican opponents have been elected to sensitive law enforcement positions in the county and state in recent years, they were able to accomplish very little. These Republicans included Benjamin Adamowski, once a Democrat and part of the inner circle of one-party politics, who turned Republican in 1956 and was elected Cook County state's attorney, a post he held until 1960; Richard B. Ogilvie, later to become governor of Illinois, who served as sheriff of Cook County from 1962 to 1966; William J. Scott, who was elected attorney general of Illinois, with authority to pursue civil and criminal cases anywhere he chose in Illinois; and Bernard Carey, who was elected Cook County state's attorney in 1972 and 1976. A quick review of their individual careers in these positions gives a better understanding of the environment Republican-appointee James Thompson worked in as district attorney from 1971 to 1975.

Adamowski's name recognition as a longtime figure in Chicago politics—stretching back to the early 1930s—made election possible as a Republican in 1956, not because there were large amounts of Republican votes. Actually, he had been a Democrat until just before seeking the prosecutor's job. During his four years, Adamowski developed a number of cases designed to undermine the Democratic political system. At the end of a first term in 1960, Daley was determined to remove Adamowski, and he succeeded.

Ogilvie in his four years as sheriff did little to uncover political corruption for prosecutors. His defenders say the deputies under his hire were appointed by Democrats and could not be removed, and the U.S. and county prosecutor positions were held by Democrats unwilling to buck the friendly political system. Because of his isolation, Ogilvie's term is discounted as a reflection of Republican strength.

Scott has carefully chosen his legal confrontations in Chicago, publicly acknowledging that the Democratic-controlled circuit and appellate court systems in Cook County virtually preclude any widespread cleanup drive. Scott receives broad support in Chicago and Cook County at election time.

Carey has edged cautiously into political corruption cases but has not waged open warfare on the Chicago system. Defenders say he is handicapped much the same way as Scott, with a Democratic-dominated court system and a Democratic sheriff.

The lessons are clear to Republicans who want to make a career of holding law enforcement offices in Cook County: You can't win on Republican votes, because most of them are "shadows" that can be turned on or off by Democratic precinct workers; the only way to stay in office is to act "with the best interests of Chicago at heart." Translated, that means: Don't rock the boat.

From reviewing the history of these other Republican law enforcement officers in Cook County and Illinois, one can begin to see some of the elements that gave Thompson his opportunity. While his appointment as U.S. attorney required the backing and support of Republicans who understood the Chicago political system, once in office he was responsible only to Washington and was restrained in Chicago only by the degree of public support that could be generated. The political environment did not restrict nor inhibit him, as it had done others, and he seized that opportunity. The likelihood of elected Republican law enforcement officials being able to break away from the chains of one-party domination and indulge in continuing prosecution of political corruption is no greater than before, because the party in the city and most of the county suburbs remains largely imaginary and exists at the whim of the Democratic organization.

The future of that environment was not a concern of Thompson as he headed toward a gubernatorial contest in 1975. He knew the reality of a paper party in Chicago and was determined to collect the necessary votes in the suburbs and downstate to offset it. But there is a relentlessness to Illinois politics that never lets a state official forget Chicago. The story of Jim Thompson after 1975 is the story of a man coming to grips with his own city in an entirely different way than as U.S. attorney.

Candidate for Governor

Addressing a conference of political writers in 1978, Jack Germond, nationally syndicated columnist and political expert for the *Washington Star*, said of Jim Thompson: "He doesn't know much and he knows it."

Thompson might have disagreed with Germond at that point—more than a year after becoming governor—but at an earlier time Thompson not only admitted his ignorance of public affairs and state business, he wore it as a badge of courage.

That was during the first months of Thompson's candidacy for governor, roughly from June, 1975, until the end of that year. As he traveled across Illinois, much of it for the first time in his life, Thompson readily admitted a lack of knowledge about the job and the issues. In one interview he said, "If I had concentrated on state issues while I was a prosecutor, I wouldn't have been a good prosecutor."

Surprisingly, the media in Illinois—considered by many to be unrelenting in pursuit of politicians' foibles—accepted Thompson's plea for understanding. After all, some editorialists argued, the candidate had resigned as U.S. attorney only in July, and he needed time to become knowledgeable. Few newspapers questioned his lack of experience, or suggested it as a liability.

From his earliest days as a prosecutor, Thompson acknowledged his political interests, and the two routes most likely for him to follow: mayor of Chicago or governor of Illinois. The mayor's job tempted Thompson first. Daley, perhaps physically damaged by a stroke in 1974, faced re-election in April, 1975, and if Thompson wanted to run for mayor, a decision had to be made in the fall of 1974.

Close associates, friends, and acquaintances advised against it. Senator Charles Percy was among them. "I did nothing to encourage him. We were desperate to find a good candidate, but he was too valuable to waste on that. We needed good candidates for mayor, but you can't throw away a real prize when you get someone like Jim Thompson. They don't come around everyday."

At least one Chicago columnist, Michael Kilian of the *Chicago Tribune*, said Thompson would find the mayor's position a political dead end. He wrote: "Thompson might have a clear road to the governor's mansion, and from there it could lead to the United States Senate or even that large, white house in Washington that every politician (however wistfully) dreams of. But the road doesn't go through City Hall." Thompson agreed and decided against the contest.

If the governorship offered Thompson the better route, it was not without roadblocks. One was the peculiar two-year term beginning in 1976. Until 1976, governors of Illinois served four-year terms coinciding with the terms of the president of the United States. A full term beginning in 1976 would have ended in a presidential election year, but changes in Illinois law mandated that terms end in nonpresidential years beginning in 1978. Thompson, if elected in 1976, would have to run a second statewide contest before having a first chance at national recognition.

Despite his decision not to enter the mayoral race, Thompson continued in the public eye. Irv Kupcinet, *Chicago Sun-Times* columnist, wrote a few days after Thompson's refusal to run: "...Jim Thompson has announced he will not be a candidate for mayor. Then what's he doing riding an elephant in the traditional Ringling Bros. and Barnum & Bailey Circus parade on Wednesday? That's a typical ploy of a candidate."

Thompson's refusal left Republicans with two names on the list for governor: Bill Scott and Jim Thompson. To avoid intraparty strife, party leaders attempted to turn Thompson toward the attorney general position or Cook County state's attorney. Their eyes focused first on Scott, recognizing his seniority in party affairs.

Scott always seemed destined for something higher than attorney general. That was the public expectation of him, but those who knew Scott were aware of his reluctance to risk job security for higher office. Richard B. Ogilvie once referred to Scott as "a professional politician who likes to be in office and really doesn't want to do anything else." About Scott as governor, Percy said: "I'm not so sure Bill wants to be tied down to that detailed a job, accountable for every instance, every second, every minute of the day. That's why the attorney general fits him so beautifully. It fits his personality."

Scott's first brush with elective office was in 1962 when he won the state treasurer's position. Two years later, urged by conservatives, including leaders of the *Chicago Tribune*, he challenged Percy for the gubernatorial nomination in a no-holds-barred primary campaign. Scott lost to Percy and served out the balance of his term as treasurer. Unable to succeed himself because of a constitutional prohibition, Scott "retired" in 1966 to the private practice of the law.

In 1968, Ogilvie won a primary contest for governor against John Henry Altorfer, and Scott, Ogilvie's friend from the days they served together as assistant U.S. attorneys, got the attorney general nomination. Characteristically, Scott waged a relentless and highly partisan contest, defeating Francis S. Lorenz, a candidate handpicked by Mayor Daley.

Although Ogilvie moved to the center of attention, Scott's light seemed undiminished. Frequent articles speculated about his future, first as a possible primary candidate against Percy in 1972, then as a possible primary candidate for the U.S. Senate against Adlai Stevenson III in 1974. Denying ambition for higher office, Scott turned away from both challenges. "I'm not in this job for the money, not in it for license plate 3 or 1," Scott said. "In good conscience I can't walk out on the cases I have going."

Republicans began grumbling over Scott's refusal to leave the comfort of the attorney general's office for a head-on clash with a Democratic giant. Still, heading into 1975 many party officials were ready to nominate him for governor. He had earned respect as a popular candidate who could help Republican candidates at the local level.

In what many observers saw as a preliminary to 1976, Scott battled head-to-head with Democratic Governor Dan Walker on such issues as public disclosure of campaign contributions and the jurisdiction of state-employed lawyers. These skirmishes inspired Jerome Watson of the *Chicago Sun-Times* to write: "Scott's private and public pronouncements make clear his abhorrence of Walker and Walker's top aide, Victor DeGrazia." Walker's political mastermind, DeGrazia, could smell the candidates coming as early as the fall of 1974 and dared them to come, citing Thompson's decision not to challenge Daley and Scott's reluctance to fight big game; he called them "chicken" and said neither had guts enough to challenge Walker.

Public accounts indicated undeniable momentum for Scott toward the governor's race. In later years, however, key Republicans, including Scott himself, have said they doubted the attorney general's interest all along. Although there were no such indications at the time, Thompson, Percy, and Ogilvie all say now they didn't think Scott would run.

Meanwhile, Thompson enjoyed great success as a prosecutor in 1974 and early 1975. Indictments, trials, and convictions fell in a downpour and the accompanying publicity pushed Thompson's name to the tips of Chicago's lips. The evening news hardly passed without his appearance, as the press noted his movements, thoughts, statements, and social activity. One Chicago writer caught the flavor of Thompson's popularity: " 'Big Jim' can't walk down a block of a city street without having somebody come up to him to shake his hand or just talk to him." Everything seemed to come together for Thompson. He rode the crest of popularity in the area of greatest population concentration in the state and party officials liked him and saw his potential.

On May 30, 1975, Scott called a press conference—described as "sudden"—to announce he had no interest in seeking the governorship, clearing the way for Thompson. With the field clear, Thompson waited. While he had done his political homework before the Scott announcement (at least one suburban Thompson committee already was in action), details of his campaign had to be worked out, and his affairs as prosecutor put in order. Thompson feared being caught in violation of the Hatch Act—which prohibits political activity by a civil servant—and he hemmed, hawed, hedged, and dodged questions about his intentions. Pressure built so much that Thompson issued a memo telling his staff not to be upset by the rumors and to continue their work.

Thompson's suspected candidacy met with minor opposition. George Lindberg, state comptroller, said he would wait to see if Thompson caught fire in the 1976 March primary. If Thompson failed, Lindberg hinted he would be available. The right-wing splinter, represented by suburban Republicans who organized the Illinois Conservative Union, looked for its own candidate.

Michael Kilian, carrying Thompson's banner in the *Chicago Tribune* before the official announcement of candidacy, commented, "If he runs he will do so free of any debt, obligation, or backroom loyalty to any party leader." Kilian noted that Thompson's independence made him unpopular with some officials who wanted a candidate in tune with patronage needs at local government levels.

On July 1, Thompson announced his candidacy, a few hours after resigning as U.S. attorney. He wept at the resignation. All elements of surprise wrung from the announcement, Chicago newspapers and television stations were ecstatic. Thompson received rave reviews of his prosecutor performance and prediction of great success.

In his statement of declaration, Thompson struck mildly at Walker. "The theme of this campaign will be that Illinois needs leadership. We need politics to make government work and not politics for its own sake...." Thus, with no money, little name recognition outside the Chicago area, and few political acquaintances among party people at the grass-roots level, Thompson took a first step toward the governor's mansion.

Neophyte or not, Thompson had worked the political angles well. Ogilvie, Percy, and Scott (although reluctant) stood firmly behind him. Percy provided Thompson with a mailing list of contributors, and they all made calls in Thompson's behalf. Untried and untested on a state scale, Thompson came to the campaign with the stamp of approval of the Republican hierarchy.

Why did Thompson, a political beginner, think he could defeat incumbent Walker? He believed Walker was vulnerable and had some data to support the conclusion. One poll taken before he announced as a candidate for governor showed Thompson leading Walker in name recognition by 12 points in the Chicago suburbs. That encouraged Thompson.

Also, he did not fear Walker or his campaign techniques. In campaigning against Paul Simon for the nomination and later against Ogilvie in the

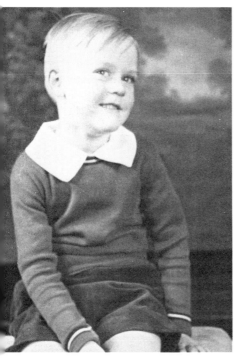

ABOVE: Thompson at age 5. ABOVE RIGHT: Thompson at age 17.
BOTTOM: Thompson at age 20.

TOP: Thompson, Cook County assistant state's attorney, carries box of evidence in October, 1960. BOTTOM: From left, Otto Kerner, Theodore Isaacs, and Thompson are pictured on day jury returned guilty verdicts in 1973.

TOP: U.S. Attorney's key staff members early in the 1970s included, from left, Samuel Skinner, Martin Lowery, Joel Flaum, Arthur D. Connolly, Thomas Huyck, Sheldon Davidson, and John Simon. BOTTOM: U.S. Senator Charles Percy congratulates Jim Thompson after the Illinois Republican gubernatorial primary in March of 1976.

Jim Kutina, Elgin Daily Courier

TOP: Gerald R. Ford and Jim Thompson campaigning together in northern Illinois prior to the 1976 elections. BOTTOM: Thompson gives "thumbs up" cheer after winning election as governor of Illinois, Nov. 2, 1976. With him are Lt. Governor Dave O'Neal (L) and Attny. Gen. William Scott (R).

United Press International

1972 general election, Walker intimidated his opponents with confrontation politics, aiming at the opponent's programs and personality. He caught Simon unprepared and scared Ogilvie with the technique.

After his courtroom successes, Thompson had confidence in holding his own against any Walker tactic. The prospect of two image-conscious candidates banging away at each other on television excited political observers.

Walker's poor standing among Chicago Democrats made him vulnerable in that Democratic stronghold, and Thompson thought a Republican with popularity in Chicago and Cook County, strength in the suburbs, and with traditional Republican help downstate could erase Walker's incumbency advantage.

Finally, the possibility of a Daley-backed candidate—Neil Hartigan, Michael Howlett, or Alan Dixon—running against Walker in the primary lightened Thompson's risk. If Walker survived a primary, he would be tarnished from a bruising battle with Daley. If Walker failed, Thompson liked his chances against any other Democratic possibility.

Not all of Thompson's hope rested on the ailments of the enemy. He had strengths, including the blessing of Chicago's media. Jerome Watson, *Chicago Sun-Times* political editor, wrote: "Thompson is one of the hottest new political properties the Republican party has in Illinois or anywhere in the country, emerging as he does from a much-heralded career as the nation's top corruption-busting prosecutor."

Rather than offer himself as a Chicago product, Thompson tailored his appeal to the shifting population patterns that were altering the political face of Illinois.

Shifts of population to the suburbs and rural areas nearby had begun decades before, as Chicago's population dropped from 44 percent of the state total in 1930 to 30 percent in 1970. The numerical impact, however, was not felt until the 1960s and early 1970s. The drift away from the city was more than displacement. The people rediscovered themselves and changed life patterns to reflect the new environment. Many of those leaving Chicago for the suburbs brought along Democratic party voting habits, but it was respectable to vote occasionally for Republicans. Then it became fashionable to be an "independent," and finally the old ways of the city gave way to a sense of affluence, freedom, and personal renewal. People found alternatives to grime and bolted doors, and they looked for alternatives to the tired faces and ethnicity of Chicago politics. Then, along came Thompson. White, fresh, and clean, he looked and sounded like a suburban neighbor.

It may be an oversimplification to describe Illinoisans in the mid-1970s as bent on escape, but the trends were undeniable. White flight from the cities was documented, and with the United States withdrawn from foreign wars, people found it easy to ignore problems and seek personal gratification. Also, with the trauma of Richard Nixon's resignation behind them, people wearied of national political quarrels and sought solace in entertainment and gossip.

These factors made Thompson all the more appealing, but they were not restricted to dwellers of the Chicago suburbs. Identical trends occurred among urban families in other Illinois cities, including Rockford, Springfield, Decatur, and Peoria. Residents there wanted to get away from life and its problems, too. Many looked outside the urban centers, and suburban developments blossomed.

One effect of the shift in population and attitude in Illinois was to destroy the old tripartite political theory. This theory held that Illinois could easily be divided into three entities: Chicago, suburbs, and downstate. Further, almost any political contest could be predicted by analyzing the individual characteristics and voting patterns of each area and providing a campaign style and message that would appeal to each. The visibility of candidates through the media—particularly television—destroyed this theory, however, and Thompson was among the first to realize it.

In his book, *Illinois: A History*, Richard J. Jensen talked about the changing urban picture. He wrote of the 1970s: "Indeed, the very term *urban* no longer connoted sophistication, wealth and diversity; instead it was reserved for the chronic problems of poverty, welfare, crime, and disorder in the inner city black ghettos of Chicago, East St. Louis and Cairo."

No matter how appealing Thompson was considered in the Chicago suburbs, hard-core conservatives were not interested. They sought an alternative in Richard Cooper, a millionaire who had developed chapters of Weight Watchers, Inc., and had interests in banking and real estate. Conservatives persuaded him to drop his candidacy for Congress in the 10th district and seek the Republican nomination for governor. Confident of his chances and abilities, Cooper scoffed at reports that he could not raise enough money to beat Thompson. Cooper planned to spend up to $500,000 of his own. He became Thompson's opponent in the primary.

Thompson had an immediate advantage over Cooper because of his exposure in northeastern Illinois, but he had no standing at all in the traditional Republican reaches of the state. A poll taken for him to determine the scope of the task revealed only 14 percent of the population downstate knew his name. He brought that up to 30 percent by the 1976 primary election.

Traditionally, Republican gubernatorial candidates had relied on a strong downstate showing to offset Democratic strength in Chicago and a nonexistent Republican party in Cook County. Jealous of the growing suburbs as an influence in party affairs, downstate county chairmen posed a challenge for Thompson. He could not ignore them because of Cooper's presence, and he knew Walker's victory in 1972 had eroded Republican strength downstate. With Walker still the target in the summer of 1975, Thompson recognized the importance of converting downstate party chairmen.

They were skeptical of the city slicker and waited for him to demonstrate his political abilities. The first chance Thompson had after declaring his candidacy was to tour county fairs during the summer. The visits gave him a chance to campaign one-on-one and also to demonstrate his willingness to hustle votes in the heat and the dust. He passed the test.

Appearing to enjoy sweating in Illinois summer heat, Thompson walked in the dung and fawned over children with cotton candy smeared across their faces. On one day he appeared in Galesburg at the Knox County Republican party barbecue. He worked the crowd, granted interviews, and spoke the generalities that were characteristic of his early campaign days. Asked to state the prime plank in his platform, Thompson said it would be to get people back into government and to end artificial divisiveness. "We will fill in the rest of it later," he added.

In the next month, Thompson's itinerary included barbecues, fish fries, and county fairs. After Thompson appeared at the Champaign County Fair in central Illinois, newspaper editor D. G. Schumacher wrote, ". . . Big Jim walked the fairgrounds and easily met people. He negotiated the livestock tents without getting dirty, which is an accomplishment." Political drudgery or not, he liked the work. "I'm one of those people who fits within the broad Lyndon Johnson definition of liking to get out and 'press the flesh,' " he said.

Thompson stressed everywhere that he was "learning" to campaign, "learning" the issues, "learning" to work the streets and meet people. "I've been a highly visible U.S. attorney, but I'm learning about campaigning now," he said at many stops.

Thompson quickly made moves to strengthen his campaign. At the recommendation of Percy, he hired the Washington political consulting firm of Bailey, Deardourff, and Eyre. The firm's credentials included development of Percy's 1973–74 presidential strategy. In 1976, the firm plotted gubernatorial strategy for James Rhodes of Ohio, William Milliken of Michigan, and Christopher Bond of Missouri. The most important client of Bailey and Deardourff in 1976 was presidential candidate Gerald Ford.

With the help of Bailey and Deardourff, Thompson established a goal of $2 million for financing the primary and general election campaigns. The figure sounded large, but other gubernatorial campaigns, including Ogilvie's and Walker's in 1972, had cost more. Thompson spoke freely of the difficulties in raising money and openly solicited funds, against the advice of political veterans such as Ogilvie. Most candidates referred donors to aides or finance chairmen, but not Thompson. "It gives me a chance to talk about their motives," he said. Thompson emphasized an openness about money by making daily disclosures of campaign contributions through his Chicago campaign headquarters, although this was not necessary under Illinois disclosure laws.

During the campaign Thompson maintained an association with the law firm of Winston and Strawn, one of the most prestigious in Chicago, for which he received $50,000 a year. Thompson declared that barely adequate to keep him going. "I need a job like anybody. . . . They will pay me $50,000 a year, a fairly modest figure, judging by current standards on LaSalle Street."

While his staff and strategists worked on campaign themes, Thompson himself was the author of a theme that stuck for the entire campaign. He recognized early that Walker and the Democrats would jump on him if there were any sign he favored increased state taxes. Therefore, from early on in the campaign Thompson backed away from talk of taxes with declarations of "no promises." Mostly, he avoided serious discussion of issues.

Thompson added trusted associates, such as Gary Starkman, his former assistant in the U.S. attorney's office, to his campaign staff. Starkman first worked in the campaign as director of research on issues; after the election he was appointed Thompson's chief legal counsel. As summer ended, Thompson made other key appointments; some of these people would remain after the election. James L. Fletcher, thirty-two, a former parliamentarian in the Illinois General Assembly, became campaign manager. A law associate of George Burditt, the unsuccessful Republican candidate against Adlai E. Stevenson III in 1974, Fletcher came highly recommended by Percy. Fletcher stayed on after the election as deputy governor. A third aide without previous campaign experience was David Gilbert, thirty-five, who began as press secretary. Gilbert, transportation editor at the *Chicago Tribune*, became Thompson's press secretary in the administration.

The quest for downstate votes continued. Thompson did not sweep downstate off its feet the first trip around, but initial press reports were favorable. Unlike their Chicago cousins, skeptical downstate editors withheld adoration, but they liked the engaging young man who seemed at home in any setting. The hustle was different, easier, more relaxed than with Walker or Ogilvie.

Thompson usually arrived at a newspaper office with his suit coat off and slung over one shoulder. He had loosened his tie. Breaking into a broad grin, Thompson entered the room boldly with long strides and reached for the editor's hand. He filled up the interview room. Tossing his coat over one chair, he sprawled in another. If it seemed appropriate or permissible, Thompson leaned back in the chair and swung his feet up on an adjacent table or desk. He laughed, joked, and usually once during the interview turned to serious talk. Thompson stayed as long as the questions came, even if it threw his schedule off track. He never appeared bored or impatient.

Thompson exuded a sense of candor that went over well with the media. Many editors were not used to that approach. After disarming his interviewers, he often entered a plea for patience and understanding. When Thompson admitted his ignorance of state issues, editors were understanding.

Thompson also acquired a campaign helper from Winston and Strawn in Thomas A. Reynolds, Jr. A partner in the firm, Reynolds became chairman of Citizens for Thompson, and in 1978 he served in the same capacity. Reynolds said of the Thompson association: "We first met late in April or early in May of 1975 and agreed on the association. I figured we'd either have him as governor or a successful lawyer in our firm."

Thompson's pledge of "no promises" held up without much serious questioning until early fall, when he made his return visits to downstate localities. The declaration drew more attention than any other two words from Thompson. As a kind of open-end campaign pledge, "no promises" had considerable public impact. Many applauded it as a frank approach and a contrast to trite campaign promises by other candidates. Some editorial writers called it an attempt to avoid comment on issues.

Thompson said there were semantic differences between "promise" and "propose." He explained he would make specific proposals for action, but he would not promise that they would be enacted as proposed or that they "would solve all of the state's problems." Thompson said the two-year term was too short to tackle a long list of issues. To pile up promises for the sake of promises would be "irresponsible," he said.

After three months of campaigning among downstate party bigshots, Thompson told writers for the Lindsay-Schaub newspapers his effort to win over Republican officials had mixed results. "I'm trying to convince them that I won't put all Republicans in jail," he said. His opponent, Richard Cooper, made the same calls but failed to impress the county chairmen.

Thompson worked hard because he wanted an easy primary election victory. Also, a victory without rancor made it easy to rally the party behind him. However, some party members tested his tolerance, especially his old friend, Bill Scott.

Back to running for re-election as attorney general, Scott seemed to go out of his way to irritate Thompson. One episode occurred in November of 1975, as the rumbles of Mike Howlett's possible candidacy for governor grew louder. Howlett had scheduled a dinner to raise money for his re-election campaign for secretary of state. The affair drew bipartisan support, reflecting Howlett's popularity with all manner of politicians.

Scott, a friend and associate of Howlett, showered pleasantries on the guest of honor, saying he would support Howlett for any office he pursued. A week later Scott spoke at a Thompson dinner but did not endorse Thompson's candidacy. Scott declared it was a practice of his not to endorse candidates in a primary.

The Howlett comments had irked Thompson's supporters and staff, but Scott's refusal to endorse Thompson burned them. Scott tried to explain his actions: "I would be for Howlett over Walker. I would be for Dixon over Walker." The target of his comments, Scott said, was Walker, not Thompson. He still did not endorse Thompson until after the primary. He refrained from further public praise of Howlett, but the memory lingered with Thompson, providing one more irritant for future relations between the two Republicans.

Meanwhile, Cooper's campaign fizzled and died. Despite an occasional perfunctory mention in the press, Cooper attracted little attention. In a moment of political kindness, Thompson offered his eulogy for Cooper: "He is a serious candidate, but not a serious threat."

In the spring of 1975, a year before the 1976 primary election, Lieutenant Governor Neil Hartigan counseled a reporter not to count Howlett out as a challenger to Walker for the Democratic gubernatorial nomination. The suggestion was preposterous. Howlett insisted he wanted only to seek re-election as secretary of state so he could glide comfortably toward retirement.

Howlett, then sixty-one, had earned consideration for his wishes. He had waged six previous statewide campaigns, one for treasurer (1950), four for auditor of public accounts (1956, 1960, 1964, 1968), and one for secretary of state (1972). His first victory came in 1960, and he had not been out of office since. Over the years he carried the Democratic torch to countless service club luncheons, fish fries, and chicken dinners across the state. His profile was familiar to thousands: No one could miss the portly Irishman with the broad grin and boisterous laugh. As a storyteller he had few peers.

Howlett had wanted to run for governor in 1968 and 1972, but Daley ignored him. In 1968 Daley blessed Samuel Shapiro, who lost to Ogilvie; and in 1972 the nod went to Paul Simon, who lost to Walker in the primary. Howlett thought he could have won either time, and the memories hurt. Although a loyal Chicago South Sider, Howlett never enjoyed a chummy relationship with Daley, and it had cost him earlier chances to be governor. They remained friends, but not confidants. Now, in the twilight of a public service career that had covered nearly two decades, Howlett wanted only to be slated by the organization for another four years as secretary of state.

Howlett's wishes did not influence Daley, however, as the mayor wanted to even scores with Walker. In 1972, Walker ran as an independent Democrat for governor against Daley's choice, Paul Simon, and won. Throughout his successful campaign against Governor Ogilvie and for the next four years Walker waged personal war with Daley, despite the mayor's attempts to bring the governor into the regular party fold. By 1975 Daley had given up on reaching any accommodations with Walker and made up his mind to do all possible to defeat Walker in the 1976 Democratic primary. He wanted Howlett, the party's most popular officeholder, as his candidate.

Howlett's determination to remain as secretary of state was not an endorsement of Walker. Howlett never cared for Walker personally or professionally, although he tried several times to welcome Walker to that unofficial, exclusive club of high officeholders in Illinois, where political differences occasionally are settled over thick steak and martinis.

Walker shunned the friendly advances of Howlett from the beginning. After Walker's inauguration in January, 1973, Howlett made a point of crossing the political bridge to congratulate Walker and establish a working relationship that could transcend the pettiness of Chicago-downstate politics. The governor said no deal, and Howlett never forgot it.

By late summer of 1975, the rumors of Howlett's candidacy for governor appeared regularly in the Chicago media. Nevertheless, after receiving private word from Howlett that he still wanted only to be secretary of state, Treasurer Alan Dixon said he would challenge Walker in the primary. And although unannounced, Hartigan stood ready to run for almost any position other than lieutenant governor.

Thompson, meanwhile, watched with interest, for as 1975 wore on it became clear there was a possibility that he could be pitted against one of his closest friends in politics. The campaign would be an extra strain if the Democrats nominated Howlett.

The Howlett-Thompson friendship began in the early 1960s, when Thompson worked for Cook County State's Attorney Benjamin Adamowski and his assistant Francis X. Riley. Howlett and Riley were longtime chums and that friendship led to an introduction of Thompson. When Thompson traveled to Springfield to argue appeals before the state Supreme Court in the early 1960s, he often stopped to see Howlett. In the 1970s, Howlett and Thompson became frequent lunch and dinner associates, often joined by another longtime friend of Howlett, Marshall Korshak. A familiar name to Chicago politics, Korshak had served in the state legislature, had been a ward committeeman, and was a successful Chicago lawyer. Thompson enjoyed their company. "They are two of the state's most fabulous political storytellers, and I learned a lot listening to them." They continued to meet regularly until Howlett became a candidate for governor.

Before 1976 ended, the Thompson-Howlett friendship would come under severe strain. In the meantime, persons who valued the friendships of Thompson and Howlett often found it difficult to walk the line so as not to appear to favor one over the other. One such case involved Don E. Reuben, a Chicago attorney noted for participation in high political and public intrigues. Through the years Reuben and Thompson have had casual associations with each other, usually of a legal nature, but sometimes in a social setting. Reuben recalls one such instance on a guest boat that he owned, and another at a dinner party at Reuben's home. Reuben, considering himself a supporter of Thompson, intended to take an active role in the 1976 election campaign until it developed that Howlett would be a likely opponent. Reuben's friendship with Howlett was closer.

Reuben declared he would stay neutral in the contest and perhaps not even vote. But during the primary election contest between Howlett and incumbent governor Walker, Howlett needed a spokesman on questions of alleged conflicts of interest. Reuben, coming to his friend's assistance, recalls representing Howlett in a "free-swinging style in an effort to protect him as much as possible from the disaster I perceived was looming. I received no fee for representing Howlett." From that point the story reflects the lack of communication that occurs so often in political contests.

After Reuben's representation of Howlett, two persons, one a former law partner, told the attorney his involvement with Howlett had angered and displeased Thompson and "he wanted nothing further to do with me as my conduct was an embarrassment to him." Further, Reuben said, a spokesman for Thompson said Reuben could "balance the books" if Reuben made a sizable campaign contribution. Reuben refused, and taking that as Thompson's final word, ended the association. The relationship rested on that basis until later in 1978 when Reuben related his version in a letter. A mutual friend relayed the episode to the governor and Thompson called Reuben to deny any injured feelings from the 1976 campaign. The two declared the matter ended.

Daley did not need polls or professional advice to tell him who should be the 1976 primary candidate against the despised Walker. He wanted Howlett, the only person in the field who could be trusted completely and whose popularity in Chicago and the state would sink Walker.

Daley had a long memory and his enemies seldom got a second chance, but not many remember Daley detesting anyone as thoroughly as he did Walker. Daley wanted him out of the picture because Walker had embarrassed the state, the party, and the mayor. Daley had tried to bring Walker into the party orbit, leaving him room for some independence, but the governor resisted. He twitted Daley at every opportunity.

Daley's single-mindedness about defeating Walker led some observers to declare Howlett a throwaway candidate in the general election. In view of the 1976 election results, that theory looked good. At the time, however, Howlett's popularity across the state was thought to be sufficient to make him a strong candidate against Thompson. Thompson still had not shown any ability to run away with the gubernatorial contest.

Nevertheless, the historical pattern of Democratic mayors playing ball with Republican governors is strong enough to suggest Daley might not have cared whether Howlett or Thompson won in November. Governor Dwight Green and Mayor Edward J. Kelly collaborated in the early 1940s, and Daley had Republican Governor William Stratton eating out of his hand during the 1950s. Although Ogilvie projected an independent image, he and Daley struck early bargains on a number of issues, including a state income tax.

Daley preferred a docile Democrat, such as Kerner or Shapiro, and he certainly did not want a Democrat like Walker who acted independently. Howlett, although able to speak up to Daley, would have played ball most of the time. On the eve of the Democratic State Central Committee's slating meeting in Chicago, the Democrats battled, traded, and made deals. The committee slated Howlett for governor, Hartigan for lieutenant governor (a decision that embittered him), Dixon for secretary of state, and Michael Bakalis for comptroller.

The slating process, and the manuevering required to get Howlett chosen for governor, brought predictable criticism from Walker, who had always refused to appear before the slating committee. Thompson, meanwhile, speaking at Illinois State University two days after the slating meeting, offered a hint of his campaign theme:

> If you look at the ticket they [Democrats] put together, I don't think it is too partisan a characterization to say it is a Daley ticket from top to bottom with only a bone thrown to downstate—Alan Dixon—because that is the only way they could back him off the governor's race . . . .
>
> If that ticket is successful there is a very grave danger that the governor's office, the mayor's office, and the state legislature, and indeed the state judiciary, will all be in the hands of one man. And I don't think that's healthy for Illinois, whether you are a Republican or a Democrat.

Thompson campaigned dutifully for the primary even though he was assured of victory. He had lost nearly forty pounds and the ever-watchful press called him "Slim Jim." Also he watched as the Democrats slugged it out in one of the state's dirtiest primary elections. Accusations came from both sides about alleged misuse of money, conflicts of interest, special interest skullduggery, and flaws of character. Walker started behind and fought like an alley cat. Howlett resisted overwork, saying: "I'm out meeting people 365 days a year. I've met everybody in Illinois at least ten times now. Anyone who thinks they're going to get votes by shaking hands is deluded."

Several issues arose in the primary that haunted Howlett through the general election, but none so much as "news" that he had been paid $15,000 a year for fifteen years by the Sun Steel Company of Chicago Heights. He denied any conflict of interest, despite rumors he had supported legislation that had favored the steel firm. Although the public considered the information new material, Howlett had disclosed the additional income several times before the campaign, and it had passed without mention. Walker made it a fresh issue. "It came as a great surprise to me that anyone didn't know it. It was not 'uncovered.' I brought it out," Howlett explained.

Asked what work he performed for Sun Steel to earn the $15,000 a year, Howlett described the work as consultation on such issues as labor negotiations. He admitted needing the money. "How are you going to raise a family of six children and take care of a ninety-year-old mother-in-law?" he asked.

Howlett successfully shrugged off the Sun Steel revelations and Dan Walker, winning the primary by 115,431 votes. Thompson stomped Cooper by more than a half million votes, constituting 86 percent of the Republican total.

St. Patrick's Day is special for the Irish, of course, but for millions of other persons of ethnic origin in Chicago—Poles, Croatians, Germans, Jews, Italians—it is also a noteworthy day, highlighted by a mammoth parade along State Street. Leading the parade for as many years as persons could remember was Daley, the city's No. 1 Irishman. On St. Patrick's Day, 1976, a day after the primary election, Howlett stood next to the mayor, reviewing the parade.

Resembling two aging, overweight leprechauns in their traditional green hats, they smiled, laughed, and waved to the crowd. Their prominent jowls and protruding stomachs made them look like twins of the auld sod.

Little did either man realize that pictures taken of them at the event— and published widely in newspapers across the state—would play into the hands of Thompson and Republicans who were prepared to make the link between Howlett and Daley a major campaign issue. Then and later, Howlett never denied his friendship with Daley. "I don't make it a secret that I'm a friend of Dick Daley's, and I never knew anyone who ran for office who didn't want his support." But denials did not work, as Howlett found out later.

While Daley savored victory, Thompson plotted strategy, much of it based on information from past elections and some rather obvious observations about the Howlett victory. "Downstate will be the key in the fall," Thompson said. "He'll [Howlett] carry Chicago, I'll carry the suburbs, and downstate will provide the balance either way." Although that analysis required no special wisdom, it did focus accurately on the battleground. Election statistics from 1968 and 1972 made the point more dramatically.

In 1968, Ogilvie won election over Sam Shapiro by 127,794 votes, having received 51.4 percent of the total votes cast. In 1972, he received only 49.3 percent of the total, losing to Walker by 77,494 votes. The difference between victory and defeat for Ogilvie was his showing down-state and in the suburbs outside Cook County.

In both elections Ogilvie received about the same percentage of votes from Cook County: 46.2 percent in 1968 and 47.7 percent in 1972. In the five metropolitan area suburban counties (DuPage, Lake, Will, McHenry, and Kane), Ogilvie received 63 percent of the votes in 1968. Walker reduced that margin to 59.5 percent. Downstate's swing was critical. In 1968 Ogilvie received 56.7 percent; in 1972 Walker whittled that to 50.4 percent.

If the past was reliable, Thompson had to work the suburbs and downstate hard to overcome the expected large Chicago turnout for Howlett. Political experts say a Democrat must build a 250,000 vote lead in Cook County to offset Republican strength downstate.

Primary election returns revealed Howlett's vulnerability outside Cook County. Although Howlett defeated Walker by 115,341 votes and took 53.8 percent of the Democratic primary votes, Walker stomped Howlett outside Cook County. Walker received 113,434 more votes than Howlett in the rest of Illinois's 101 counties. Downstate—outside the collar counties around Cook—Walker won some counties by as much as 75 percent of the vote. In losing, the governor won 86 counties, Howlett only 16.

Election results exposed the myth that Howlett enjoyed strong down-state voter support. Friends of Howlett and the press built that story over several years' time. In fact, in only one election—the 1964 race for auditor—did Howlett carry downstate.

Howlett came away from the primary with other liabilities, too. One was the chasm created by the bitter contest with Walker. Name-calling between Howlett and Walker went beyond the bounds of even the toughest Illinois election battles (Howlett once called Walker "a jalopy spewing dirt"), presenting Howlett with the monumental task of reconciling party factions.

Thompson saw the advantage for him. "The bitterness of the Democratic primary will help me. There will be substantial Democratic defections in the general elections. I would have gotten more defections if Howlett had lost. But I'll get a lot of defections anyway."

Issues from the primary campaign vanished quickly. Thompson was not interested in using smears generated by the Walker campaign, especially the Sun Steel episode. First of all, Thompson did not question Howlett's ethics; but more practically, Walker had been unable to use the issue successfully, and Thompson doubted if it would help him. He wanted to generate his own issues.

Instead of painting a picture of Howlett as an undesirable character, Thompson worked on images that strategists told him would have a more lasting impact on voters. He hammered away at Howlett's link with Daley and took every opportunity to create in the public's mind the contrasts between Howlett and himself in speech, manner, style, dress, and levels of energy.

Daley was not the only issue, Thompson said frequently, but the specter of the mayor stood out above all other issues. Shortly after the primary, Thompson watered the seeds of doubt planted by Walker and others before him, saying: "I do believe that if Mike Howlett were elected the governor of the state of Illinois, the mayor of the city of Chicago would have a vast influence in his administration. And I think every rational person in Illinois believes that as well."

Thompson revealed further rhetorical skills on the Daley subject when confronted once by a reporter about his Chicago origins and background. "Sure, I'm from Chicago, too, but I'm my own man and would be the governor of all the people. I won't be under the control of the man on the fifth floor of Chicago City Hall. You can count on that."

Howlett counterattacked with his own issue: experience. He said, "The job of governor is managerial. Experience is the big issue. You have to have somebody for this unique two-year term who can start operating government right away.... This is no time for rookies.... Inexperience breeds mistakes." On another occasion Howlett said, "In football, you know, I don't care if a quarterback is an All-American in college, it takes five years to learn to run a pro team. A young quarterback is going to make errors. We can't turn it over to a rookie."

The electorate did not swallow Howlett's experience line. Voters had heard too many similar speeches from politicians who did not deliver results. Nixon, Kerner, and Lyndon Johnson all had experience but they had trouble running their professional and personal affairs, too. Thompson played on that doubt and fear when he replied, "What's he administered? The auditor's and secretary of state's offices? Well, so could my mother. Sure, he's done a good job, but what did it consist of? Making sure the auditors audited and the license plates got out."

From the early stages of the contest, the two candidates seldom discussed particular issues of government. Neither felt comfortable with specifics, so they avoided them. The issues of education, highways, aid for cities, the environment, welfare, and business development were largely ignored while the two argued over Daley's influence and Thompson's naivete.

Such discussions of issues were not necessary as long as Thompson expanded his lead in the polls. The strategy called for imagery, and Thompson gave that his best shot every day. Howlett expressed his attitude when he told a reporter, "Issues are bullshit."

Thompson presented the picture of a young, vigorous, hard-working, playful candidate in contrast to the overweight, sedentary Howlett. Percy created the same illusions in 1966 by displaying his youthful appearance in contrast to the older and slower Senator Paul Douglas.

On June 19, 1976, in the midst of the campaign, Thompson paused long enough to marry his former law student, Jayne Carr, in a fancy Chicago ceremony that was acclaimed as the highlight of the social, political, and media season. Until their engagement on May 8, Thompson had remained coy about the relationship and parried questions about marriage. Afterward he said, "Actually, I regret not doing it earlier."

It is easy to see why the two were attracted to each other. They share a similar geographic background—Oak Park and Chicago's West Side—and each attended Northwestern law school, although ten years apart. Above all else they share a deep interest in the law, on the prosecutor side, and in Jim's political career. Jayne once told an interviewer, "A prosecutor has a duty to see justice done—to bring a charge and also to see that the wrong person doesn't go to trial."

Jayne Carr always wanted to be a lawyer—since age eleven, the story goes—and made a career as a prosecutor. She liked to work long hours, weekends and nights, and did not worry about a social life. "I never said I had to be married," she told an interviewer. "In the abstract, it was never important to me. I'd rather be single than be unhappily married and it didn't bother me to stay home on Saturday nights working on a legal brief." Thompson stated his feelings for Jayne this way: "She's good looking, smart, friendly, with a good personality. And I fell in love with her after the fifth or sixth year that we knew each other."

Thompson is responsible for bringing Jayne Carr to the attorney general's office, in 1969, when he served as an assistant to Bill Scott. He left for the U.S. attorney's office and once tried to hire her, but she preferred work for the state and remained there until resigning in 1977. Eventually she became deputy chief of the criminal justice division and earned a reputation as a tough, fair prosecutor.

Thompson and Carr dated with increasing frequency after 1970, and signs of seriousness began to appear. She attended Thompson's announcement for governor in July, 1975, and after that campaigned with him occasionally. They announced their engagement on May 8, 1976, Thompson's fortieth birthday.

Because Jayne Carr worked for the attorney general and Thompson was campaigning, they made hasty plans for the wedding. The Presbyterian church they wanted in Chicago was not available, so they "borrowed" the Episcopal Cathedral of St. James. The bishop permitted Jayne's Presbyterian pastor to perform the ceremony. They entertained more than 500 persons at the reception, in one of the large rooms at the McCormick Inn, not far from McCormick Place on Chicago's lakefront.

There was not much time for a honeymoon and, after a few days in New York, they were back in Illinois to resume the push toward election day. Meanwhile, if Howlett needed more reminders of Thompson's uncanny knack of attracting media coverage, he had only to follow the lengthy accounts of the wedding in the press and on television.

Thompson took his traveling show to county fairs where his uniform often consisted of jeans, boots, and a checkered shirt or a T-shirt (one of his favorites said "I'm a Country Boy"). As the campaign wore on, media representatives asked more questions about the calculated emphasis on clothing. Thompson said he wore the clothes mainly for comfort. "Most of the people who go to county fairs would have thought that I didn't have good sense if I wore dress shoes through all the mud and manure."

On one of his trips to southwest Illinois, Thompson stopped in Monroe County and bought a red Irish setter puppy, which he named Guv. Going everywhere the candidate went, the dog received an incredible amount of media attention. Thompson insisted he would have bought the dog even if he had not been a candidate for governor. "I haven't had a dog since I was fifteen, but I have to admit that Guv has added a nice touch to my campaign."

While Thompson spent much of his time downstate that summer, Chicagoans and suburbanites learned of his travels in Chicago newspapers. In one unflattering article, the *Chicago Daily News* labeled his rural style a "beer can image." Readers got this glimpse of Thompson on the stump: "There is the beer can he carries in almost every parade, the slight drawl he develops when speaking downstate, the Southern Illinois vocabulary . . . like 'I've been takin' quite a lumpin' from Daley and Howlett.'"

The same approach, with slight variations, worked well in most places. At universities he drank beer with students and faculty. If he arrived in town for a newspaper interview, often as not he and reporters would end up having a beer in a nearby tavern. When those present were industrialists or bankers, Thompson wore business suits and kept his shoes off the boardroom tables; and he drank whiskey on those occasions. Thompson knew his way around the country club as well as the countryside, and he charmed the guests at dinner parties and cocktail parties where the subject, in addition to Jim Thompson, usually was money.

While downstate or in the suburbs, Thompson never let up on Daley. Thompson repeated over and over again in Benton, West Frankfort, Herrin, Anna, and Jonesboro that "Daley handpicked Howlett to run for governor," or "Most people—Democrats and Republicans—don't want a governor who is under the influence of the mayor of Chicago."

As the one liners about his opponent rolled off Thompson's tongue, his simplified campaign rhetoric flowed. He promised an "open and decent and honest" administration. He dropped these generalities across the state: "I'll build roads where the traffic need is, not where the votes are . . . ." "People see that government has grown too large, too unloving, too complicated, too unproductive." Neil Mehler, then political editor of the *Chicago Tribune*, called it "a Jimmy Carter style." In one of its articles

Time magazine called Thompson's appeal "Carterish."

No matter where Thompson went, someone seemed sure to say, "Keep putting those crooks in jail." During an interview with a *Chicago Tribune* reporter, Thompson reflected on the phenomenon of being remembered as a prosecutor:

> Many people seem to assume that if you've been a hotshot prosecutor, you can be a hotshot mayor, senator, or whatever. Many prosecutors have fallen victim to this notion themselves.
>
> But politically, nobody's against a prosecutor. Unlike politicians, prosecutors don't have to take controversial positions on civil rights, busing, the economy, and the plight of the cities. Prosecutors put people in jail for committing crimes, and the public favors that.

By early September it appeared to some observers that Thompson led almost by accident; more because of the ineptness of Howlett's campaign than the caginess of Thompson's. What looked like a sometimes chaotic, and always informal, campaign operation was a carefully disguised blitzkrieg. Thousands of dollars rolled in each week to finance a carefully planned media campaign. Bailey and Deardourff, the paid strategists, had a master plan in effect, although Thompson threw them an occasional curve by testing his own instincts. That seemed harmless with such a large lead, and he usually returned to the plan. Thompson's campaign hit its stride about Labor Day and ground on toward election without pause.

Playing catchup in an Illinois gubernatorial campaign after September 1 is an almost hopeless task, doomed without some miracle or scandal. If a candidate for major office is not close to his opponent by midsummer, the contest probably is over. That is the position in which Howlett found himself as private and public polls showed him trailing badly. Making matters worse, Howlett's disposition reflected his plight. He became more surly with the media and less accessible and showed signs of tiring.

Howlett failed to develop an issue of substance on which either to base his own claim for the governorship or to use against Thompson. On the other hand, Thompson did not need to develop issues because he led comfortably, and his image campaign showed no signs of slowing down. Taxation came closest to being an issue for the two, but they both were so cautious that they did not seem to be far apart. Given some license with the language, Howlett and Thompson made it clear they did not intend to raise taxes if elected. Thompson sometimes hedged more, saying he couldn't predict what might happen in the future. Howlett originally left the door open to a tax increase if the level of state services demanded it.

Walker had made rational discussion of the taxation issue difficult, or at least politically risky, and neither candidate was inclined to take risks. By using his "no tax increase" pledge skillfully from 1971 through 1976, Walker threatened to bludgeon any politician who inferred that higher taxes might someday be necessary. He ruined the gubernatorial careers of Paul Simon and Richard Ogilvie with it. Therefore, Thompson stuck to "no promises."

To accusations that he shied away from answering direct questions about taxation, Thompson said: "I don't know how much more candid a candidate can be. My staff already quakes when I talk about taxes."

In one frank discussion of state finances, Thompson acknowledged a potential future need for more taxation. "Someday taxes will go up. I don't know when, how, or how much, but that's the historical trend. I've pointed out that Illinois now has gone seven years without a tax increase, and it has never done that before."

Thompson and his aides revealed the flabbiness of their issues program frequently during the campaign, but that did not bother many persons or organizations. With Thompson so far in front, few groups seemed interested in exploring issues. Newspaper editors, the Independent Voters of Illinois, and the League of Women Voters put on their traditional push for statements on issues, and the candidates responded halfheartedly. Fletcher outlined Thompson's campaign as based on these points: ethics in government, independence from interest groups and powerful political brokers, and economic improvement. Thompson did propose specific ethics legislation in one of his periodic position papers. He suggested

- Giving jail sentences to politicians and lobbyists who violate the peoples' right "to an honest, impartial government."
- Reshaping the Illinois Governmental Ethics Act by increasing the amount of financial disclosure and tightening registration for lobbyists.
- Creating a seven-person board of ethics to examine all disclosure forms.
- Changing lobbying rules to include greater disclosure of expenses, and prohibiting former legislators from appearing as lobbyists.

These ideas formed the backbone of ethics proposals Thompson made to the General Assembly in 1976 and 1977, but the legislature never took any action.

In consultation with Bailey and Deardourff, Thompson and his staff issued a series of position papers to convince voters and the press of Thompson's sincerity in addressing the issues. The papers helped create a favorable image. In contrast, Howlett issued no papers, and did not bother to hire an outside strategist. His staff, said Howlett, would comment on a full range of issues without special statements.

Some of Thompson's position papers dealt in details, others passed over serious subjects with generalities. One Thompson paper dealt with the issue of the Crosstown Expressway. Howlett supported Mayor Daley's plan for a north-south freeway to relieve existing highways from congestion.

The paper declared Thompson as opposed to all plans for a Crosstown Expressway, but left the door open to a future plan that could get his approval. While some read the paper to mean he opposed the Crosstown, the carefully worded statement gave Thompson room to negotiate with Chicago interests.

Background papers appeared on ethics, child welfare laws, proposed dams and reservoirs, the environment, agriculture, and railroad crossings.

While no single paper could be cited as typical, Thompson's positions on the environment, covering thirty-one pages, provided an illustration of how the candidate approached ticklish public issues. The paper adequately reflected Thompson's "no promises" pledge.

Thompson tried to reassure environmentalists and business development interests that he would consider their respective positions on major issues. As an example, he called for upgrading water quality standards for lakes and rivers from which drinking water was taken. To balance the picture, he said industries that installed antipollution equipment should have a ten-year guarantee against having to install new equipment to meet higher standards.

On the other hand, he called for "effective land use planning" to protect prime farmland. He added that such planning must have the "voluntary cooperation of the landowners involved." Casual readers might have missed the contradictions of the statement. Landowner opposition had blocked previous attempts at land use planning in the state, and "voluntary cooperation" hardly seemed likely.

The paper was filled with examples of loose rhetoric without specific suggestions. He called the delay in regulating use and transport of hazardous materials "intolerable" but offered no new solutions. In fact, such regulations did not materialize for almost two years after he became governor. Thompson called for "responsible legislation" on regulation of transport by rail, but offered no specific program.

As the candidates went through the motions, signals appeared everywhere that Howlett's campaign had not gained public acceptance. Campaign funds continued to flow to Howlett, but at a reduced rate, and the Democrats knew that borrowing would be necessary to finish the campaign with a media push. For instance, the Illinois Education Association, more philosophically in tune with the Democratic party than the Republican, endorsed Thompson and contributed generously to his campaign after he voiced support for collective bargaining by public employees.

Losing ground rapidly, Howlett dramatized his positions. He began with a change in his taxation position and followed with an accelerated personal attack on Thompson.

Wanting to appear tougher on a "no tax increase" pledge than Thompson, Howlett promised to veto any tax increase bill in the two-year term beginning in 1977. "I promise . . . the 11 million people of Illinois I will not seek a second term if state taxes are increased during the next two years."

Thompson called the hardened Howlett position a "phony promise." Speaking at Illinois State University in Normal, Thompson said he would do everything possible to keep taxes from going up. "It's irresponsible for a candidate for governor to stand there and make that desperate kind of eleventh hour pledge." Undeterred, Howlett called Thompson "soft" on taxes.

An attempt to link Nixon and Thompson in the public's mind gathered momentum. Howlett said: "Make no mistake about it. He's a Nixon Republican. When he is speaking with Republican businessmen, the truth comes out." Following Howlett's lead in a rare appearance, Walker said: "When the State Chamber of Commerce comes and says business and special interests want this but the people don't, there isn't any doubt, Jim Thompson will sign it. Mike Howlett will veto it."

Neil Hartigan, running for lieutenant governor on Howlett's ticket, picked up the theme and called Thompson "Nixon's lawyer." This prompted editorial comments in Chicago newspapers, with the *Chicago Tribune* seeing the attempt to link Thompson and Nixon as a Daley idea. "This one has been a dry well ever since Mr. Daley started pumping it.... This claptrap will not convince anybody who isn't already convinced.... We can only say, 'Come off it, Mike.'"

Echoing those thoughts, the *Chicago Daily News* called the Democratic strategy "the old guilt-by-association trick." The paper said: "None of the mud slung by Hartigan and the mayor bears on the question before the voters: Is Thompson or Democratic nominee Michael Howlett the better man to lead Illinois as governor for the next two years?"

In a final barrage, the Democrats launched a broad attack on Thompson's record as a federal prosecutor. Responding to the pleas of Democratic friends, Tony Kerner, the late governor's son, made a series of statements in an effort to paint Thompson as having conducted a political vendetta against his father.

Thompson accused Kerner and the Democrats of starting a "dirty, personal" campaign. Acknowledging the increased emotional level of the campaign, Thompson said: "In the last year and a half it has taken a sharp, suddenly dirty, personal turn." Howlett rebutted: "What does he think he's in, a powder puff contest where everybody will bow to him in hopes of getting immunity?" Howlett implied Thompson received financial support from persons who were given immunity from prosecution for their testimony in federal cases.

Early in October, on a campaign swing through Evanston, Howlett used the word "fix" in connection with a political contribution to Thompson from Albert E. Jenner, Jr., a partner in the Chicago law firm of Jenner and Block. Jenner defended a wealthy industrialist who was given immunity by Thompson in a legislative corruption case. The "fix" accusation ignited a series of statements from the two candidates. Temperatures soared with each comment.

The Associated Press quoted Howlett as saying: "I don't pass judgment on what a jury did, but there's something wrong with the system when you let all the millionaires go, you let Marje Everett go, you let Bill Miller go, you let the Crowns, you let the millionaires that testified against Eddie Barrett ... and they gave immunity to Material Service Corporation and there isn't a lawyer in the country that can justify giving immunity to a corporation." Then Howlett mentioned the $5,000 contribution from Jenner, "an attorney for the Material Service Corporation."

By using the word "fix" to describe an immunity agreement and Jenner's contribution, Howlett deliberately attempted to excite the public with a word that engenders negative reactions. Thompson recognized the ploy and said he resented any implication of a fix.

Further confusing the issue, Howlett offered a definition: "...Fix, that is to determine the course of action in the cases prosecuted by the office. He determined for whom immunity was sought, who he would ask the grand jury to indict.... It is in this context that he fixed the Material Service case—by seeking immunity for the corporation and its officers...."

Thompson responded that Howlett "is a kid from the West Side, and so am I. And in the city of Chicago the word 'fix' in the way he expressed it has only one meaning."

Doing what he could for a friend, Daley jumped on the immunity band wagon a few days later. He too mentioned the Material Service case, saying: "Do you have to give immunity to forty or fifty people in a corporation? Why wasn't immunity given to the fella who took 100 or 200 bucks to the legislature? You check, in every case, immunity was given to the man who proposed corruption to the official."

Thompson said the mayor had been "yelling about immunity for years. The people haven't paid attention to it before. I don't think they're going to pay attention to it twenty-nine days before the end of the campaign. All Daley's attack does is to show what we've been saying up and down the state. That is, Daley and Howlett are one and the same." Daley then accused Thompson of granting immunity to tavern owners in order to convict policemen in shakedown schemes and of leaking information to the press in his prosecution of Kerner.

The exchanges strained the ties of friendship between Howlett and Thompson. Newspapers reported that Thompson was so disturbed over the attacks that he planned to "re-evaluate his past friendship with Howlett." Thompson said Howlett "used to be" his friend. "He's the one doing the cutting, but I refuse to bleed," Thompson said. About the friendship: "I think we ought to re-examine that after the election.... I'm not going to make any final judgments now.... It's not the Mike Howlett I know."

Howlett's forces had two surprises yet to pull. Both were doomed to misfire because of timing and desperation.

In October, aides to Howlett began calling in person on newspaper editors to plant rumors of Thompson's homosexuality. At one point a Springfield Democrat mentioned the subject at a dinner party. The rumor never got widespread distribution, but it was not because Howlett helpers did not try. One newspaper editor virtually threw the emissary out of his office. Howlett disclaimed any responsibility for the personal attack, although he knew it happened. He apologized to Thompson.

The story first surfaced in Chicago during Thompson's service as U.S. attorney and before he married. Respectable publications, including *Time*, have alluded to the rumor. Thompson says the story grew out of his bachelorhood until age forty, and the political environment of Chicago where enemies will spread any story if they think it will damage a person's reputation. Thompson says he is not a homosexual and never was. Friends of Thompson who have known him at all stages of his life say they never saw any behavior that might be associated with homosexual activity. Those who have accused Thompson of being a homosexual have not offered any proof or accounts of specific incidents.

The other last gasp occurred on the Sunday before the election. In full-page newspaper advertisements across the state, Howlett shouted: "Don't cast your ballot for governor without reading the truth about Jim Thompson." The ads reiterated accusations that Thompson had been involved in a bribe arrangement with Marje Everett for her testimony against Otto Kerner. The ads said Thompson helped Everett get a racing license in California by not testifying against her during hearings on granting her a license.

The final desperate shot fell flat; the accusation had never been proven before and there was no new evidence to give it life.

All that remained were the election returns, and applause for Thompson. Even before a vote was cast, some national publications were proclaiming a new Republican savior in the midlands.

By election day, November 2, 1976, most Illinoisans who cared knew the next governor of Illinois would be James Robert Thompson. They did not know what kind of governor they were getting. The only impressions they had were from his television appearances, campaign gimmickry, and his statements on the emotional issues of the campaign. If they cared about his understanding of state government, or his philosophy toward public affairs, or how his personal tastes would jibe with his leadership style, they were in the dark. Illinois stood on the threshold of having its third Republican governor in the last twenty-five years (Stratton and Ogilvie were before him), a political rookie, unproven but fun loving.

The two candidates for governor retained their senses of humor long enough to pass this verdict on the campaign:

HOWLETT: I should've bought a dog.

THOMPSON: I said he could have one of the puppies.

Interregnum

On the day after he lost the gubernatorial election to Jim Thompson, Mike Howlett spoke as if he were making a farewell appearance at Yankee Stadium. "It's not my last hurrah, it's my last candidacy," he said. "I've got a lot of hurrahs left."

For immortality, Howlett's last words hardly compete with those of former governor Adlai E. Stevenson, but they weren't bad for a public servant whose memorable speeches and phrases would barely fill an envelope.

They also seemed appropriate for a man who had held statewide elective office sixteen years and who for uncounted years before that had devoted time to partisan politics and public affairs.

Howlett failed in a test between young and old, between old standards and new principles of politics. With those few words, he left public life and Jim Thompson moved in. Thompson could not wait to move into the governor's mansion and assume the governorship. Some persons thought he already looked well beyond Springfield. To such persons Thompson countered:

> The number one lesson I've learned is, you don't go anywhere else until you've first done a good job where you're at, and Jim Thompson isn't moving along anywhere—sideways, backwards or forwards—until he's first been the best governor this state's ever had, or tried to be .... I'm just going to put talk of national leadership, or a national role or national prominence behind me, until I've got a handle on my job as governor of Illinois and can demonstrate some achievements.

Howlett said goodbye in fewer words than Thompson said hello, but both messages came across. Thompson had beaten the Democratic party's best by almost 1.4 million votes, an incredible political feat in a state that has known few runaway elections for governor in its history.

Thompson's election-night celebration in Chicago's Palmer House was an appropriate ending to the campaign and a beginning for the new administration. Workers tallied votes in one room; on another floor Thompson mingled with those who received special invitations (one reporter called it "the money room"). Thompson's staff partied elsewhere.

Faithful workers, friends, hangers-on and even some gate-crashers crowded together in the main ballroom amid deafening dixieland music, waiting to see the candidate and hear his victory speech.

Thompson and company did not disappoint the crowd. After a slide show saluting Thompson's staff, Dave O'Neal, lieutenant governor-elect, was introduced. Then came Thompson, accompanied by thunderous applause and surrounded by banners and signs. Twice during the reading of a prepared statement Thompson broke down, as one observer wrote later, "with sincere emotion, overwhelmed by the movement." Kilian of the *Chicago Tribune* offered another view: "He cried. Cook County politicians never cry, not even when they're sent to the penitentiary." But Thompson did cry, and this was not the first time nor the last.

Borrowing from Churchill, Thompson told the crowd: "This is not the end, nor even the beginning of the end, but it is the end of the beginning."

The beginning ended with a stunning victory for Thompson. He won 100 of the state's 102 counties, and the two counties Howlett won were by narrow margins. In Alexander County, Howlett won by 323 votes; in Gallatin County, by only 31. Downstate figures showed Thompson with 71.5 percent of the vote (including figures from the suburban "collar" counties); in Cook County, Thompson led with 57.6 percent. The final embarrassment for Howlett came in Chicago, where he won by about 160,000 votes—far from the plurality a Democrat needs to carry the whole state. Thompson won twenty of Chicago's fifty wards, certainly a moral victory. Outside the city, Thompson clearly ranked as the suburbanite's man. In the five suburban counties surrounding Cook County, Thompson won by 318,196 votes or 79.5 percent of the total.

Beyond the figures, political speculators looked for surefire explanations for Thompson's triumph. They argued that Thompson had victory handed to him with the selection of Howlett—an ineffective campaigner—as his opponent. They said Thompson rode the crest of a national mood that sought escape from the dilemma and disappointment of Vietnam and Watergate. That explanation, too, had merit. They said the public search for fresh personalities explained victories by Thompson and Carter. In Illinois that parallel did not hold up: Thompson won handily, but Carter lost the state in a close match to Ford.

There were other explanations for Thompson's success which most political observers missed, such as the influence of Governor Walker on the campaign. Although beaten in the Democratic primary in the spring, Walker had almost a full year left to serve in office. He made an easy target. When Thompson wanted to cast himself as a contrast to Walker, the culprit was handy, still residing in the governor's mansion and trying to keep the state's finances in order. Thompson did not have to refer to a vanquished governor or remind the public of his antics. Walker could not avoid controversy, and he obliged Thompson all year long. Thompson told voters he would be quieter and more civil and would give them a "needed rest" from Walker.

While to some observers it appeared as though unpredictable forces had swept Thompson into office, the evidence is strong that Thompson skillfully managed to read public sentiment and devised a campaign that minimized his inexperience. "Crafty" is what Thompson might have been called in an earlier time. "Cool" is more appropriate in the modern lexicon.

Thompson stole and borrowed successfully. He stole Walker's anti-Daley and anti-Chicago theme and refined it. He borrowed Charles Percy's Washington strategists (he paid for them, too) and selected out their best advice. He literally borrowed Percy's and Ogilvie's donor mailing lists. He studied the successful voter coalitions assembled by Percy and Scott and discovered a vote potential well beyond the Republican party.

He used the media, as he had during his prosecutor days in Chicago, to build an image of the independent public servant beholden to no special interest, while he raised more than $2 million for the campaign and incurred enormous political debts. He managed to do this so well that much escaped the eyes of reporters and editors across the state. The public was in a buying mood, and Thompson sold purity and independence, a potent mixture when delivered smoothly.

Always the artful dodger, without appearing to be so, Thompson skillfully played the role of an innocent in the early days of his campaign. The technique kept the media off balance and bought time for the candidate to become acquainted with grass-roots politics and with a passing knowledge of state business. In contrast to the arrogance of Walker and the smugness of Howlett, Thompson sounded refreshingly honest when he admitted that he didn't know everything. And when Thompson talked about the limitations on the power of a governor, as he often did, it was music to the ears of a public weary of officials who abused their authority.

Then, with the media and the public persuaded of his sincerity, Thompson shifted gears, revealing a well-cultivated sense of timing. In interviews early in 1976, Thompson began to demonstrate a newfound self-confidence and familiarity with issues. This new posture coincided nicely with the Democratic primary election, which gave Thompson an opponent with a political record and name recognition.

Occasionally Thompson's inadequacies showed through. Questioned once about his familiarity with higher education policy in Illinois, Thompson nodded knowingly and said he was familiar with Master Plan IV for the state's colleges and universities. Thompson implied knowledge of the strategy and long-term policy for higher education. When it was pointed out that many policies from plans I, II, and III still were in effect, Thompson admitted he had not read them. Such episodes were rare, however, and Thompson slid through the campaign without the thinness of his knowledge becoming apparent to the general public.

With the help of Bailey and Deardourff, the firm he hired almost immediately after becoming a candidate in 1975, Thompson avoided the pitfalls of discussing the issues. In the first year of use, Thompson paid the firm about $100,000 for its services. From Douglas Bailey, Thompson got ideas for the campaign; from John Deardourff, information on how to budget and plan. To criticism that Thompson relied too heavily on consultants, the candidate replied: "I didn't even follow the campaign plan. It recommended that I spend considerable time in the suburbs because there were many swing precincts there that might go either way. But I decided to campaign downstate instead because I wanted to increase my name recognition percentage there." Supporting his boss's independence of outside manipulation, campaign manager James Fletcher said, "Anybody who knows Jim would know it is preposterous to think that he is in the hands of someone else."

The expectation level of the electorate is a major factor in an election, and the successful candidate must recognize and satisfy these expectations. In 1976 the public was receptive to what Thompson could offer: inexperience and a different face. Carefully packaged and presented, Thompson's liabilities—which in another time might have doomed him— became assets. The process astounded professional politicians and political scientists. They were not confounded by the victory, but by how easily Thompson destroyed a political veteran.

Another explanation of Thompson's success was his careful planning and his use of an instinct that had served him well at almost every major crossroad in his life. When tradition and standards of decorum dictated certain behavior, Thompson often ran counter. His behavior irritated traditionalists—just as it did during the campaign when some Republicans thought his campaign manners were unbecoming a candidate for governor—and occasionally got him in hot water. But his actions always separated him from the pack. The pattern started in law school, continued in the state's attorney office, at Northwestern law school, and as prosecutor in Chicago. At every turn, he demonstrated an uncanny feel for the expectation level and tolerance of the public.

Further, the public's expectation level may have been at an all-time low in 1976. Consequently, Thompson appeared to respond to this by promising little more than a balanced budget, a tougher attitude toward crime and punishment, and something called "no promises." Although problems of government and society existed everywhere, the public wanted relief from them and Thompson offered a two-year lull.

In order to satisfy public expectations raised by his campaign, Thompson would have to deal with special interest groups professing to represent society's needs as well as those who simply wanted a larger slice of government funds for themselves. While Thompson succeeded in leaving the impression that he was free of pledges and promises, the inferred commitments could be found in the lists of contributors to the Thompson campaign. One organization that analyzed Thompson's finances was Common Cause, the citizens' lobby, which concluded, "It is obvious . . . that big money and special interests play the dominant role in the way we elect our chief executive in Illinois." The organization said contributors had their hooks in Thompson. An analysis of financial information confirms the existence of a broad special interest coalition from which Thompson received the bulk of his $2.6 million campaign chest.

The 1976 gubernatorial campaign was the first one to be covered by the Illinois disclosure act and the Illinois Board of Elections, which oversees implementation of the law. The board said Howlett spent almost $3.4 million on the campaign, including $1.6 million that he spent to defeat Walker in the primary; Thompson spent less than Howlett, mainly because of the lack of a serious primary contest. Thompson's total expenditures reached $2.4 million. With last-minute contributions from persons and organization wanting to get on the victory bandwagon, Thompson finished with a surplus of $250,000 on which to start his 1978 campaign.

Thompson took a personal interest in collecting, reviewing, and acknowledging contributions. He determined policies under which some contributions were refused. Thomas Reynolds, chairman of Citizens for Thompson in 1976 and 1978, said: "We couldn't deposit a $5 check without his approval. He made decisions on an ad hoc basis, and I never knew the reasons why he returned some checks." With Thompson making all decisions on acceptance, no rules were written to guide Reynolds or his fund raisers. Thompson maintained a defiant attitude about the expectations of donors for favors. "If the highway contractors think I'll pay off on contributions they might as well vote for Howlett." Contractors, among others, were not deterred by Thompson's talk.

The list of major benefactors for Thompson was headed by Ray Kroc, chairman of the board of McDonald's Corporation, operator of the fast-food chain. He gave $46,500, which was more than any other contributor. Kroc gave in spurts of $10,000 and $15,000, apparently in response to telephone calls from Thompson during which the candidate asked for more money. Thompson admitted making frequent requests of Kroc—"You bet I'm going to ask for more"—but the amounts were up to Kroc. "I never ask for a specific amount," Thompson said.

Kroc said he liked Thompson and wanted to help him become governor. Thompson explained: "He took a shine to me. He believes in me. He gave Richard Nixon over a million dollars, so the contributions to me are relatively small in comparison." To questions about Kroc's someday asking a favor, Thompson replied, "I've not made a single promise. Besides, what could I do for Ray Kroc?"

One answer might be "free advertising." During the campaign, Thompson frequently said that the McDonald's "quarter pounder wit! cheese sustains me on the campaign." "Access" is another. Thompson made it clear to individuals such as Kroc and organizations like the Teamsters that he would be accessible, and he would listen. In that limited sense money "talks," because most of the individual contributors to Thompson could not reach the governor by telephone or in person under any circumstance. Contributors who give enough to gain access have opportunities to make their cases for pet projects, a political appointment, or Thompson's support of an issue.

Perhaps, as is often said by those who make large financial contributions to politicians, some donors want only the satisfaction of being at the top of the contributor list. W. Clement Stone, the millionaire insurance tycoon and Republican benefactor, makes such a claim. By his own accounting, Stone has given in excess of $7 million to Republicans. He laid a large portion of that on Nixon. Illinois Republicans Percy and Ogilvie fared less well. Stone's contribution to Thompson's election totaled $37,632.

Other familiar Illinois names were among Thompson's contributors, including Gaylord Donnelley, chairman of R. R. Donnelley & Sons Company, a huge printing company in Chicago. James Bere, president of Borg-Warner Corporation, served as Thompson's finance chairman and contributed, too. A. Watson Armour, III, descendent of the meat-packing family, gave, as did Edward McCormick Blair, Sr., managing partner in William Blair & Co., an investment firm. Blair was a director of Field Enterprises, publisher of the *Chicago Sun-Times*. Leo H. Schoenhofen, board chairman of Marcor, Inc., at that time the parent company of Montgomery Ward, offered funds, as did Edward Carlson, board chairman of United Air Lines.

The Percy mailing list may have helped with the likes of William B. Graham, board chairman of Baxter-Travenol Laboratories, Inc., and a longtime supporter of the senator; and Robert W. Galvin, chairman of Motorola, who has supported Percy's political adventures since the early 1960s.

Cash flow to a campaign is important, especially during the last two months when media advertising must be paid for, and candidates will do almost anything to avoid the tag of "loser" before September. The word was out on Howlett by Labor Day, and contributions began to slip. After running well ahead of Thompson in receipts till midyear, Howlett did poorly during the critical period from July to October. Thompson's political committees reported $1,083,750 in that period and Howlett's $805,723.

Once Thompson became the acknowledged front-runner, organizations stampeded to get aboard. No special interest group wanted to be absent from the contribution list when the election was over. Therefore, it was no surprise that the largest single contribution to Thompson after October 1 came from the Illinois Education Association, which represented 80,000 teachers. Admittedly late in its declaration for Thompson, the IEA's support came after he pledged full funding of the school aid formula. Another late contribution came from the United Auto Workers.

Historically, some of the biggest money in gubernatorial campaigns is contributed by contractors who do business with the state, especially those involved in the construction of highways and state buildings. Their habit is to play both sides of the fence until the contest appears to be turning decidedly in one direction then to unload large amounts of cash on the apparent winner.

Early in the campaign, Howlett held a large edge with contractors, mainly because they are traditionally more generous to Democrats and also because Howlett was believed to be willing to continue old methods of spreading contracts across the state. Through June 30, Howlett's largest contributor was E. A. Bederman, president of Arcole Midwest Corporation, a paving firm which at the time held $49 million in state road contracts. Bederman contributed $20,000 through midsummer.

Until July 1, Howlett received $98,900 in contributions of $500 or more from contractors; Thompson's total was $4,450. The trend changed dramatically toward the end of the campaign. Between July 1 and October 1, Howlett led Thompson $142,000 to $35,000 in contributions from contractors; in the final month of the campaign, however, almost all contributions from contractors went to Thompson. Assessing the last-minute switch among road contractors, Donald Hoagland, Thompson's financial aide, said: "At first, a lot of people figured Howlett could not be defeated. Finally, they decided he could be beaten and they would not be throwing away their money by supporting Thompson."

In its analysis of campaign contributions, Common Cause linked Thompson closely with special interests known to be active lobbyists with Illinois governors and legislatures. Part of Common Cause's effort was to build a case for public financing of elections, so the organization drew conclusions accordingly. One Common Cause statement concluded, "As the cost of campaigning continues to skyrocket...we can expect that big money and special interest money will become ever more important."

In the Common Cause report on large contributors, the organization computed that more than $1.4 million, about half the total, was contributed in amounts over $500. Business interests topped the list with a total of $299,834, which should not have surprised anyone familiar with donations to Republican candidates. Four other categories showed contributions of $40,000 or more: medical groups, $48,981; construction contractors, $47,250; partisan political committees and individuals, $47,079; and labor organizations, $41,500. Only the contribution by labor was a surprise, because of labor's historic leanings toward Democratic candidates. However, Thompson paid the debt by appointing an official of the United Auto Workers to be the director of the Department of Labor. Thompson also received $30,484 from the legal profession, mostly from friends in the Chicago area.

Badgered by Common Cause to make clear his position on public financing of state election contests, Thompson understandably ducked the issue. In less than two years, he would face another, probably more serious, political challenge, and he had to begin almost immediately to plot 1978 financial strategy.

With campaign memories, celebrations, and analyses behind him, Thompson drifted into the awkward period between election and inauguration when decisions need to be made about the new administration's directions, but the election victor has no authority and limited resources. Traditionally, transition time had been quiet in Illinois politics, unlike the presidential interregnum, when the White House press corps records every whisper.

Thompson's transition period began in the normal pattern with establishment of committees to study the old ways and think of new ones. Before the two months ended, however, Thompson's world had turned upside down: critics had thumped the governor-elect with harsh words, and Thompson's first attempt at influencing the legislature had fallen with a thud.

Election dust hardly had settled when Thompson began to make personal appearances outside Illinois. State capitol press corps representatives joked that Thompson would be making all important announcements from foreign locations so the citizens of Illinois could read about them first in the New York Times. Wire services and newspapers began taking note of the governor-elect's absences and travel schedule. The Associated Press reported early in December that Thompson had made three trips outside the state and was planning a fourth. In the space of a month he had not appeared formally before any major organization or group in Illinois. His smashing victory and the rarity of being a Republican governor—there were only twelve in the nation in 1976—made him popular outside Illinois, but taxed his popularity at home.

Three days after the election, Thompson spoke in Washington, D.C., to a group of campaign consultants and corporate lobbyists on political tactics. Then came a seminar for new governors held in Pinehurst, N.C. Two weeks later Thompson was back in Washington for the National Republican Governors' Conference. Thompson's fourth out-of-state speaking invitation was to address the National Conference on State Government Relations in Fort Lauderdale. Before he left on the Florida trip, grumbles began appearing in print.

Thompson smarted under criticism of his travels. "I'm the governor-elect," he told the *Chicago Sun-Times* in December, 1976, "but I'm not on any state payroll. I have to spend my days doing state business without compensation and practice law at nights in order to pay the mortgage." Thompson felt he "should be entitled to attend conferences and [make] speeches" at any time.

Thompson denied he had been away from Illinois too much in the transition period. He also noted that he could have been away a lot more. "I've gotten maybe fifteen requests to speak at Republican fund raisers all over the nation, and if I were running for president, I could have instant visible exposure all over the place. But I turned them down." Thompson explained the sniping by editorial writers and politicians by saying, "Now I understand the psychology of this. Neither the press nor your fellow politicians like to see anyone win that big, so they're going to chop at you a little bit, just to let you know you are mortal."

Unexpectedly, Thompson cancelled the Florida trip. Aides said he needed to be in Illinois for the "veto" session of the General Assembly, a period of a few days during which the legislature attempts to override vetoes by the governor. The timing of the legislative session and criticism of his travels obscured the exact reasons for Thompson's decision not to go to Florida.

The legislature and lame duck Governor Walker were locked in a battle over appropriations passed the summer before. Walker, using the amendatory veto power which permits a governor to reduce appropriations subject to confirmation by the legislature, had irritated legislators with what they called indiscriminate action. Walker said the state's financial stability was at stake.

The question of overriding Walker's vetoes was important for Thompson because of the state's tenuous cash flow situation, mostly the result of spending without much restraint by the governor and legislature in the early years of Walker's administration. If Walker's vetoes were overturned, the first six months of Thompson's administration might be awash in financial troubles.

Thompson plunged headfirst into the veto session with a blitz campaign to save the state from more financial headaches. He met with legislative leaders in Chicago and issued a public statement at one of his rare public appearances in Illinois since the election. "I will use every means at my disposal as governor-elect and as governor to prevent the state of Illinois from going into bankruptcy," he proclaimed. That was an obvious exaggeration, made more for drama than for the record. Unable to resist the forum, Thompson added: "I will similarly use all my power to prevent a tax increase in this or the next fiscal year in order to pay for the reckless consequences of any override."

Those were strong words from an untested governor-elect who had no authority and even less experience in dealing with the legislature. He was using what leverage he had as an incoming governor who could get some measure of revenge once in power if the legislature did not heed his advice. Legislatures are not easily dissuaded by a rookie, however, and by the time Thompson entered the picture the override process had begun. It continued unabated.

A few days later, Thompson again appealed to legislative leaders and appeared at a closed-door Republican caucus in Springfield. He asked Republican legislators, a distinct minority in both houses, to sustain the vetoes of Walker. In effect, Thompson asked his partisan colleagues to reject the temptation to make Walker pay one last time for his transgressions. The legislature wanted to punish the lame duck governor who had whipped senators and representatives unmercifully for three years.

One Republican legislator expressed the sentiment of many. "By the time he came down here Wednesday morning, just about everybody was already locked in on how they were going to vote. Most of us were impressed with his appeal, but it came too late." A convenient excuse no doubt, but convenient or not that is how matters turned out. The legislature overrode Walker's vetoes and restored $69 million in appropriations.

Thompson could not win. While his efforts to defend the unpopular Walker may have been a sign of statesmanship, Democrats saw no reason to be gentle with the incoming Republican governor. Legislators decided to teach a lesson to the new kid on the block, the kid who had whipped Howlett, one of Springfield's favorite politicians. Another Republican legislator put Thompson's dilemma in perspective: "I don't think he knows just how rough they can play around here. If he thinks that he can win legislative battles with speeches and statements to the press, he's got a lot to learn."

Thompson learned the hard way, but he learned just the same and created a helpful image for himself in the process. State income in the next six months more than covered additional expenditures. In the minds of some citizens, Thompson had shown a willingness to enter the Democratic lions' den without fear of the consequences. Actually, he had little to lose.

The skirmish reinforced Thompson's feeling that accommodations with Democratic leadership in the legislature and with Mayor Daley would be imperative in 1977. Citing Democratic domination of the legislature and his status as a minority party governor, Thompson feigned executive impotency in order to head off criticism by the media for not having a specific program. Thompson said: "There's a finite limit to the powers of a governor to persuade. A governor can rarely do things by himself."

The protest of limited power meant that Thompson had no intention of bulling his way through the first six months of his term and leaving behind a trail of confrontations and political liabilities. The mandate from the electorate—as Thompson interpreted it—was to chart his course carefully. In the end, events of December made it easier for Thompson to satisfy public demand with modest legislative goals.

The public got little impression during the transition period of what Thompson had in mind for his administration. Occasional tidbits with little substance surfaced in Thompson's rare public statements and press conferences. During an interview at the Pinehurst, N.C., governors' meeting, for example, he pledged to overhaul state government structure, with priority to be given to reorganization of the law enforcement agencies. That seemed more of a casual comment than the outline of plan.

Much of the governor's energy and that of his transition staff went toward preparation of the first Thompson budget, due for release in March. Thompson's campaign pledge to balance the budget, control spending, and avoid a tax increase telegraphed his punch. "There is a simple set of alternatives," he said. "One, you can cut spending growth below revenue growth to build up your balance. Two, you can go broke. Three, you can raise taxes. Only number one is acceptable to me."

While Thompson waited for his inauguration, Illinois Republicans, who had been out of the mainstream in Springfield since 1972, rubbed their hands in glee, anticipating an outpouring of patronage. Thompson considered patronage his number one headache during the transition and during his first two years in office. As grumbles were heard from county chairmen, Thompson noted, "This is still a patronage-oriented state and Republicans are impatient with us for not filling jobs with Thompson people and throwing out Walker people." He claimed there were not as many jobs as politicians thought.

County chairmen longed for the good old days of the forties, fifties, and sixties when a new governor marched into office and fired people wholesale, then replaced them with loyal workers in his own party. That was done as late as the Ogilvie administration, but changes occurred, altering the way patronage was handled. Court decisions restricted the absolute right of governors to remove state employees, and Ogilvie and Walker had put thousands of state employees under protection of civil service codes.

Complicating the patronage picture was an overt effort by Walker and his staff in their final days to fill scores of vacancies, especially those from which persons could not be removed for political reasons. The cumulative effect reduced patronage opportunities for Thompson. In Chicago, for example, where patronage is as much a part of life as the trash collector (and they are often related), gubernatorial hiring opportunities were severely restricted. Local politicians made no effort to understand Thompson's explanations.

As if patronage troubles were not enough, Thompson found filling key executive positions a slow, frustrating task. He appointed a special Committee on Executive Appointments to develop a hundred or so names from which he could choose the thirty-five top aides he needed, as well as scores of persons for lesser positions. Chairman Gene Croisant, a thirty-nine-year-old Chicago banker, took longer than expected to build a list of candidates. Combing Illinois and elsewhere, Croisant developed a list of one thousand names and files. Even with that list, hiring went slowly. Croisant blamed the failure to lure executives from other locations in Illinois on "inadequate" salaries. The two-year term also affected the search. Croisant found persons entrenched in the Chicago area, for example, who were uninterested in uprooting families for less than two years; no one was willing to bet in advance on Thompson's re-election in 1978. As a result, the job of filling most executive positions in the administration drifted into 1977.

Despite a balky legislature, criticism of travels to other states, nervousness over a first budget, and the pressures of starting a new administration, the governor-elect retained much of the personal thrill of victory and anticipated running one of the nation's largest and most influential states with enthusiasm. He was prepared to take the giant step to governor and enjoy it.

Then, with the festive air of Christmastime upon Illinois, the state's political basket was overturned. Richard J. Daley, mayor of Chicago since 1955, died on December 20.

Daley, Democrats, and Deals

In Chicago, during the final days of his campaign for governor, Jim Thompson listened as a citizen reminded him of the city's reputation as a Democratic stronghold. "This is my city, too," he said. The defiant tone reflected Thompson's determination, before and during the campaign, to stake a claim on Chicago. His roots were too deep to deny self-interest, and as a politician he knew the importance of Chicago to any success as a governor.

To fathom the relationship of the governor of Illinois and the mayor of Chicago requires an understanding of practicality, accommodation, and communication. Talk has been cheap throughout Illinois political history. Most governors before Thompson delighted in an occasional attack on the city's reigning monarch as a means of declaring independence. The true test of making the politics work was in being available for a telephone conversation or a dinner meeting to talk business. Most mayors would ignore an occasional public outburst in return for the privilege of accessibility. Thompson planned to be accessible.

The practical governors of the last sixty years—Lowden, Green, Stevenson, Stratton, Kerner, Ogilvie—learned to work effectively within the system. Occasionally one came along who could not or would not, and he suffered for it. Henry Horner, in the 1930s, and more recently Dan Walker defied the mayor of Chicago publicly and privately. Horner beat the system, serving two terms from 1933–40, but Walker paid the price for his "independence" when Daley did all he could to defeat him in 1976.

The practicality exhibited by the governors mentioned grew from common experiences, experiences that were shared to some extent by Thompson. First, all except Stratton were from Chicago or environs. After their political careers ended they planned to return to Chicago to work—among the politicians. None of them wanted to be an outcast. Further, each had had experience with elective politics in the city, either personally or in behalf of another. Thompson's upbringing on the West Side and his work as U.S. attorney provided him with the background to understand how his predecessors had handled the governor-mayor relationship.

There was irony in Thompson's position. Daley and his associates remembered the prosecutor years when Thompson ignored the tradition of winking at political corruption and sent the mayor's friends to jail. If the

tradition that Thompson ignored constituted part of the Chicago system—
as it did—then the hound was about to sit down to dinner with the fox.

Thompson knew an accommodation with Chicago had to be struck.
As an overture, he leveled off criticism of Daley and the Chicago interests
when the campaign ended. Daley suffered several setbacks in the election—
not just Howlett's loss—and he needed time for licking his wounds. Also,
there were bridges that had to be built between them. Daley remembered
Thompson's prosecuting record; and their ages—Daley was seventy-four,
Thompson forty—put them in different generations with vastly different
styles. As prosecutor and candidate, Thompson did not depend on Daley
for anything—friends, clout, or protection. The game would be played
differently starting in January, 1977.

Everyone who studied or knew Richard J. Daley over the twenty-one
years of his mayoralty understood what came first: Chicago. Maybe in a
personal sense his family ranked higher, but that was subject to debate.
Some of his early comments, uttered upon becoming a candidate for mayor
in 1955, reveal the strong commitment to religion and family that burned
in him. His roots—personal, religious, political—were in the Bridgeport
neighborhood on the South Side where he lived and on the fifth floor of
city hall where he worked. "I would not unleash the forces of evil...,"
Daley declared. "I will follow the training my good Irish mother gave
me—and Dad. If I am elected I will embrace mercy, love, charity, and
walk humbly with my God."

Performing one of the greatest balancing acts in the history of American politics—sometimes in the name of good, but always in the name of
Chicago—Daley developed Chicago into "the city that works." Chicago's
interests prevailed over almost all others, Daley's biographers have concluded, and that priority in turn dominated his involvement with Springfield politics. Daley understood Springfield because he had served in the
state house and senate from 1937–46. He knew firsthand the leverage
needed to make sure Chicago got its share of state money. In most sessions
of the legislature, Daley could deliver 20 of 59 votes in the state senate
and up to 50 of the 177 in the house. If they were not always enough to
swing approval, they were almost always enough to deal defeat. The
legislature never met without the Chicago presence felt.

Using that as a base, Daley spent two decades getting funds to build
Chicago. Also, he had phenomenal success keeping the monster of reform
from the door. A good example of this was the issue of judicial reform.
Numerous times during Daley's tenure as mayor legal interests in Chicago
and downstate combined to propose merit selection of judges, knowing
that that would strike at the heart of Daley's influence with the court
system in Cook County. Daley's forces beat back each attempt, because the
Chicago political system could not afford to relinquish judicial control.
The result, for Illinois as well as Cook County, was a statewide judicial

system based on the elective process, and in Daley's domain that meant that justice depended on political considerations.

With leverage in the legislature and influence with a major portion of the state judiciary, Daley needed only an accommodation with the executive branch to complete the triangle of control. He achieved that in some instances by treating a cooperative governor with political consideration at election time. Stratton is a case in point.

William Stratton, a Republican, might never have served beyond a single term if it had not been for Daley. First elected in 1952, Stratton had a disastrous first term. Corruption in his administration threatened chances for his re-election in 1956. However, a characteristic of Stratton's first term had been sympathy toward Chicago's interests.

Daley controlled the selection system for statewide Democratic candidates. Through the party slating process he chose Cook County Treasurer Herbert C. Paschen to run for governor in 1956. Paschen dropped out of the race when a "flower fund" scandal arose. Democrats wanted someone to run against Stratton who could take advantage of the corruption issue. Daley chose a virtual unknown, Richard B. Austin, a judge from Chicago, who had no charisma, no name recognition, and no chance. Political observers have concluded that Daley tossed Austin to the wolves, thus assuring Stratton's re-election and the Republican's eternal gratitude. That gratitude paid off for Chicago in help from Springfield for building the extensive system of expressways and tollroads in the Chicago area.

After a period of eight years, during which Democrats Otto Kerner and Samuel Shapiro served in the governorship, Republican Richard B. Ogilvie, a former sheriff of Cook County and president of the Cook County board, became governor in 1968. Those looking for Daley's hand in that election pointed to the mayor's choice of Governor Shapiro, a weak campaigner, to run against Ogilvie. The arrangement was to Daley's advantage. With Ogilvie as governor, the presidency of the Cook County board returned to the Democratic party. Furthermore, Ogilvie had worked to build a legitimate Republican party in Cook County; with his removal, those efforts were set back.

Before the Ogilvie administration had been in office six months, the governor and mayor made one of the most spectacular arrangements in state history. They agreed to push a state income tax through the legislature. The state needed a new source of revenue and Daley could see the value to Chicago in light of the percentage that would come to the city. Chicago interests steered the tax issue through the General Assembly and the bill was signed by Ogilvie.

When Daniel Walker became governor in 1972, Daley made several attempts to reach accord with him, but most of them fell through. Walker would not modify his anti-Daley, anti-Chicago theme song. They met, talked, and even agreed on some plans that benefitted Chicago, but Walker resisted the big plans, most notably the Crosstown Expressway. Even Ogilvie supported the expressway, but Walker refused. While Daley's anger toward Walker developed from several experiences, the Crosstown stood as the largest monument to the failure of the governor-mayor system from 1973–77.

Evidence is undeniable that Daley liked working with Republican governors, especially if the alternative was a maverick Democrat. That is why Daley never gave Adlai E. Stevenson III, Walker, or Sargent Shriver the chances they wanted to run for governor. Stevenson chose the U.S. Senate instead; Walker defied Daley and ran on his own; and Shriver left Illinois for other political pursuits.

Deterioration in Daley's ability to control all he touched was inevitable. Some marveled that he delayed it as long as he did. By 1976, signs of weakness had been detected—enough for an occasional cry from the hopeful that Daley's influence was crumbling. Insiders laughed, but they saw plaster falling.

In the primary election, Daley's triumph over Walker received the headlines, but it obscured setbacks. One came in the city's first congressional district on the predominantly black South Side. There, longtime black leader U.S. Representative Ralph Metcalfe defied Daley once too often and the mayor slated an opponent against the congressman. Metcalfe won in a bruising battle, providing impetus for talk that Daley had lost his longtime hold on the city's black vote. Daley's biographer Milton Rakove, a political scientist, disagreed. "...Metcalfe's victory, which has been interpreted by some a harbinger of a successful black reform movement, is no such thing." True to the code of Chicago politics, Rakove said, Metcalfe's win meant blacks wanted more of the pie, not reform. Daley could keep the blacks if he would give up some territory.

In other primary elections, Rakove saw a growing dilemma for Daley. The victories of two independent Democrats for the state supreme court from the Cook County district revealed a suburban vote that eluded Daley. Rakove observed that "...suburbanites will support quality machine candidates, will vote against traditional party hacks, and will cross party lines for issue-oriented candidates who support suburban interests. The machine's power at these levels will diminish, even as its power in the city remains stable."

Ominous results came from the general election, too. Thompson's victory over Howlett hurt, although it was inevitable. Closer to home, and more important to Daley, Republican Bernard Carey defeated Edward Egan, Daley's choice for Cook County state's attorney, a powerful position in Daley's backyard. Republicans had not held that office since 1960.

On the more visible side, Daley's national stature suffered when Gerald Ford won Illinois, despite an all-out push by Democrats for Carter. The Illinois result decreased the state's influence with the new administration in Washington. The Associated Press concluded: "Daley still retains his control over the city and can still deliver Chicago votes. But his state and national power seems to be draining away."

Not so, declared Andrew Greeley, a Roman Catholic priest and syndicated columnist living in the Chicago area. The conclusions reached by political writers were old stuff, he claimed. "After each defeat the national press and some of the local press cheerfully announce that the organization is dead. Anyone reading such headlines should be wise enough to suspect that reports of its demise may be premature." The Greeley explanation: Illinois Democrats never do well in the gubernatorial contests; Carter's loss was a "suburban loss," not a city loss.

As always in the free-wheeling Illinois political atmosphere, there was another voice just as loud waiting to be heard. It belonged to Studs Terkel, a writer and Chicago media fixture who never gave Daley an inch, in life or death. In Terkel's eyes, the 1976 election pattern provided final denial of the Daley myth. "As a figure of national importance, Richard J. Daley died on election night, 1976," Terkel declared. "Again, it need not have been, and none would have been the wiser. Autistically, he chose a handpicked hack, Mike Howlett, as his party's gubernatorial candidate against a highly popular young Republican."

Implying that Daley had his head in the sand, Terkel declared that "Jim Thompson swamped Daley's choice by an unprecedented majority and thus carried Illinois for Gerald Ford." Terkel believed Daley should have slated State Treasurer Alan Dixon to run against Thompson. "Thompson would have been given a real run for his money.... The myth of the kingmaker would have been intact."

Myth or not, as Thompson approached inauguration—and the day when he and Daley would hold the two most important positions in Illinois—he faced the imperative of three important words: Deal or die.

That time was only a few days away when, on December 20, the mayor showed up in the office of his physician, Dr. Thomas Coogan, complaining of a pain in his chest. Coogan said: "He told me he had a very brief episode of pain in his chest which lasted a few seconds. When I examined him I found an atrial fibrillation, which is an abnormal rhythm in the upper part of his heart, and I felt he should be in a hospital."

Coogan left Daley alone to make hospital arrangements. "When I returned," the doctor said, "he was on his chair but unconscious and with a heartbeat." Coogan summoned fire department paramedics and a Catholic priest. The mayor's wife Eleanor and several of the couple's seven children came quickly. The family prayed the Rosary in Coogan's office as doctors tried to revive the mayor. Daley was pronounced dead at 3:40 p.m. by Dr. Coogan.

The outpouring of sentiment began immediately and did not abate for days. It revealed what had been known before: Daley was respected by Chicago businessmen, party professionals, and precinct workers; all would dearly miss the Irishman. They also worried about who might take his place. As the city mourned, the scramble began to determine his successor. Daley had not anointed anyone because he had no particular reason to fear death just then. Also, Daley knew a chosen successor would still have to fight for the job, and Daley would not be able to help.

Early speculation on a successor ran the gamut of those close to Daley, including Michael Bilandic, the city's chief legal officer and alderman from Daley's Eleventh Ward; Wilson Frost, a fifty-year-old black attorney and presiding officer at City Council meetings when the mayor was absent; George Dunne, president of the Cook County Board; and State Senator Richard Daley, the mayor's son.

The death caused reverberations not only in Chicago but in Springfield as well. Representative Michael McClain, Democrat from downstate Quincy, said: "If I were Jim Thompson, I'd be nervous right now. Before you could deal with one guy. Now you may have to deal with forty-two." He referred to the number of state representatives from Chicago.

That prospect had occurred to Thompson and his aides. Zale Glauberman, Thompson's legislative adviser, commented: "The big unknown is what this means in terms of the influence of the delegation from Chicago. It will embolden the guys trying to break the Irish Mafia. . . . I don't think there will be a show of solidarity unless someone can grab the reins quickly." Glauberman could see an ethnic war for Daley's empire developing among the Irish, Poles, Italians, and blacks.

James Fletcher, soon to be Thompson's deputy governor, took a nervous view of the city-state relationship without Daley. "It will be difficult to have a program for the city with the mayor gone. Our commitment to the city will remain strong, but the way in which we approach the city will in large part be determined by the leadership that emerges." In other words, Fletcher said, we'll wait for you to make the first move, but we're still willing to talk. The message got through. Thompson, speaking in vague terms, implied there might be an expanded role for him in meeting the needs of Chicago interests, such as development of business and industry.

Daley not only had not tapped a successor in Chicago, he had not indicated a preference for new leadership in the legislature. While Chicago politicians played their marbles for an interim mayor, the legislature, scheduled to begin in less than a month, remained without leadership. The vacuum existed because Gerald Shea, Daley's man in the house, had retired. Cecil Partee, the senate president, had given up his seat to run as Daley's candidate against Scott for attorney general.

A few days after Daley's death, officials reached a consensus on an interim mayor: Michael Bilandic. News stories described the fifty-four-year-old Bilandic as "colorless, single, and quiet." Of Croatian descent, a lawyer, a Daley confidante and neighbor, Bilandic was reported to be lacking legislative experience and knowledge of Illinois outside the metropolitan area. What few persons knew was that Bilandic had spent twenty years working with the mayor, learning his methods, and studying the results. He put that knowledge to use in the political skirmishing that led to his selection. Eight days after Daley's death, Bilandic took over as interim mayor, saying he would not be a candidate in the special election for the unexpired portion of Daley's term, which was to end in 1979. Furthermore, Bilandic said he would return to the practice of law after serving in the interim post.

Bilandic's plan to step down changed when quarreling factions in the party could not agree on another candidate for mayor. Inspired by the sons of Daley, the factions reached a compromise, and Bilandic declared his candidacy for mayor in the April primary. Various elements of the party threatened to oppose Bilandic, but no major threat surfaced. Bilandic won easily over four opponents.

The primary victory was for all purposes the general election, as the Republican party barely existed in the city. Only a candidate whose appeal could cut across party lines might have a chance. That conclusion led to speculation about Ogilvie, but he declined after studying the possibilities. Democratic factions had submerged their differences behind Bilandic, and Ogilvie saw no opportunity to splinter the forces.

Bilandic's Republican opposition in the June general election was Alderman Dennis Block, a little-known city politician handpicked by Thompson to make the sacrificial run.

Before the primary, Thompson made visible contributions to Block's campaign, leaving no doubt of his support. Thompson's campaign committee, Citizens for Thompson, donated $10,000 to Block and loaned a political operative from the Thompson staff to coordinate and plan Block's effort. Citizens for Thompson paid the director.

During the general election campaign, from April to June, Chicago newspapers criticized Thompson for what they felt was a half-hearted effort in behalf of Block. In an interview, Thompson explained the understanding he had with Block. "I told Block when we started that I wasn't going to sever relations with the city of Chicago or do anything in a political way to hurt the city or the interests of the state for his benefit. He understood that." Thompson felt an obligation to support a Republican, rather than let the party go unrepresented.

The campaign languished. No one expected Block to win, but Bilandic needed to roll up a big vote spread to establish his claim to Daley's empire. The bombshell came on May 12, when Thompson and Bilandic jointly announced from city hall that the state would help finance a major expressway project. Thompson had approved a deal to bring about the long-discussed Crosstown Expressway. To avoid the old term, Thompson called the plan the Burnham Corridor.

The announcement jolted Block. Thompson left a campaign trip with him to make the announcement with Bilandic. Block had not known of the announcement until just before the press conference. It became obvious as the story of Crosstown unfolded that Thompson valued Chicago Democratic help in the legislature more than he valued anything else politically at the time, including Block's campaign. More was at stake than saving face with a Republican mayoral candidate.

Daley had proposed that the Crosstown Expressway run north and south through the western portion of the city. He had bipartisan support, including Ogilvie's, for the project until Walker became governor. Claiming the expressway would displace too many citizens along the route, Walker refused to work out a deal with Daley. Crosstown became a symbol of the tug-of-war between Daley and Walker, but Daley never gave up.

Prior to the 1976 primary, Howlett had announced support of a modified Crosstown, but Thompson opposed Howlett and Daley's plans, leaving the door open for another arrangement. In January, 1977, he told the Economic Club of Chicago that Crosstown "is an idea whose time has gone" and state funds should be used for other projects. Thompson suggested the money be used for highway improvement, an extension of the Chicago Transit Authority elevated line to O'Hare airport, and a Franklin Street subway in the city. That was a come-on, for Thompson knew that Chicago did not plan to give up on Crosstown even with Daley dead. The statements notwithstanding, Thompson and Bilandic began talking about a Crosstown arrangement. Each needed to make a quick record for himself, and Thompson especially needed help in balancing the state budget.

In agreeing to Crosstown, Thompson had reversed his field slightly. "I felt a certain amount of discomfort," Thompson said, "because I had condemned Howlett's half-a-Crosstown, as I called it, pretty strongly during the campaign. . . . Some people have pointed out that [Crosstown] bears a remarkable resemblance to Howlett's proposal which I attacked. To that extent, it appears I'm going against my campaign position."

Thompson said if the Crosstown proposal he and Bilandic approved was built in the same fashion that Howlett's highway was proposed "then I have gone back on the campaign promise." If that occurred, he said, and if the public saw that as wrong "I'll be punished politically, or at least there will be the opportunity to punish me politically." Thompson believed the public has a short memory, and he doubted if Crosstown would be a liability.

Thompson worked hard to sell the plan across the state. While most of the funds for Crosstown, and for the other road projects in the same package, were to come from the federal government, some state funds were required. Without sufficient funds in the treasury, Thompson had to get authority from the legislature to issue bonds. Although a number of downstate legislators grumbled and spoke against the "deal," the sale of $162 million in bonds was approved.

To quiet downstaters, Thompson said: "Downstate's got nothing to complain about; they got their money first. The Burnham Corridor will be a long time building." He pointed out that Crosstown had to go through environmental impact studies and court proceedings. "It takes time to plan a highway of that magnitude, and I don't know where it's going to go or how long it's going to be, but I know I got my money for downstate." The package of highway projects, of which Crosstown was one, totaled $1.5 billion in state and federal money.

A deal had been cut and everyone knew it. Thompson, therefore, spoke of the arrangement openly. It became clear that legislative cooperation was part of the bargain. "Democrats organized the house and senate," Thompson said. "They had the votes; they had the horses. You have to accommodate them to get your program passed. So you have to make agreements that give them some of what they want to get some of what you want."

Until the Crosstown agreement, the legislature had dawdled and refused to accept Thompson's budget requests. After the Crosstown deal, most appropriations fell in line with Chicago impetus and Thompson got his balanced budget.

The trade-off meant Thompson could campaign for re-election in 1978 having made good on a promise to balance the budget. Crosstown gave Bilandic a needed boost in the mayoral campaign, and he ran up huge margins of victory across the city on election day. Bilandic passed the test of whether or not he would fill Daley's shoes.

Again the practical side of Thompson prevailed. He made good on a pledge to be accessible and was amenable to a proposal affecting Chicago. In an interview with columnist Neal Peirce after the Crosstown announcement, Thompson stated his philosophy toward getting along with Chicago that would be used again during his administration. "Where we can't get along, we'll fight. . . . But that doesn't mean that I refuse to recognize that an entity called the Chicago city hall exists; because it certainly does."

The First Year

In the first six months of his term as governor, Jim Thompson made it clear he understood what the people wanted. They wanted a rest, and he had the sleeping pill. In a series of statements, he declared:

> Save money and get off the people's back. I think maybe that is the issue. Give us a little peace and quiet . . . .
>
> The newspapers keep wanting me to be an activist governor. I think most people would like two years of being left alone . . . .
>
> I said maybe the mood of the people of Illinois—after four years of Walker, fighting, and confrontation—was to have two years with nothing happening to them . . . .

Carefully drawn from his campaign experience and from his research findings, those opinions represented Thompson's elixir for the state's ailing condition. He added a balanced budget, but little more; he believed the public did not want much more.

The Thompson administration began with symbols and contrasts, reflecting the campaign in its superficial nature. Thompson opened his inaugural with a speech devoid of specifics and full of slogans:

> There will be no jobs bought; there will be no favors sold.
>
> Impropriety will be treated firmly by the law; the appearance of impropriety will be treated firmly by me; the need for public confidence will tolerate neither.
>
> No citizen seeking help will be asked his or her party allegiance or political loyalty; this is a government for all the people.
>
> Promises will not be made if they need someone else's help to fulfill; and promises made will be promises kept.
>
> Every budget will be examined . . . .
>
> Higher taxes will never be justified if today's taxes are misspent . . . .
>
> All of Illinois is our constituency; there will be no tactics of confrontation; there will be no politics of division.

During his first months in office, Thompson planned to concentrate on giving the impression of governing less while balancing the budget, holding the line on taxes, and reminding people of his commitment to tougher

118

penalties for criminals, ethics for public officials, and restraints on spending.

Thompson went from "no promises" to "few programs."

As appealing as that sounded to a weary electorate, Thompson could not stop there. He had to be visible, and that is where the "politics of personality" came in. This political style got him to the governor's mansion, and Thompson believed it would keep him there. He was prepared to sell to the public the image of a physically fit, mentally sharp young governor wrestling with the complexities and frustrations of government.

Thompson's public appearances could be compared to a ten-second television commercial. He spoke simply and in declarative sentences. He gave quick, easy answers to most questions. He presented an array of kaleidoscopic impressions to be soaked up by those watching. Responses to his simplifications reinforced the imagery, as in the case of radio commentator Paul Harvey, who on inauguration day, January 10, 1977, declared of Thompson: "At least there is one honest politician left."

Only one other politician appeared in early 1977 to be as successful with imagery as Thompson and that was President Carter. Watching the inauguration ceremonies on television, Thompson must have wondered, as President and Mrs. Carter walked from the Capitol to the White House, "Why didn't I think of that?"

Thompson did not have much time to bask in the glory of his inauguration. The next day the legislature was ready to begin its work and the numbers looked bad for the Republicans. Of the 177 members of the house, 94 were Democrats and 83 Republicans. In the senate, Democrats held 34 seats and the Republicans 25. Normally, Mayor Daley and selected officials of the majority party chose the leadership for the two bodies. Occasionally the house or senate rebelled (as it did in 1975 when it took 86 ballots to name a speaker of the house), but Daley got his way most of the time, and he was careful to provide balance by including some downstate Democrats on the leadership team.

Without Daley to make the decisions a drawn-out contest appeared likely in one chamber or the other. Speaker of the House William A. Redmond, from the Chicago suburbs, retained his position for two reasons: He usually did what the Chicago interests told him to do, and if he didn't, a Chicago strongman could hold the No. 2 position—majority leader—and steer legislation around him. That position went to Michael J. Madigan, an efficient and loyal state representative from Chicago, generally popular among other legislators.

With the state house squared away, eyes focused on the senate president's job vacated by Cecil Partee. He left no "natural" successor. Chicago legislators backed Thomas C. Hynes, an attorney representing the South Side of Chicago. One of Hynes's principal supporters was Senator Richard Daley, the late mayor's son. Hynes needed more than Chicago votes to win, however, and a stalemate developed. Downstate senators balked, not because they objected to Hynes but because they wanted a bigger piece of the leadership pie than had been doled out under Partee. Hynes refused and the senators held firm; a compromise eluded them for 186 ballots, a record for the state senate. The tussle paralyzed the legislature, and pre-occupied Thompson until it ended on February 16, 1977.

The stalemate also affected Thompson's job performance. By constitutional provision the governor presides over the senate until a president is chosen. Thompson, therefore, had to be present or on call for each of the 186 votes. It restricted his movements and distracted him from business. He later blamed the preoccupation with slowing his appointment of key personnel in the administration.

Thompson had no apparent role in the selection process, although the decision was important to him. He stayed out of compromise efforts, but it is unlikely he would have had much influence with Democratic senators anyway, and Republicans were disinclined to vote for a Democrat just to break the deadlock. As a final vote neared, Thompson told the Republican senators: "I am not going to use my voice to dictate to anybody who the senate president ought to be. I have made no suggestions and I have offered no demands."

Finally, Hynes gave in to downstate holdouts, placed three of them on the leadership team and, in return, was elected president of the senate. Breathing a sigh of relief, Thompson said: "I have learned a great deal from this process. I shall take it back with me to the second floor [where his office was] where I more properly belong."

The link between legislative leadership and the Chicago Irishmen who formed a coalition behind Bilandic was unmistakable. *Chicago Sun-Times* political editor Basil Talbott, Jr. identified the persons who muscled their way into the vacuum as "the Irish Six." Hynes and Madigan were included, along with young Daley, Chicago Park District chief Ed Kelly, Assessor Tom Tully, and Neil Hartigan. With Bilandic out front, they became the deal makers and Thompson knew with whom he would be talking.

No one mistook the mission of Madigan and Hynes in Springfield. Hynes said, "Our basic job is to make sure that Chicago and Cook County get our fair share of the state's $10 billion largesse." Madigan bluntly added, "Money is the name of the game." Clearly, unless an issue had direct impact on Chicago, Madigan and Hynes would be unlikely to mobilize Chicago votes for support.

Thompson's greatest concern was the state budget and Democratic acceptance of the balanced-budget approach. Immediately after the election, Thompson began calling for a "year of sacrifice" to restore the state's financial security. No other projects exceeded the budget in importance, Thompson later told *Chicago Tribune* columnist Neal Peirce. "We had been deficit spending in the state for three years," Thompson said. "Our financial rating was in jeopardy. If we had another year of deficit spending, we would have been bankrupt. . . . So, I submitted the first balanced budget in four years. It attended to the needs of the people of Illinois but may not have met everybody's expectations."

Walker had indeed overspent, putting the state in poor financial condition. He had inherited a small surplus of funds from the Ogilvie administration, not enough to tempt a big spender, but the state income tax passed in 1969 under Ogilvie generated more revenue than ever before. By 1974 the state had a cash reserve of $453 million. Walker spent it and, when recession softened the growth of state revenue, he issued bonds to maintain the spree. Taxpayers would be paying debt service on the bonds for years to come.

Professor James Heins, a University of Illinois economist, commented later on what forces Walker set in motion. "The problem with spending $400 million excess cash in three years lay in the resulting anticipation for more spending." Having already rejected a tax increase as a means of relieving pressure, Thompson could not feed the anticipation. He had to say "no" to agencies and departments that had not heard a governor say that for years.

Anticipating special interest disagreement, Thompson took pains to create an atmosphere of "crisis" as he unveiled his budget and began the sales pitch for it. Heins analyzed the governor's overstatement. "The term *fiscal crisis* grossly misleads," he said. "It was not a crisis and the problem was not fiscal. The problem was political and of less than crisis proportions." Heins and other revenue experts agreed that proposing a balanced budget is a governor's job and should not become the most time-consuming chore of an entire administration.

The politicking involved in the 1977 budget prevailed over what appeared to Heins and others as routine business. Thompson still called it a "crisis" and hardened his line on additional tax revenue to relieve the dilemma. "If a tax increase is needed, I'll be the first to say so, but I'm darn sure the people don't want it."

Thompson submitted to the legislature a "conservative" $10 billion budget in March. Taking the offensive in what he knew would be a "get Thompson's budget" free-for-all, he toured Illinois cities with a "dog and pony" show complete with charts and graphs to illustrate the "crisis." He talked to legislators, newspaper editorial boards, and citizens' gatherings.

". . . I made twenty-one speeches around the state defending my budget," he recalled. "Twenty-one god-damned grinding speeches, over and over again, with the charts, until I was sick of them and was seeing them in my sleep. But they had an effect. It's the only way to do the job." Thompson was not the first salesman for a budget. Walker began the practice with fireside chats at the mansion.

Thompson and his budget director Robert Mandeville determined the state would have about $300 million in new revenues for spending in the fiscal year beginning July 1, 1977. If the legislature followed Thompson's spending suggestions, there would be a small surplus to bridge the gap from one fiscal year to another.

Thompson allocated about $100 million of the amount to pay debt service and other commitments. The remaining $200 million included about $125 million for education—Thompson said it was his budget priority—and $75 million in increases for dozens of other state agencies and departments. Many received no increase at all and, with inflation eating away the previous year's allocation, they in effect suffered a reduction.

Howls of protest went up immediately, mainly from educational interests, which said that being the priority in an inadequate budget was still inadequate. In previous years had such a budget been proposed, Chicago school officials and politicians would have led an assault on Springfield to dismantle the plan and pump more money to their districts. But it did not happen in 1977. There were whimpers and threats, but by the time the amounts for education were determined late in June, Thompson and Chicago had made their peace and schools took their medicine.

The Associated Press reported with understatement late in the Illinois legislative session, "Chicago Democrats, noted for their aggressive demands for more school aid and their attacks on Walker's budgets, allowed Thompson's conservative $10 billion spending package to pass basically intact."

Thompson's budget and pledge for legislative restraint drew support from the *Chicago Tribune*, the state's largest newspaper. An editorial noted reductions in social services, then concluded: "All this looks like what is needed; a tough, even painful program designed to pull the state back from the fiscal windowsill from which it was teetering and to avert any need for a tax increase. . . ." The less-adamant *Chicago Sun-Times* praised the budget under a headline "Prudence and the Budget." The newspaper said the budget "sets the right tone, considering Illinois's economic condition and the public mood."

Alone among Illinois newspapers, the Lindsay-Schaub group downstate said the budget shortchanged levels of service—especially the social services—and urged Thompson to consider a tax increase.

The *Chicago Tribune* found one glaring exception in Thompson's austerity budget and called him to task for it. The newspaper said it agreed with the broad strokes of the budget "except for a jarring exception: his strange generosity toward his own office." The governor asked for a 53.8 percent increase in expenses for the executive office. The *Tribune* listed some of the unnecessary expenses: ". . . funds for a new turboprop airplane, the leasing of a large imposing auto, and an expanded state radio-TV service that provides news about the governor and state business to broadcasting stations throughout Illinois." Inferring that Thompson had a penchant for empire building, the *Tribune* advised: "Forget it." Many of the items were dropped from the budget.

As the legislative process developed in March and April of 1977, Chicago had other priorities besides Crosstown, and Thompson obliged. He guaranteed that McCormick Place, Chicago's gigantic exposition and meeting complex, would continue to receive a share of the revenue from the state cigarette tax. Additionally, the legislature authorized $10 million in new bonds for expansion of the Port of Chicago, and granted increases in tax rates for the Chicago Park District and the Metropolitan Sanitary District, all without referendums. Chicago got most of what it wanted.

Technically a legislature session begins in January, but the process is slow to start. Not until a governor offers his budget for inspection in March does the legislature begin serious consideration of bills, and discussion and debate don't begin until April or May. That leaves a little more than two months of hard work before the legislature is supposed to adjourn on July 1.

In Thompson's first year as governor there were some unusual delays that caused the legislature to stall. In addition to the senate leadership deadlock and Thompson's budget proposal, the Chicago primary election in April distracted legislators. Thompson's temperature began to boil, and he made his disappointments known publicly, apparently to create the picture of an embattled governor. He told F. Richard Ciccone of the *Chicago Tribune*, "When I was out there last year, I was frustrated because I wasn't the governor and couldn't do the things I knew needed to be done. Now that I'm the governor, I'm frustrated because I can't get everything done that I want to." On another occasion he complained, "I find that a lot of problems just are not soluble, or if they are, they're not soluble very quickly. It's a difficult job."

These protests baffled political veterans, who presumed Thompson had learned the facts of political life before becoming governor. But the governor persisted, and the legislature made a useful target. "I'm disappointed at the skepticism with which my programs have been greeted.... My other disappointment was with the legislature. I knew that politics play a major role in decisions of state government, but not the extent I discovered." Any political primer would have prepared him for such difficulties.

About the time of the Crosstown announcement in May of 1977, Thompson hardened his attitude toward the legislature, calling its members petty and narrow. "Everything seems to be tied to a job or a position on a commission," he said. Yes, he told an interviewer, the culprits often were Chicago legislators, but "I can't even get my own party in line much."

As questions came before the legislature, Thompson's positions became clearer. He reaffirmed his support of the Equal Rights Amendment, although the legislature again refused to ratify. He also said he would not work the legislative aisles for the amendment because it was an issue for the legislature, not the governor. The approach angered pro-ERA forces. Nevertheless, Thompson never denied his support: "I favor the amendment. I favor its ratification. I favor the ratification now."

He signed a new capital punishment law which complied with U.S. Supreme Court guidelines. While the issues stirred some criticism, he never wavered in support of the death penalty as an effective deterrent to crime.

The deteriorating condition of Illinois roads and a rapidly diminishing road fund inspired Thompson to support a state gasoline tax increase. While he carefully avoided specifically proposing a gas tax, he talked with legislators and citizens about such an increase. Critics of a gas tax charged that an increase was part of the Crosstown Expressway arrangement. Before the legislative session ended, almost every controversial proposal had been credited to the Crosstown "deal." By the end of April, Thompson decided to drop the gas tax subject. "I admit there is no great enthusiasm in the legislature for a gas tax hike."

Later, Thompson said he talked with legislative leadership in both parties about joint support of a gas tax increase to insure sufficient road fund revenues. They turned him down, and he vowed not to bring the question to them again. "If they want a gas tax increase later, let them come to me."

Contrary to criticism that Thompson had no legislative program beyond the budget, the governor brought two specific subjects before the legislature: ethics and criminal justice. Neither was a new subject, but Thompson had talked at length about them during the campaign, and on one occasion unveiled a specific ethics proposal. A proposal related to criminal justice was a natural outgrowth of his background and experience. On familiar ground Thompson could be a tenacious fighter, as the legislature learned. He wanted changes in the criminal code more than improved ethical standards, but early in the session he called an ethics bill his second priority after a balanced budget.

In April, Thompson dropped an ethics proposal on the legislature. His press release said it would "plug loopholes, add teeth to existing conflict-of-interest laws, and strip the secrecy from lobbyist spending to influence public officials." The proposal was similar to what he offered in a campaign position paper: a state board of ethics, prohibition of commissions, tougher financial disclosure for officials, and expansion of lobbyist registration requirements.

Democrats led members of both parties in denouncing the plan. Hynes called the bills poorly written and added, "This is nothing more than trying to get a roll call on a package of bills labeled 'ethics' which is synonomous with motherhood and apple pie." Chicago Democrats wanted nothing to do with either.

After reading the signs, Thompson backed away and did not press for consideration. His unwillingness disappointed ethics advocates. Later Thompson explained: "People have asked me why I didn't try to arouse public opinion on that. Well, sometimes a governor can successfully arouse public opinion in support of a legislative proposal, but it has to be done carefully, deliberately." Thompson did not feel the subject called for sticking his neck out. "It's got to be an issue the people can understand and rally to," he said.

Persons less charitable of Thompson's practicality said he feared retaliation from Chicago Democrats on the budget. After only a single hearing, the bill died in the senate executive committee, a graveyard for bills not favored by Chicago. Thompson called the defeat "sad and strange." Later he said, "I bit off more than I could chew and thus violated one of my cardinal rules of a rookie governor: Don't bite off more than you can chew."

If ethics legislation did not excite the public, Thompson knew an issue that would; and, in the case of crime legislation, he was willing to take it to the public if necessary. About his package of crime bills Thompson said: "This is one I'm willing to go to the people on. They can understand it. It's very simple, it's tough. It's what they want." And he wanted it, too, to maintain the image of a two-fisted prosecutor and to deliver on the promises he had made during the campaign to put more criminals behind bars.

The crime package did not sprout from Thompson's brow, although the public might have thought so. For two years before his election Democrats had worked on a package of bills that addressed the subject of flat-time sentences for all crimes. Authors of the legislative package introduced bills about the time Thompson introduced his.

The governor's package included eight crime bills, involving a number of issues ranging from authorization of the attorney general to convene statewide grand juries to creation of a new category of crimes called Class X. He proposed that seven heinous crimes, such as rape and use of a weapon in the commission of a felony, be subject to sentences of at least six years each in prison without parole.

With two proposals on the table, a compromise was necessary for one to be passed. Thompson offered to combine bills, but the Democrats refused. In the final days of the legislative session, Speaker Redmond prevented action on Thompson's package by invoking an obscure parliamentary procedure, and nothing passed. Redmond's action and the unwillingness of Democrats to cooperate infuriated Thompson.

He blamed Chicago newspapers for jumping on the Democratic bandwagon and creating a stampede among legislators. "They said it's been a pretty good session with the exception of Thompson having his glamorized version of Class X in there, you know, Thompson should mend his ways. Well, Thompson's not going to mend his ways."

Editorial comment on Thompson's personal project varied. Some newspapers said Thompson's view of criminal justice was too narrow. Critics attacked the idea, saying it dealt with the result of crime but not the causes. Thompson responded: "Those [the specifics] were called harsh. What I say is 'Well, crime is harsh.' Crime is just as tough on its victims as this legislation may be on criminals."

Various pieces of the package died in committee before adjournment, but Thompson wanted only Class X. He spent an enormous amount of personal and staff time on the plan, making it clear he intended to fight to the last. His behavior in pushing Class X revealed a tenacity not previously seen in the governor.

Determined to get a crime package passed, Thompson called a special session of the legislature in the fall to deal with the subject. The *Chicago Tribune*, uncharacteristically nasty with the governor, called on him to merge his ideas with those of the Democrats and quit "grandstanding on this issue." The newspaper pointed out that Thompson "has time before the special fall session to work out some compromise with the sponsors [of the Democratic bill]. But we urge him not to oppose an excellent bill just because it isn't his." The Lindsay-Schaub newspapers said Class X "would do little about psychological and social forces that push so many people into crimes against people and property."

The special session became a free-for-all with Redmond and Thompson at each other's throat. The necessary compromises did not cause as much trouble as Thompson's determination to label it "Class X" and take credit for passage. After public and private wrangling, a bill emerged and passed. Its main provisions included:

- Creation of a category of ten serious crimes, labeled Class X. Class X crimes called for a mandatory minimum six-year jail sentence with a maximum ranging from thirty to sixty years in some cases. The ten crimes were aggravated kidnapping; rape; deviate sexual assault; heinous battery; armed robbery; aggravated arson; treason; armed violence; hard narcotics transactions; and conspiracy to sell, produce, or distribute hard drugs.
- Establishment of a provision designed to put three time losers away for good. Persons convicted three times of a Class X crime would be sentenced to mandatory life in prison with no chance of parole.
- Elimination of the Parole and Pardon Board along with the concept of parole. Prisoners would get a specific release date instead of having to take a chance on persuading the parole board to release them.
- Establishment of a system of determinate sentencing, with fixed terms for defendants and less judicial discretion in setting sentences.

Surrounded by legislative leaders, Thompson signed the bill in December and it became effective in February, 1978. A relieved *Chicago Tribune* wrote that Class X was "an impressive showing for the year in crime legislation. In advance of an election year, that will be useful for both sides."

Although Thompson sensed correctly that the public wanted tougher crime laws—public opinion polls on the death penalty were a tip-off—murmurs continued after passage of Class X legislation that the administration's crime fight had narrow dimensions. Sociologists, criminologists, and some newspaper editorial pages hedged their enthusiasm for Class X by calling for a crime fight that tackled the causes, not the results.

Thompson read that criticism as an intellectual put-down of his theory. Fighting crime and correcting social ills might blend together in another generation or two, he said, but they are separate subjects now.

> To say that until we eliminate poverty and ignorance and lack of employment and lack of adequate housing, we're not going to do anything about putting bad guys in jail is just plain nuts. And I'm not going to have any part in that. We've got to continue our social programs to try to alleviate what people think are the root causes of crime, but at the same time we've got to treat the symptoms, the hitting over the head. The only way I know of doing that is to take those people out of society and put them into jail.

In these days no legislative session is complete without at least one emotional issue which generates rallies at the statehouse and gives the public an opportunity to blow off steam. In 1977 there were two. One proposal prohibited the use of state money for abortions. The other legalized sales of the so-called cancer drug laetrile. Both passed the legislature and both were vetoed by Thompson.

Opposition to the use of laetrile by the American Medical Association apparently convinced Thompson to veto the bill, but he sympathized with persons who had exhausted acceptable methods of fighting cancer. "It is an extremely difficult thing to tell a terminal cancer patient he can't have something he believes will help him." The legislature overrode the veto.

Expecting to incur the wrath of the powerful antiabortion lobby, Thompson vetoed the bill prohibiting state funding of abortions, but he baffled pro-abortion forces by not pressing Republican legislators to uphold his veto. When asked why he accepted legislative override without a fight, the governor said: "I know the individual legislators fear the antiabortion lobby more in their individual districts, and I can sympathize with them. They aren't going to vote against this bill for that reason, if no other. On the other hand, I have a constituency of 12 million persons, and the special interest lobbies are less of a threat to me." He said the bill was not a partisan issue and Republican legislators "wouldn't pay any attention to me anyway."

In vetoing the antiabortion bill, Thompson turned his back on advice from campaign strategist Douglas Bailey, who felt a veto was an unnecessary political risk. The veto did anger those opposed to state spending for abortions but delighted Chicago newspapers. The often conservative *Chicago Tribune* agreed with the decision and the *Chicago Sun-Times* offered some of the strongest support for Thompson's action by calling it a "courageous veto."

Politicians were less charitable. Michael Bakalis, by then a candidate for governor in the 1978 race, criticized the veto. Lieutenant Governor Dave O'Neal, looking for noneconomic issues on which to disagree with Thompson for the sake of his "independence," said he preferred a prohibition on use of state funds. Jesse Jackson, the black leader from Chicago, compared public aid payments for abortions to approved genocide for blacks.

What irritated Thompson the most, however, was a concerted effort within the Roman Catholic church to override his veto and to criticize his actions. In an interview Thompson said he knew that many priests and the bishop of Springfield had taken him to task from the pulpit and in denominational publications. Although the Catholic population is a distinct minority in Illinois, Thompson acknowledged that when it combined with other antiabortion forces, it became the best-financed and most pervasive lobby in the state.

During the summer, Thompson vetoed another measure passed by the legislature that could have affected the economy and quality of life in the state. Under pressure from Illinois coal interests and the state Chamber of Commerce, the legislature passed a bill which stated that air quality laws in the state could be no more restrictive than those at the federal level. Illinois had air pollution standards considerably tougher than those passed by Congress, and the effect would have been to lower air quality.

Environmentalists argued that lowering standards would result in damaged crops, a reduced quality of life in rural and urban areas, and contaminated rainwater. The state Chamber of Commerce argued that maintaining tough standards inhibited industrial use of Illinois coal and gave business and industry another reason for leaving the state for more favorable business environments. Thompson rejected the arguments of business interests and vetoed the bill. The legislature did not override.

If Thompson's signals to the legislature were not always clear, signals to the public about the manner and style of his administration created confusion, too. Supporters liked his relaxed approach to life and business, but critics, including some members of the Springfield press corps, called him lazy and disorganized. When he wore a T-shirt, jeans, and thongs to a Republican party picnic in central Illinois, many present thought slacks and a shirt would have been more appropriate. More than once he lacked dignity. His taste for the good life encouraged accusations that he lived in "regal splendor," but this criticism did not slow him down. At solemn moments, Thompson could be downright emotional. Almost always his words, prepared or spontaneous, were appropriate. He presented a veritable panoply of sights.

Thompson moved in circles not frequented by governors before. For example, no one recalls any previous governor who dressed in jeans, sneakers, and a Farrah Fawcett-Majors T-shirt for a visit with disc jockey Larry Lujack on Chicago radio station WLS. But Thompson did that in April.

Lujack, who held down the early morning spot on the rock music station, was never less than No. 1 or No. 2 in the popularity ratings. Considering Lujack's draw, and the station's coverage in Chicago among teenagers and young adults, Thompson's voice and antics were heard by an audience the governor could not put together any other way.

Thompson jokingly accused Lujack of snubbing him by not attending the inaugural ceremonies. To make the point, Thompson presented Lujack with a black tie, a T-shirt with the inaugural invitation printed on the front, and a new pair of jeans. The repartee was dazzling. When Lujack offered Thompson a Farrah Fawcett-Majors poster, the governor replied, "Is it the one with the wet bathing suit? I've been looking for that one."

The conversation closed with Thompson giving Lujack a snapshot of his dog's home in Springfield. Lujack rejoined, "When you become president, will you remember me? Let me do a show on the White House lawn, maybe?"

Thompson wasted no time after his election in providing snips and tidbits of gossip about his lifestyle. Often the items were reported with a hint of wrongdoing or at least a suggestion of impropriety. An example occurred when a former friend of Thompson, Michael Kilian, reported in the *Chicago Tribune* about Thompson's first days in Springfield: "One of Thompson's first acts as governor was to move his office to a larger, more grandiose chamber. Another was to move up the planned redecorations of the governor's suite." Similar reports throughout the first year were good for cocktail party conversation but said little about whether the governor's habits were good or bad. Thompson never promised to serve his term in a pantry, but for some people his occasional extravagances were disturbing.

Some reporters thought Thompson got carried away at his inaugural. Private donors contributed $65,000 for the governor's "little get-together," which included two inaugural balls. (One of the persons in charge of planning the festivities was Michael Dunn, a twenty-four-year-old campaign worker from Rockford who was to become Thompson's patronage chief, and later a major embarrassment to the governor.) To avoid accusations that Thompson invited only large contributors to the campaign, those who arranged the party drew names in a lottery to see who got the 20,000 invitations. Thompson's reason for having two identical inaugural balls was to mix the crowds geographically at each. Persons from Chicago and southern Illinois attended one ball, and persons from northern Illinois and central Illinois the other. The governor and his wife attended both.

Although a little self-indulgence by a newly elected governor was no crime, it sometimes was difficult to limit the indulgence to "little." The episode of Thompson's official car illustrates this difficulty.

In 1973, Governor Walker put down some populist roots for his administration by rejecting the large, black limousines associated with a governor's privilege. He chose instead to ride in Chevrolets. In 1977, Thompson did not think much of Walker's choice. "These Chevys, which get horrible gas mileage and are expensive to maintain, were bought by Walker in a great display of economy when he got rid of Ogilvie's limousine. The net result is that Walker's Chevy . . . costs more than Ogilvie's Lincoln. . . ."

Thompson complained more than once about the leftovers. "I saw nothing but Fleetwoods and limousines at Daley's funeral," he said. "I arrived in the back seat of a beaten-up state police squad car that had lousy shocks and bad springs and I kept hitting my head on the roof every time we hit a bump and my knees were up around my neck. But if I go buy or lease a new car, Walker will jump down my throat and say 'Aha, the limousine governor. . . .' "

Thompson wanted to lease a Lincoln Continental and a Chrysler at a combined cost of $3,700 a year. "I'm a big man," he appealed. "I need the room. How am I going to be an effective governor if I have to ride around in the back seat of some small car with my knees up to my chin?"

The financial arrangement did not seem out of the question, but the Springfield press corps badgered the governor. Finally, in a bizarre press conference, reporters became advocates of smaller, more economic cars for the governor. Thompson backed down from the Chrysler-Lincoln idea and began using leased Checker autos.

When Thompson was not defending his right to live a little better than the next guy, he was showing up on television or in newspapers wearing some strange garb performing a ceremony usually not associated with a governor's routine. On one such occasion, he was photographed in a sport shirt and visored cap operating the gasoline pump at a self-service gasoline station shortly after he signed legislation permitting self-service.

Before many weeks had passed, Thompson's flirtation with racquetball made news reports. He played racquetball an hour or so each day, and pictures appeared of him in violent, sweaty battle with a friend or aid. (In the previous four years Walker's tennis game had gotten some notoriety.) Soon Thompson's car sported a bumper sticker that read: "I'd rather be racquetballing," and the public got the message. Thompson's activity "peaked" in May when he appeared on the cover of the national racquetball publication, which was published in suburban Chicago. The story of how Thompson made the magazine's cover is illustrative of the tangents he was capable of taking.

A couple of months prior to appearing on the magazine cover, Thompson received three racquetball sets from Robert W. Kendler, president of the U.S. Racquetball Association. In a thank-you letter dated March 30, Thompson wrote: "I have been telling everyone that I am going to be on the cover of your magazine and if I am not, I will have to leave the state of Illinois. That would make Lieutenant Governor Dave O'Neal governor and he hates racquetball . . . and therefore could not possibly be governor. So, you will have to help me keep my promise and put me on the cover." Five hundred copies of the magazine were delivered to Thompson's office after he appeared on the cover.

An irony of Thompson's racquetball activity is that it represented a rare adventure into the athletic world. He seldom participated in any sport, as a child or an adult. "I'm not very well coordinated, so it never was much fun for me," he said. "Besides, I wasn't any good at whatever sport I tried." Racquetball died an unnatural death in Thompson's life when it aggravated a back ailment.

Nevertheless, there were times when Thompson's unorthodox approach won new friends for the governor. An example is the story of the Chadwick Slab, as reported for Lindsay-Schaub newspapers by Fletcher Farrar in 1977. The tale caught the flavor of Thompson's charm, glib manner, and down-home appeal.

A busload of angry rural families had met the governor on one of his trips near Springfield. They wanted Thompson to do something about repairing the Chadwick Slab, a road project the state had postponed for some time. Thompson had been briefed in advance by his staff, Farrar reported. "He [Thompson] stepped into the middle of the crowd of angry farmers who were standing in a covered walkway, sheltered from a pounding rain," Farrar wrote. "He was taller than the others, and it was difficult to imagine a short governor speaking with as much authority."

The governor was quoted as saying: "I've told I-Dot [Illinois Department of Transportation] to give the Chadwick Slab a high priority. I've told them it's just a god-awful mess." Then, Farrar said, Thompson began talking about the cost of road repair and how the slab didn't qualify for federal aid. "Fixing that road sounded more impossible by the minute," Farrar wrote. Thompson's skill paid off before the angry group dispersed. A woman moved almost to tears said, "We have faith in you, governor."

Calculated or spontaneous, politically inspired or innocent, Thompson's style got the public's attention. He tried to explain the appeal: "My style is open, candid, forthright, friendly, and natural. The people want to feel comfortable with their public officials. They want to identify with them. . . . Most people just want to feel that the government is running honestly and efficiently and isn't doing anything bad to them, and that it's run with some common sense."

Once in awhile common sense eluded Thompson. The saga of his membership in private clubs became one of the most embarrassing and senseless episodes of his first year in office.

The story began with an interview in the *Chicago Sun-Times* that grew out of a conversation at a governors' conference in Detroit. Thompson told a reporter that he held memberships in the "men-only" Butler National Golf Club in Oak Brook, and the Union League Club of Chicago, a club that attracted Chicago's leading lawyers, bankers, and businessmen. In the interview Thompson attempted to justify his membership in the two clubs by differentiating between clubs that bar women and clubs that bar persons because of religious preference or racial background. He said private clubs have the right to exclude various groups, including women, blacks, and Jews, but that he did not "approve of organizations which bar people on the irrational ground of religion or the color of his skin and I don't associate with those who do."

Apparently anticipating the inevitable criticism, Thompson appeared to grope for an explanation of his behavior. "I can't square belonging to a club which excludes women with my feeling about clubs which bar people on racial or religious grounds. I suppose it's a generation gap." He did not say which side of the gap he was on. The governor said he would resign from the golf club (which he did) but would retain his membership in the Union League Club and work within the organization to change its rules. Thompson did not explain why he waited until he was months into his administration before confronting the membership issue.

The media were not gentle with Thompson. The Lindsay-Schaub newspapers called on him to resign the Union League membership, too, and asked him to provide leadership on the issue in a broader sense across the state. The *Chicago Sun-Times* called Thompson's action a "step-and-a-half in the right direction." The newspaper said going an extra mile to satisfy the wishes of women concerned with equal rights was "not too far for leaders in 1977." Thompson did not, however, resign his Union League membership, and he did not work to reform the club's rules either.

Finally, in January, 1978, Thompson resigned from the club in a letter to its president. "... I regret even more that I did not follow through on my public promise to attempt to persuade my fellow members to open membership to women on an equal basis with men. That omission was inexcusable and I offer no excuse." Thompson said he concluded "that it is not right for the governor of the state of Illinois to accept membership in a club which excludes women from membership solely because they are women." A month later, Thompson notified three other private clubs of his resignation because they discriminated against women. They were the Tavern Club in Chicago, the Oak Park Country Club in west suburban River Grove, and the Mid-Day Club in Chicago. It took Thompson six months to clear the membership issue.

While Thompson avoided major scandals during his first year in office, he tripped several times over minor episodes that kept his record from being absolutely clean. A vigilant press created instant headlines and editorial comment, regardless of the seriousness. Judging from records of governors in Illinois, and other states, one would say that peccadilloes are inevitable; they only become important in a cumulative sense, and Thompson accumulated his share of them in 1977.

In May, Thompson opened his "gift book" to the press and public. This book recorded gifts received by Thompson, the name of the donor and, in some cases, disposition of the gift. No other governor had kept such a book, or at least none was ever made public. Thompson made the gesture to demonstrate his openness. Most of the items were curiosity pieces and provided examples of what people will send to governors, whether they know them or not.

For example, Thompson received two books from Ralph G. Newman, a Chicago rare books dealer, convicted in 1975 of lying to the Internal Revenue Service and filing a false affidavit in connection with Richard Nixon's 1969 income tax return; American League and Chicago White Sox season baseball passes from Sox management (Thompson is a lifelong Cubs fan); a dozen T-shirts from Uncle Dennis T-shirts of Chicago; a dozen beef steaks from Rocke's Meating Haus, in Morton; a plane flight from Washington to Illinois from Gould Inc., a Rolling Meadows electronics corporation.

Those items hardly created a ripple, but a tidal wave of criticism developed over one listing: a free trip to the Kentucky Derby as guests of the Chessie System, a railroad holding company with lines in Illinois. Chessie owns the Baltimore & Ohio Railroad and the Baltimore & Ohio Chicago terminal. The Thompsons and a state trooper accepted the flight to Louisville in a Chessie jet. Chessie also provided $83 Derby seats for each. An aide to Thompson said the governor went at the invitation of James O'Keefe, a Chessie director and personal friend of Thompson.

From Louisville, another Chessie jet flew the group to Peoria, where Thompson presented a posthumous award to former Governor Kerner at the annual Lincoln Academy Ball. Ironically, Thompson did not see the Kentucky Derby, because he left early to make the Peoria appointment.

Thompson denied any impropriety. In fact, he thumbed his nose at insinuations of unethical behavior. "If they invite me next year, I'll go again," he said defiantly. "If it is proper and legal to take campaign contributions from regulated industries . . . I can't understand why it is different than accepting a modest gift in the form of a trip to the Kentucky Derby." The *Chicago Sun-Times*, in an editorial entitled "No Favors, Please," told him what was wrong. First, the paper complimented him for opening the gift book for public view. Then it said the public would be "more reassured if Thompson refused favors from now on and pays his own way." After criticism from other quarters, Thompson swallowed some of his earlier remarks at a fund-raising dinner a couple of weeks after the first stories. "I still think I did nothing wrong in taking that trip," he said, "but I'm afraid my initial response might have been a bit arrogant." He apologized to friends and supporters who voiced displeasure with his acceptance of the Chessie gift.

While no evidence existed that Thompson knew of Chessie System requests then before the Illinois Commerce Commission, or that he had made any attempt to influence the commission's decision, the potential for conflict existed. Chessie had a rate-increase request before the regulatory commission and awaited decisions on other subjects, including requests for permission to abandon station buildings and cases involving the railroad being required to improve protection at grade crossings.

Gifts flowed without pause, and they were recorded in the gift book. The Associated Press reported later in the year that the Thompsons had received a United Auto Workers jacket from a UAW official, a basketball from the president of a Springfield hardware firm, and a box of "Jayne and Jim" monogrammed matches from a Chicago match corporation.

Thompson never apologized for accepting gifts. He said to refuse gifts would be awkward and might insult the donor. He recalled an instance when a Ukrainian couple from the Chicago area tried to give President Carter a handcrafted wall hanging of the seal of the United States. "They called up the White House and said, 'We've got something for the president,' and somebody said, 'The president won't accept gifts,' click."

The most serious abuse revealed in Thompson's first year came to light during June in a series of articles by reporter Carol Alexander of the Lindsay-Schaub newspapers on the misuse of the state airplane fleet. Her articles explained abuses by legislators; Lieutenant Governor O'Neal; Speaker Redmond; Melvin Rosenbloom, Thompson's director of the Division of Aeronautics; and Michael Dunn, an aide to Thompson. At about the same time, a reporter for Gannett News Service in Illinois published reports on an investigation of executive office use of the planes.

The most serious accusations were against Rosenbloom and Michael Dunn, Thompson's patronage chief. They had abused the privilege, and apparently Dunn had attempted to conceal his use of the planes.

The reports said that during the first three months of 1977 Dunn and his wife used state planes to make at least sixteen personal trips between Rockford, Dunn's home, and Springfield. On several of the trips, Dunn or Dunn and his wife were the only passengers. On about half the flights, state planes flew empty one way. The normal procedure would have been for Dunn to have the Division of Aeronautics bill him for the trips. He made no payment. In addition, Dunn was accused of falsifying records to cover up some trips.

Dunn said, "Before my wife and I bought a house in Springfield I had to commute between our Rockford home and my Springfield job. My wife came down to help look for a new home in Springfield. It's hard to buy a house without your wife." Thompson ordered an investigation of the records and said the state would be paid for Dunn's trips. Under fire, Dunn resigned. Ironically, he had been a member of a special task force appointed in February by Thompson to investigate abuses in use of state aircraft and propose remedies. Dunn's name would surface again in 1978 in connection with alleged fraudulent signatures on petitions.

On June 9, Alexander reported that Rosenbloom "regularly used state airplanes for personal business between airports near his suburban Chicago home and Springfield." Rosenbloom said, "There were times when I took state planes to Chicago for no other reason than to go home." Less than two weeks later, Thompson fired Rosenbloom.

During the melee, a report suggesting curtailment of the state fleet and tougher regulations for use of planes sat on Thompson's desk. Not until March, 1978, more than eleven months after receiving the report, did Thompson order changes in operation of the state fleet. Thompson said he delayed action until a new director of the Division of Aeronautics could review the matter.

Dunn's misadventure hurt Thompson, not just because of the public embarrassment, but because the two were friends. Dunn had worked his way into the inner circle of Thompson's "whiz kids." After announcing Dunn's resignation, Thompson told a *Chicago Daily News* reporter, "He was a bright young kid who had a dirty, rotten job to do [as patronage chief]. And he had two big problems. He wanted to please everybody and was an airplane nut."

Before the summer passed, Thompson had an ethics problem which flared temporarily in headlines. It involved receipt of a campaign contribution from Thrall Car Manufacturing Company, a Chicago Heights railroad firm whose president, Richard L. Duchossois, was a benefactor of Republican politicians. The conflict arose because Duchossois was an officer of the Illinois Thoroughbred Breeders and Owners Foundation, a nonprofit organization which was granted racing dates by the Illinois Racing Board. It was illegal for any organization with racing connections to make contributions to political candidates or their campaign committees.

The contribution came from the Thrall firm, not directly from Duchossois. Thompson defended receipt of the funds: "As I read the law...there is no prohibition for a non-licensee [for racing] holding corporation to make a political contribution. Under the circumstances I would accept the same money again." No one claimed that Thompson had done anything more than brush the edge of illegal activity.

The bane of 1977 for Thompson was the continuous sniping. Besides the press's picking at his exclusive men's club memberships, the trip to the Kentucky Derby, problems in the Division of Aeronautics, or possible racetrack contributions—persons in the governor's own political party were griping.

On the "outside" in Springfield since 1972, Republicans grumbled when Thompson played ball with legislative Democrats, cut deals with Chicago Democrats, appointed Democrats to key cabinet posts, and romanced Democratic leaders, such as Secretary of State Alan Dixon. Thompson put down the rebellions saying, "Politicians just love to grouse...." But the critics were not that easily discouraged. Republicans at the local level throughout Illinois expected to reap a harvest of jobs when Thompson moved into the governor's mansion, and they wanted action. Thompson warned them that he did not have as many jobs as party officials thought. Thompson said: "There are no spare jobs floating around. There aren't any $25,000-a-year jobs in Cook County. Most are in Springfield and most are tested under civil service."

No one in his party heard him. Displeasure with Thompson's patronage program arose early, prodded by a succession of patronage chiefs, none of whom satisfied the feisty veteran politicians. By the end of 1977, four different persons had been in charge of patronage. The most infamous was Michael Dunn.

Edward S. Gilbreth and Robert G. Schultz, political reporters for the *Chicago Daily News*, reported that Dunn's resignation pleased most Republicans. "In Springfield, after news of Dunn's departure speeded through the legislative halls ... many Republican lawmakers were ecstatic. One after another, they'd stop and whisper to a reporter how delighted they were because 'that know-it-all' wouldn't be around anymore."

Gilbreth and Schultz told of an occasion when Dunn spoke at a meeting of the Illinois State Republican Central Committee. "Afterward, a state central committeeman reported that most of those who heard Dunn were outraged by him. 'He was arrogant, obnoxious. He presumed to tell us that despite his youth, he knew far more about political patronage than any of us, and he was going to run things his way.'" Pinpointing the validity of complaints about patronage was hard to do, because politicians reacted with generalities. No one was sure why Dunn failed, except that the politicians did not like him.

Republican party anger grew steadily through the year. Appointments of two Democrats to key cabinet posts, including the Department of Transportation, which dispenses hundreds of patronage jobs, prompted much of the anger. Thompson inherited Langhorne H. Bond as director of the department. Bond later left to join the Carter administration as head of the Federal Aviation Administration. Serving Bond as deputy was John D. Kramer, twenty-eight, a Democratic appointee of Daniel Walker.

Thompson wanted Kramer for the position, despite his youth and party credentials. With a Democratic administration in Washington and Bond in the federal Department of Transportation, Kramer had the connections Thompson wanted. He intended to announce Kramer's appointment early in June.

Republicans heard of the plan and forced Thompson to postpone it while they tried to change his mind. They argued against the appointment on political grounds and cited Kramer's inexperience. Kramer is a Los Angeles native and a graduate of Stanford University. He worked for Carter's transportation task force during the 1976 presidential campaign.

Finally, after a month's delay, Thompson announced his choice: Kramer. Republicans howled across the state. The appointment still remains a sore point with Republicans. Thompson's support of Kramer never sagged. About the Republican sentiment the governor said, ". . . I understand that feeling and I'm not putting it down. Republicans have a right to expect that when they nominate and elect a governor that some of their people will be put into sensitive policymaking positions. . . . And it's been very frustrating for the Republicans of Illinois to see so many holdovers. . . . I thought John Kramer was the best person available to me in the nation." A year later, with party criticism still in the air, Thompson said, "Kramer's appointment has not cost the Republicans jobs."

Republicans grumbled, too, over Thompson's choice for director of the Department of Labor. William M. Bowling, thirty-seven, of Carbon Cliff, Illinois, resigned as president of United Auto Workers Local 1309 in Rock Island to take the position. While the Department of Labor does not have many patronage workers, and Republicans generally have trouble finding acceptable nonlabor persons for the position, some party officials saw the appointment as a blatant payoff to the UAW for election support. Democrats encouraged the speculation.

Some irritation between Republican party officials and Thompson resulted from oversights and staff confusion, but the officials considered them personal affronts. Two such incidents occurred in the fall. Both were infractions by Thompson of the political courtesy rule, which Thompson had so carefully followed when he campaigned in 1975 and 1976. The rule states that when a party official enters a county to campaign or even to conduct business, he informs the county chairman. It is one of the first rules new politicians learn.

Aides of Thompson tried to plan fund-raising events in the fall of 1977 in Peoria and Decatur. Each conflicted directly with a local fund-raising event. Peoria Republicans were planning a gala for U.S. Representative Robert Michel and had invited a number of luminaries, including former president Ford. Decatur's Macon County organization had most of its 1978 election financing plans at stake in a dinner featuring former California governor Ronald Reagan.

In both cases Thompson cancelled plans for his events, but in the case of Macon County, he did not back off until several telephone calls and veiled threats by the county chairman, H. G. "Skinny" Taylor. Taylor, a longtime party worker, threatened to make the subject a public issue at the Reagan dinner if Thompson persisted. Mary Alice Erickson, chairman of the Peoria committee, said bitterly, "I think Governor Thompson has chosen not to really work with the Republican party."

To show their irritation with Thompson, the Republican County Chairman's Association, which had flexed its muscles since the early 1960s, snubbed Thompson by not inviting him to address a meeting in Springfield. The group did invite Senator Percy, and a Thompson aide attended. Taylor, one of the organizers of the association, said, "That will show him that we don't need him to have a successful meeting."

County chairmen are important to a governor, and not just at election time. For a governor with presidential ambitions, as Thompson is, it will be important to send a united delegation to the Republican National Convention in 1980. Much of the work of selecting candidates for delegate is done by county chairmen. Taylor indicated he would work to elect an independent slate of delegates to the convention and use that as leverage with the governor on patronage.

Thompson further irritated some state Republican leaders when he gave a *Chicago Tribune* reporter his slate of candidates for Cook County offices in October, 1976, while attending the Republican Governors' Conference in Bretton Woods, New Hampshire. Thompson had not discussed these choices with Ogilvie or the Cook County Central Committee. Moreover, Thompson's list of names included two former employees from the U.S. attorney's office, and critics envisioned the governor stacking Cook County offices with old friends. The two he wanted to slate were Dan Webb for sheriff, and Ty Fahner, Illinois director of law enforcement, for Cook County board president. Ogilvie had held both positions in the 1960s and had his own candidate for sheriff.

Smarting, Ogilvie let it be known he had not been consulted. A few days later, Thompson acknowledged his "off the cuff" remarks, adding: "If I have caused members of my party any offense by that, then I apologize." However, that did not mean Thompson planned to ignore Republican politics in Cook County.

In the end, Thompson kept his candidates out of the races for sheriff and county board president. Ironically, Ogilvie's candidate for sheriff, Lou Kasper, fell in the primary to Don Mulack, an aide to Attorney General William J. Scott. Mulack lost in the general election. The defeat of Ogilvie's candidate did more to strengthen Thompson's hand in Cook County Republican politics than if he had engaged in a bloody contest with the former governor. Thompson moved in after the primary and cleaned house. By April, 1978, Thompson had forced County Chairman Harold Tyrrell from office and replaced him with J. Robert Barr, an Evanston attorney.

Thompson's skirmishes with county organizations in the fall were not his only clashes with Republicans. He was drawn into discussions of a potential 1978 primary battle for Charles H. Percy's U.S. Senate seat. Phyllis Schlafly of Alton, a conservative housewife, author, lecturer, and outspoken foe of the Equal Rights Amendment, began thinking about challenging Percy in the primary. Most party officials made no public comment, but behind the scenes they tried to dissuade her from running. A wild primary—as it would have been—could injure Republican chances for major victories across the state in 1978, they argued.

Mrs. Schlafly persisted in her study, but in the meantime Thompson and Percy announced a joint election-year venture. When possible, they planned to share offices and voter-preference polls. Thompson and Percy assumed they would be on the ballot together, and cooperative activities made sense. They also shared the same campaign consultant, Bailey and Deardourff.

Amid rising expectations of a Schlafly-Percy donnybrook, Thompson announced his support of the senator and vowed to campaign for him if necessary. The statement angered anti-ERA forces, which were pressuring Schlafly to run, but helped to avoid an open clash: Schlafly decided not to run. Thompson and Percy breathed sighs of relief.

Thompson received increased visibility in party circles outside Illinois in 1977, mainly through the party publication, *First Monday*. Apparently in recognition of Thompson's presidential interest and his status as one of only a dozen Republican governors, the magazine twice featured his comments. In one article, Thompson urged the party to broaden its base—not unlike other moderate Republicans, including Percy, had done—and to develop programs based on human needs. "We have to start by admitting that the Republican party is perceived by the general public as being more concerned with dollars and cents than with people and their problems," he told the publication.

In a second *First Monday* article, which utilized excerpts of a speech, Thompson talked about the party's image with the public: "The Republican party is perceived wrong these days, and we're often on the wrong side of issues. We too often identify with ... corporate boardroom interests rather than corporate interests as a whole. A corporation is more than a board of directors. It's the employees. It's the consumers. It's the customers. It's the shareholders who may be senior citizens, working people."

Pleading for a less dogmatic and more pragmatic approach to party affairs, Thompson said: "A Republican who runs for office out in Arizona has got different problems than a Republican who runs in Manhattan, and we ought to face that and not be ashamed of that."

On some occasions when Thompson addressed fellow Republicans he stayed safely in the middle on party matters. "Straight-line party voting is dead and any political party which doesn't recognize this is courting the same fate. . . . Our party should strive to become a recruitment vehicle that

finds the best candidates and encourages them to run as Republicans."
He added some details on this broadening process. "The only way to truly
broaden the base of our party is to speak to the needs that differentiate
those groups from their fellow citizens. And if we do, I believe we'll find
that those needs aren't really so different from those of the white Anglo-
Saxon middle-class males who supposedly dominate our party. . . ." He
did not spell out what needs or what programs.

He made the same speech—with the same omissions—many times. On
the national party's attempt to recruit and campaign for black Republican
candidates—announced in 1977 by National Chairman William Brock—
Thompson said cautiously, "It depends on how well the black candidates
do. It's a gradual thing. It's not going to happen overnight."

While his statements sometimes lacked force, that did not reduce the
opportunity Thompson had to meet Republicans across the nation in 1977.
He averaged two trips per month outside Illinois and made headlines from
Arizona to New Hampshire. He lectured Republicans in Michigan and
Mississippi and conferred with Rockefellers in New York. He mixed state
business with personal exposure. These travels did not always sit well at
home, however, and some critics implied that he might be ignoring Illinois
business. Thompson snapped: "What's wrong with my going to New York
for a Saturday and Sunday? Is governor a seven-day-a-week job?"

On one such trip to New York, Thompson touched base with political
leaders, fund-raisers, bankers, brokers, publishers—"all to further the good
name of Illinois," Thompson said. "I want to bring them a message of
reassurance about Illinois's fiscal future." Two Rockefellers, Nelson and
Laurence, made the visitation list. Also included was Maxwell Rabb, one
of the party's ablest fund-raisers. With Rockefeller, Thompson said, "We
discussed the future of the Republican party and how to keep it on a
centrist course." Pictures of Thompson and Rockefeller surely were filed
carefully for future use by party conservatives.

Thompson wore a path to Washington during the year, hoping to
impress the piercing eyes of Washington society and captivate the media.
His eagerness got him in hot water with Illinoisans in the District, not all
of whom were captivated by the young governor. One incident occurred in
March at the National Governors' Conference in Washington.

Thompson breezed into town, grabbed some headlines, and left several
days later, without having contacted members of the Illinois congressional
delegation, violating the "courtesy call" doctrine. While the governor had
time to hold a press conference, he skipped a luncheon thrown by senators
for visiting governors. The Chicago Tribune's Michael Kilian wrote
later, ". . . He sent a representative to make courtesy calls on the Democratic leadership. The representative he sent was a youth whose assignment
in the campaign was to care for Thompson's dog."

One of the slighted persons, Senator Percy, gently called Thompson on the carpet. Recalling the conversation, Percy said, "I told him 'When I'm in Springfield I call the governor up, and we work together.'" He told Thompson how adamant congressmen are about respecting the courtesy rule. "Now the next time you need them and you call them together and half of them don't even show up, don't be surprised," Percy recalled saying. Percy blamed "inexperience" for the gaffe, and afterward Thompson dutifully paid his respects to Illinois congressmen when he visited Washington.

Recognition by the national press is not easily accomplished, but Thompson's media charm worked from the beginning. Actually, several writers of national affairs caught Thompson's act during the 1976 campaign, but the first major flurry of "discoveries" occurred in 1977. The tone ranged from cautious to bubbly, with only an occasional blast of criticism.

No article gushed more than the one in the *New Republic* written by Ken Bode toward the end of 1977. Bode painted a colorful picture with such statements as "Thompson's easygoing, conciliatory, aw-shucks style has gone over well in Springfield"; "Thompson's modest approach to government . . . has made him an object of interest in some GOP circles"; "Thompson is at home in flannel shirt and boots campaigning in the mud at county fairs"; and "He has been tough on crime, has balanced the budget, has whacked welfare fraud and has not raised taxes. . . ." Legends are made of such stuff.

Thompson's national activities and ambitions made news in Illinois media, too, occasionally as a result of comments by friend or foe. One episode occurred late in October, when Lieutenant Governor O'Neal said Thompson told him he would not run for the presidency in 1980. To convince his audience of the report's authenticity, O'Neal added, "I talked to him yesterday to make sure on that before I came here." Thompson and his aides spent days straightening out O'Neal's quotation. They had two messages to clarify: Tell the people Thompson is not a candidate for president now; but don't close the door on that possibility in the future.

While carving a place for himself as leader of the Illinois Republican party, Thompson never forgot re-election. He often said he began running for re-election the minute he won in 1976. Most officeholders never stop, but the two-year term forced a more calculated approach.

By summer, four Democrats had shown preliminary interest in being the party's nominee for 1978. They were Walker, Dixon, Bakalis, and Hartigan. All had name recognition across the state and well-known designs on the governor's mansion, but each knew he needed an issue with which to flog Thompson and overcome the strength of incumbency. Thompson realized that they waited in the wings for him to slip and fall, and he was determined not to make it easy for them. By working with Bilandic on the Crosstown Expressway agreement and obtaining a balanced budget in return, Thompson cleared a first hurdle. He maintained cordial relations with a variety of interests involved in the political system in order to keep his balance elsewhere.

He worked well with the press and, with a few minor exceptions, kept media sniping to a minimum. He obviously worked well with Chicago interests and effectively neutralized them for the time being. He worked closely with Democratic leaders, such as Dixon, and he ignored occasional jabs from Walker, especially when the former governor implied Thompson was not working hard.

Secretary of State Alan Dixon, who had first turndown rights on the 1978 Democratic gubernatorial nomination, clearly liked the new governor, mainly because of the contrast to Walker. Dixon said Thompson made life a lot easier in Springfield. The two liked to sit around and talk politics, drink beer, and put their feet up. There was no tension between them, and Dixon did not look for reasons to criticize the governor. Meanwhile, Walker continued a steady barrage of criticism of Thompson, first over Crosstown and then on the "hard work" issue, without noticeable impact.

Bakalis lusted to run for governor. He was elected state comptroller in 1976, but he hated it, the purely administrative job offering little opportunity for the ambitious Democrat to influence policy. He considered himself third in line behind Dixon and Walker for the chance to be a nominee—if not for governor, then for the U.S. Senate. Bakalis wanted to pull an upset, and 1978 had possibilities.

To keep his name before the public as an adversary of Thompson, Bakalis waged a running battle over predictions of state finances, and especially the year-end surplus. Bakalis implied the surplus would be larger than Thompson predicted, and he accused the governor of holding back spending unnecessarily. The subject became a near disaster for Bakalis as Thompson's budget people disproved the Democrat's claims at every turn. Embarrassed by his errors, Bakalis dropped the subject.

After his defeat in 1976, when he shared the ticket with Howlett, Hartigan entered private business and maintained his position as a ward committeeman in Chicago. As a vice-president of the First National Bank of Chicago, he earned a large salary and was given extensive responsibilities. He had not forgotten the humiliations of 1976, but the chance to run against Thompson did not look like an opportunity for him to redeem himself. He wanted revenge, but he had not decided on the victim.

The absence of a Chicago strongman complicated the selection process for a Democratic candidate. Previously Daley made the decision, often without consideration for the feelings of others, including the candidates. Slating meetings had been a farce, window dressing for the media. Now, in Daley's absence, party officials such as Bakalis and Dixon worked to broaden the downstate voice in the selection process; an elaborate series of slating meetings was designed to prove that no political boss would make the decision this time.

The factor that ultimately determined the lineup had little to do with internal Democratic politics. Thompson looked unbeatable. Walker and Dixon had quit believing in miracles unless opinion polls gave them a fighting chance. Slowly, but surely, they ducked and ran. Hartigan did not bother to make a public statement. He chose private business. On September 6, Dixon publicly declared for re-election as secretary of state. Soon afterward, Walker announced his commitment to private law practice. That left the gubernatorial contest to Bakalis, and he grabbed it. This meant the party had no one to run against Percy. Bakalis tried to lure Hartigan, Congressman Paul Simon, and others, but no one took the bait. Finally, the senate nod went to Alex Seith, a Chicago lawyer.

Thompson had decided on the main points of his re-election campaign without regard for the identity of his opponent. Thompson planned to emphasize the fact that taxes had not been raised in the two-year period; focus on the return of civility to the governor's office (in contrast to the days of Walker); and remind the electorate that he saved the state from financial disaster by balancing the budget.

Thompson faced no greater, or more important, challenge in his first year as governor than putting together the administrative team to run the state government, implement his ideas, and serve him loyally. The task took nearly all year to accomplish and, when done, the results reflected the brand of practicality so familiar to his style. There were still some Walker holdovers; a number of former assistant prosecutors from Thompson's U.S. attorney days; and many young persons. Most of these people whom Thompson brought into state government were bright, energetic, and green. They made mistakes, a few of which caused the governor embarrassment, but most of which never saw the light of day.

In conversation with columnist Neal Peirce, the governor acknowledged the strengths and weaknesses of his key employees. "I'm probably the oldest person on the staff. And there are some in their twenties and thirties, and they have strengths, enthusiasm, integrity, honesty, vitality, willingness to work hard, openness to new ideas. They also have weaknesses, inexperience, and sometimes they bump into each other or stumble over each other."

Most of the new faces were unfamiliar to the public. None was controversial, and the state senate approved the governor's choices. Thompson had no competitors under his nose who wanted to share the spotlight with him.

Of the twenty-four cabinet-level positions, two jobs went to women (Joan Anderson, who had lost her bid for lieutenant governor in 1976, at the Department of Registration and Education; and Josephine Oblinger at the Department of Aging), and one went to a black (Donald Duster, director of Business and Economic Development). All the key people were from Illinois except one—Arthur Quern, director of the Department of Public Aid, who was from Washington, where he had worked on the Domestic Council under President Ford.

As Thompson put his team together, statehouse reporters and their editors passed judgment. A *St. Louis Post-Dispatch* headline said: "Gov. Thompson Puts Together Humdrum But Capable Staff." An Associated Press story inspired this headline: "Thompson's Cabinet Capable, Nonpolitical." A *Chicago Daily News* headline declared: "Thompson Team Fumbles Often in First 100 Days." A headline in the *Champaign-Urbana Courier* read: "Governor's Assistants Have Little Power." There was some truth in all of them.

Thompson pulled some surprises in his appointments, too, the main one being Lynn E. Baird of Park Forest as superintendent of the Illinois State Police. Until Thompson reached down into the ranks for Baird, normal procedure was for the superintendent to have some rank in the department. Baird was a corporal. If he lacked experience in administering a police force, he knew the political ropes. Baird had served five previous governors as personal bodyguard. Thompson said his criteria for superintendent included wanting a good cop, a trustworthy person, and someone troopers would respect. Baird recalled the moment Thompson offered the job: "I just sat there with my mouth open."

For perhaps the most critical position, director of the Bureau of the Budget, Thompson chose Robert L. Mandeville, who the *Chicago Sun-Times* said "is acclaimed as the state's chief fiscal wizard." Mandeville, forty-three, had earned high regard as deputy to Republican comptroller George W. Lindberg from 1973 to 1977, and he had designed and set policies for the comptroller's office in the first years of its existence. Mandeville's conservatism served Thompson well and, despite the budget chief's denials, Mandeville has had considerable influence on state policies by helping Thompson determine spending priorities.

The two key personal staff positions—and ones with greatest media contact—were deputy governor and press secretary. Thompson chose persons who had been with him from the beginning of 1975.

Deputy governor is the second most influential position in state government. As developed by Walker, who was the first Illinois governor to have a deputy, the position combined political considerations and staff operations. Thompson wanted someone who was capable of keeping a firm hand on administrative business and was knowledgeable about the political ropes, too. He chose James L. Fletcher, his 1976 campaign manager.

Fletcher's selection—first as campaign manager and then as deputy governor—elicited similar responses in both instances: he was too green. Critics thought Thompson should surround himself with persons of political experience who knew where the bodies were buried in state government and who would make sure they didn't end up in the governor's closet.

Fletcher was inexperienced in running a campaign and in running a governor's office; but, putting those points aside, he was one of Thompson's most qualified appointees.

Fletcher knew the legislative process and had a surprising familiarity with state government for a man of thirty-three years. He had served as a legislative intern and then as counsel to Illinois House Speaker Ralph Smith in the late 1960s. He then served as parliamentarian for Speaker Jack Walker. Fletcher wrote several key pieces of legislation and served as director of a state commission that issued revenue bonds for higher education facilities. He had connections, too. Before joining Thompson, he worked as a member of the law firm headed by George Burditt, a former legislator and candidate for the U.S. Senate in 1974. While in that firm, Fletcher served as attorney for the influential Illinois Medical Society.

Thompson, at one point in 1977, reflected on Fletcher's contribution to the administration: "... Fletcher played a key role in the Crosstown agreement; Fletcher played a key role in the last several weeks of legislative negotiations. He is by nature and by instinct a negotiator and a compromiser, a good man to bring people together, and he's had legislative training."

Fletcher offered his own interpretation of the deputy governor's job: "I'm nonconfrontation oriented. By training and by nature I believe in problem-solving by compromise.... I'm not a hatchet man ... I see myself as a conduit to Thompson. The job could just as easily be called administrative assistant or executive to the governor." Thompson had chosen a practical man who valued compromise.

The other visible job in the administration—press secretary—went to David Gilbert, thirty-five, Thompson's campaign press secretary. Gilbert's familiarity with Chicago media and the jealousies involved minimized squabbles about access, news tips, and favoritism. He drew criticism in some quarters of the Republican party for being the author of gubernatorial publicity gimmicks, but Gilbert maintained respectability among media representatives.

With Thompson such a dominant personality, and with a staff considered to be quiet and loyal, questions about "yes-men" arose. Thompson seemed surprised at the suggestion he might surround himself with puppets. Therefore, he tested the idea on his staff. "They were absolutely shocked. I defied them to name a single yes-man. And nobody could come up with a name. You know it would be something for my ego and soothing for me because we all have egos and it would be soothing to have some say 'Yes, governor, that's right.' "

Frankly, Thompson said, he wouldn't know a yes-man if he saw one. "... I never had a yes-man when I was U.S. attorney and I can't find one on this staff.... I can't find one. I just can't."

The Second Year

Jim Thompson had a modest wish list for 1978. He wished for a chance to travel and talk about matters of national importance. He wished for a quiet legislative session and another balanced budget. He hoped for tranquility in his relationship with Chicago. He envisioned a pay increase for himself. He expected no scandals; and he wished to be re-elected in November in a landslide.

Remarkably, the major events of 1978 affecting Thompson occurred pretty much in that order. Even when occasional surprises arose, Thompson took them in stride. He remained cool.

The year began ominously with a farm strike, a coal strike, and the second harsh winter in a row; all happened within the first three months of the year and affected not just Illinoisans but millions of Americans in a dozen or more states. While the course of events was well beyond his influence, Thompson injected his comments and his presence.

Illinois had its share of dedicated and determined supporters of the American Agriculture Movement, an organization that worked long and hard at the state and federal levels for higher grain price supports. They organized a national strike by farmers designed to take commodities off the market in protest over low price support levels in the 1977 Farm Bill passed by Congress and signed by Carter. The protestors claimed that support levels were inadequate and would cause widespread bankruptcy. The organization mounted protest demonstrations in Washington, Springfield, and many other state capitals, with farmers driving their tractors to the cities in caravans, clogging roadways, and capturing newspaper headlines.

A main point of the AAM program was to force Congress to establish price supports at 100 percent of parity. Under that theory—long advocated by some farm elements, but never instituted by Congress—the government would maintain price supports according to a base year formula designed not to erode the buying power of farmers. Otherwise, with lower supports the farmers said they could not meet their expenses.

Back in Illinois, the Farm Bureau, the state's largest and strongest farm organization, echoed the position of its national parent—the American Farm Bureau Federation—by sympathizing with the farmers' plight but not backing AAM's demands for parity and higher price supports. Instead, the Farm Bureau urged Congress to enact a variety of programs designed to improve the price of commodities on the open market. That difference in approach brought the Farm Bureau and the American Agriculture Movement into conflict. At the heart of the Farm Bureau's plan were increased farm exports, a farmland set-aside program with incentives for farmers, emergency expansion and liberalization of farm credit, and relief from regulations that increase the cost of farming. Farmers in the AAM, however, wanted money, and the quickest way to get it was from Congress.

As protests grew and tempers flared, Thompson joined a delegation of ten governors from farm-belt states who called on Carter and Agriculture Secretary Bob Bergland early in February. Carter balked at higher supports because of the impact on inflation. Not all the governors at the meeting favored higher supports; but they wanted action, and they laid the responsibility for action at the president's feet. Thompson pleaded the case of young farmers who had large mortgages or who were leasing the land and trying to live off the crops. "I think something more has got to be done to rescue young farmers [who were] encouraged to go into farming when farm prices were higher," he said. Bergland promised action, and Thompson urged his fellow governors to give the government time to respond. He suggested thirty to sixty days as a time limit.

Thompson's appeal to young farmers took shape while he was in Washington. Before meeting at the White House with Carter and agriculture officials, the governor had breakfast with three striking Illinois farmers. He refused to support the strike and their demand for 100 percent parity, but he agreed to act "as their advocate." He promised to raise questions with Carter on the cost of parity, the possibility of a moratorium on farm foreclosures, and the price of federal loans. His breakfast meeting received media coverage.

Back in Illinois, Thompson continued to lament the affect of low prices on young farmers, but he stopped short of any support for the strike. On one occasion, he walked into the lions' den, a convention of the Illinois Farmers Union, which supported 100 percent parity. He threw away a prepared speech and talked for more than an hour, cajoling the farmers, massaging their pride and egos, and praising young persons. He described strikers as "young, smart, college-educated," and praised them for taking the fight to Congress.

Militant strikers thought Thompson stopped short of the support they deserved, and hard-core free market advocates at the other end of the political spectrum puzzled over Thompson's interference. But Thompson persevered, trying verbally to bring the warring factions to some common ground. He declared optimistically that "a majority of Illinois farmers are in sympathy with the goals of American Agriculture."

Thompson had planted himself squarely in the middle. He took his message to a rally sponsored by the Illinois Farm Bureau to promote its congressional action program. He tactfully avoided outright support of the

Farm Bureau program; instead, he lapsed into familiar conversation about young farmers, saying: "If they have to sell or die to get a profit then the farmers are in deep trouble." He said young farmers "may be forced off the land before they can begin."

Thompson's remarks failed to soothe the extremists, but he pleased calmer Farm Bureau elements, just as he had appealed to more moderate members of the American Agriculture Movement. Then, almost as mysteriously as he had entered the controversy, Thompson stopped talking about the strike, even though the national controversy was to continue for several months before Congress raised price supports.

At the same time, Thompson was interested in other national issues that affected his state. One was a strike of United Mine Workers, of which there were 14,000 members in southern Illinois. The Illinois union rank and file had a reputation as being tough minded and disinclined to follow instructions of union leaders. The strike began in December, 1977.

National contract talks proceeded through January and into February. Carter began applying pressure for a settlement when unsettling reports came in from states such as Ohio, which had been stricken by a deadly combination of a severe winter and a coal shortage. Utilities in Illinois, however, reported coal reserves of forty days or more. The governor remained silent.

To impress upon the public and on state officials his growing sense of alarm over the strike, Carter summoned governors of coal states, including Thompson, to Washington. After the meeting, in his first comments on the strike or its effects, Thompson said he planned to call for a voluntary reduction in electricity usage by Illinois citizens to ease the burden on coal supplies. The request involved "nonessential" services, such as outdoor lighting, Thompson said. Two days later he urged residents to set home thermostats at 68 degrees during the day and 60 at night. He also suggested that water heaters be set at 120 degrees, or medium. He mentioned that Illinois utilities had a forty- to fifty-day coal supply.

For approximately two weeks, until Carter decided to invoke the Taft-Hartley Act in the stalemated coal negotiations, Thompson was silent. He sounded surprised when Carter chose not to seize the mines and operate them with federal troops. He doubted UMW members would return to work.

Thompson elaborated on his criticism of Carter to the Associated Press. "If he closed that door [seizure] then that's a tactical mistake. He's putting all his dice on Taft-Hartley. Sometimes people obey Taft-Hartley injunctions and sometimes they do not. By delaying seizure the president may have lost time." Prior to Carter's decision, Thompson had not expressed an opinion about the choices available to the president.

At the same time, Thompson issued a new call for voluntary reductions in the state. He noted the first such call resulted in about a 1 to 3 percent

TOP: Jim and Jayne Thompson on their way to a press conference in Chicago, the day after his landslide victory for Illinois governor on Nov. 2, 1976.
BOTTOM: Governors-elect Thompson and Pierre S. duPont IV (Delaware) confer at the GOP Governors' Conference in Washington, D.C., November 29, 1976.

TOP: Governor Thompson performs with a troupe of belly dancers at Chicago's Ethnic Folk Fest during the 1978 campaign.
BOTTOM: Thompson took his 1978 gubernatorial campaign to a young people's party in Dalton, Illinois.

Thompson's ride on horse in state capitol building irked 1978 opponent Michael Bakalis.

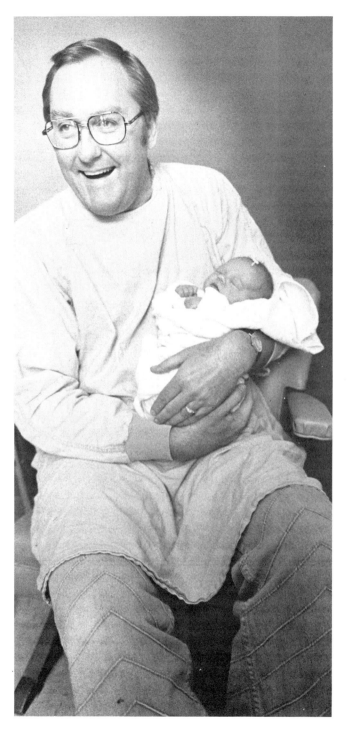

ABOVE: Jim Thompson is sworn in for his second term as Illinois governor in January of 1979, as Jayne and Samantha Jayne Thompson watch. To Thompson's right is Judge Joel Flaum, former Thompson associate. In the background, between the Thompsons, stands Dan Walker, former Democratic governor of Illinois. OPPOSITE: Governor Thompson proudly displays his day-old daughter, Samantha Jayne, who was born on August 3, 1978. The governor is quoted as saying, "She's beautiful . . . she's just gorgeous . . . she's just perfect."

Thompson's ambitions for the White House and dealings with conservatives inspired many political cartoons, such as two by Bill Campbell of *Illinois Times* in 1977 (top) and 1978 (bottom).

reduction in usage over the state instead of the 10 to 13 percent he had hoped for.

The coal strike passed without any further involvement by Thompson, and utilities across the state never felt the pinch of a reduced coal supply. No final report was made on the voluntary reduction program.

The farm and coal strikes had brought Thompson into contact with Carter three times in a short period of time. Late in February they met a fourth time when governors attending the National Governor's Conference in Washington gathered for a two-hour session with the president. Through all four meetings, Thompson and Carter never met in private and had no opportunity to establish the kind of relationship that might have helped Thompson in an emergency, regardless of partisanship. And before a month passed, Thompson most certainly needed Carter's help.

On March 24, an ice storm cut a wide swath through central Illinois, a final kick in the shin at the end of a torturous winter. The storm literally brought the cities of Springfield and Decatur to their knees and knocked out the power in hundreds of small towns. Residents were without electricity for days; business ground to a halt. When power was restored, citizens surveyed damage to trees and property; the damages totaled in the millions of dollars. Thompson reacted by declaring twenty-four counties a disaster area, and he promptly appealed to Washington for assistance.

That is when a closer relationship between Carter and Thompson might have paid off. At the least, a better rapport might have prevented later embarrassment and frustration for the governor.

The Carter administration denied aid for the counties, where an estimated 700,000 persons had been affected by the storm. Thompson smarted, professing not to know why Carter had failed to act on his request. "This is the third time that I have asked the Carter administration for disaster assistance," Thompson said. The administration had denied assistance twice before, during a blizzard in 1977 and a drought in the same year.

"I don't know whether political motivations play a part, I just don't know," Thompson lamented. The administration ruled that federal assistance is not for cases of budgetary overrun because of a storm, unless "such overruns pose a threat to life, property, public health and safety . . . ." Senators Adlai E. Stevenson III and Percy appealed on the state's behalf. Thompson asked again, and President Carter responded by telling Michael Bakalis (who was by then running for governor as the Democratic candidate) that he would personally review the appeal. He did, and he affirmed the decision. No aid came from Washington, although Thompson carried on correspondence and feuded with administration officials for weeks.

Bruised feelings over the episode surely had faded by late May as Carter and Thompson both had other business of importance. But when Carter scheduled a Democratic campaign trip to Illinois in behalf of all party candidates, including Bakalis, a minor disagreement arose over who would greet the president at the Springfield airport.

Thompson revealed with some pleasure, but in the voice of mock pain, that the White House had requested he not be present. "As a matter of common courtesy I had planned to greet the president on behalf of Illinois's 11.5 million residents. Yesterday, the White House advance team informed me that the president didn't want anyone to meet his plane."

Not all business in the first months of 1978 involved Thompson dallying in Washington or tossing dice in national affairs. The Illinois legislature pondered the governor's budget, and Democrats wondered how they could help Bakalis without disturbing their own priorities and the arrangements made between Bilandic and Thompson. The best they did was present Bakalis with a property tax rebate bill, but otherwise Thompson got much of what he asked for in the budget.

Democrats were unable to disrupt Thompson's strategy for his second budget, the priorities of which were: Give as much new money to education as possible; balance the budget; and declare no need for higher taxes.

After announcing his budget, Thompson immediately took to the road for a second series of "chalk talks" to apply pressure on the Democrats. At one budget "chalk talk," Thompson explained: "I gave about twenty of them last year and I think they did the trick to keep the legislature from increasing the size of the budget and causing another budget deficit. This being an election year I'll probably have to give forty speeches, because every lawmaker running for re-election has promised new bridges, higher school aid, or something more for his district." By conducting the fight with the legislature on turf where he knew the public was suspicious of politicians, Thompson could appear to be the protector of state finances.

Thompson played on the public sensitivity to taxes, as he had done in the 1976 campaign and during his first year as governor. In a continuation of the theme, he said, "The wolf is still at the door, but at least we have closed that door in his face."

The Thompson priority for education funds—the second year in a row—not only recognized a need, but served a sound political purpose as well. Bakalis's background as superintendent of public instruction from 1971–75 gave him a ready-made constituency among faculty and administrators of the state's elementary and secondary schools. Also, as a former professor at Northern Illinois University, Bakalis had close ties with higher education. If Bakalis had been successful in accusing Thompson of slighting education, the entire legislative session might have turned out differently.

But Thompson anticipated the Bakalis moves. The governor recommended that higher education receive $79 million more than in the previous year, or 85 percent of the requested amount of $94 million. That amount satisfied higher education officials and removed one area of potential Bakalis attack.

The other attack Bakalis made was more difficult to counter. Elementary and secondary officials had requested $185 million more than the previous year and Thompson budgeted $103 million, with the explanation that he differed with the needs as expressed by officials. Thompson gave Bakalis an opening, but the problem was where to find additional money in the budget for use in education. The Democrats spun their wheels on that issue for the entire session, shifting money around from one pot to another and threatening bodily harm to the budget.

The Democrats finally pushed through a bill calling for an expenditure of $26 million over Thompson's recommendation. The funds came from a federal windfall. Thompson avoided a fight and signed the bill, taking credit for the total and denying Bakalis the issue he needed.

Bakalis tried another issue—the repair of large potholes in pavements caused by two severe winters in a row. Winter weather not only takes a toll on tempers and patience in Illinois, it wrecks highways across the state. Dodging potholes becomes a motorist's preoccupation. Bakalis saw the subject for its irritation value, and his Democratic friends proposed spending $30 million from the general revenue fund—to be paid back out of gas taxes—to repair the maddening holes.

Thompson ridiculed the plan. "I think it's silly. The money can't come out of the air. It can't come from Washington, it can't come from printing presses, it must come from programs." Bakalis persisted. He posed for pictures near a giant pothole on a Chicago expressway. Thompson called it "the rob Peter to pay Paul loan."

Nevertheless, Thompson sensed some public appeal in the Bakalis ploy and moved to undercut the Democrat. Late in May and little more than a month before adjournment of the legislature, Thompson announced his own accelerated program for consideration. He denied Bakalis had inspired the suggestion. The measure died late in the session, Thompson having avoided pitfalls—and potholes.

The Thompson budget as approved by the legislature ignored a growing list of needs for the state. Despite its priority spending for education, many educators feared funds in Thompson's budget were insufficient to curb an erosion of quality in higher education and to prevent greater pressure on local property taxes for secondary end elementary school funding. The less spent at the state level, the more property taxes had to make up.

Recipients of public aid received a 5 percent increase in payments, but neither the governor nor the legislature indicated any interest in a systematic program of increases over time to ease the blow of inflation. Public employee pension programs continued to be inadequately financed in Illinois. A deteriorating road system received little official attention, and questions about an increase in state gasoline taxes were raised again. The governor and legislative leaders correctly assessed the public's unwillingness to develop road repair programs or to sit still for the tax increase that would be necessary to finance them.

The legislative session was not an uninterrupted series of victories for Thompson. None of the setbacks was serious, but one in particular embarrassed him. Ironically, the embarrassment did not come at the hands of Bakalis but from his own actions and those of his lieutenant governor, David O'Neal. The issue was consideration by the legislature of the politically sensitive Equal Rights Amendment.

For six years, proponents of ERA had tried to pass the measure in Illinois. Sometimes it passed the house only to die in the senate. Twice it received a majority of votes in the senate, but a three-fifths majority was required for passage. Patterns of opposition and support changed with each vote, although a constant source of opposition came from the Chicago area. As the number of states approving the amendment neared the required thirty-eight, pressure mounted in Illinois, and proponents said they would seek a vote in June.

Thompson's role in the ERA puzzle had been mystifying. An avowed supporter of ERA, he had been unable to persuade Republicans or Democrats to vote for the amendment. On the record he sounded good. "I will do my level best to use the moral and political force of my office and let the politics take care of itself," he said in June.

Staunch ERA supporters doubted his sincerity and accused him of pulling punches in showdowns. They were especially critical when Thompson followed a statement of support for ERA with a campaign visit on behalf of a legislator who opposed the amendment. To those who accused him of double-dealing, Thompson replied, "I am not one-issue oriented."

If Thompson's impotence in soliciting votes on behalf of ERA was predictable by June, 1978, so was the appearance in Springfield of the queen of the anti-ERA movement, Phyllis Schlafly, the Alton, Illinois, housewife who lobbied against ERA, abortions, and liberals with equal fervor. She was a rallying point for the opposition, and her words brought thunderous cheers and applause on the statehouse steps when she spoke. She came to Springfield leading anti-ERA forces in a show of strength, while singing new words to the tune of "Here Comes Peter Cottontail"— "Here comes Playboy Cottontail . . . trying to buy the votes for ERA . . . telling every girl and boy, you can only have your joy by becoming gender-free or gay."

Proponents of ERA made an unrestrained drive for passage by the Illinois legislature. They enlisted public support from Bilandic; the two U.S. senators, Percy and Stevenson; President Carter; and Bakalis. Eleven members of the Illinois congressional delegation sent telegrams to Bilandic and Thompson to bring out the votes. As the vote neared, Thompson tripped. First came the O'Neal matter.

The lieutenant governor was a known opponent of ERA, although he suppressed it. When the house vote neared, O'Neal made several telephone calls to lawmakers urging them to vote against the amendment. ERA sponsors learned of the end run on Thompson and told the governor. He ordered deputy Fletcher to ask O'Neal to stop making calls, to call back the persons he had contacted, and to tell them he had been expressing his own views and not those of the administration.

O'Neal backtracked. "I don't think in a confidential conversation with a few legislators it would be inappropriate for me to let them know that I've not changed my position. Unfortunately, it was not a confidential conversation, obviously, and evidently it brought embarrassment to the governor. For that I am deeply sorry." So was Thompson, who expressed "disappointment" through his press secretary.

Some observers suggested the difference between Thompson and O'Neal was contrived to demonstrate the lieutenant governor's independence, but all parties involved denied any such arrangement. Whatever the intent, O'Neal's opposition gave the administration some appeal to the anti-ERA forces, who controlled large amounts of campaign money. Gilbert, Thompson's press secretary, commented, "I don't think the governor was aware of O'Neal's lobbying."

Then came the "eavesdropping reporter" episode.

In the final minutes before a house vote on June 23, Thompson invited Associated Press reporter Bob Springer to his office to watch the governor work for votes. Apparently, the governor thought he could persuade reluctant legislators to vote for passage. If that occurred, Thompson would be the hero.

With the vote on the house floor stalled with 106 votes in favor—one short of passage—Thompson called Republicans on the floor to switch their votes. Here is what Springer recorded on Thompson's end of a conversation with Representative William Margalus, a Republican from Chicago:

> Bill, are you going to let it fail? If you go on we've got the 107. Bill, you made a commitment to me the week before. This is the only thing I'm going to ask you for forever. Bill, this is going to hurt me as a leader of the party. This is the most important thing to me. If it goes down, I've got no one but myself to blame. I can't. I can't do that, Bill. I don't want to do that to you, but if you go on the rest'll go on with 106.
>
> Do you understand what's at stake here? It's the end of me as leader of the party unless you go on. Yes it is. Yes it is. You can go from red to green that's what you can do. [Red is a no vote, green is yes.]

The governor hung up. Margalus did not switch to green. Thompson held a similar conversation with another Republican legislator while Springer listened. He failed with him, too, in front of the AP reporter.

ERA fell one vote short; Thompson's grandstand stunt had backfired. But Thompson refused to be a scapegoat. "Now, someone has decided that Jim Thompson will be the fall guy if ERA fails.... The key question is this. Why wasn't ERA passed when we had a Democratic governor, and a Democratic mayor of Chicago ... and a Democratic house and a Democratic senate.... It should have been ratified in Illinois a long, long time ago."

There were other, less publicized, issues before the legislature on which Thompson had considerable success. The beneficiaries of the 1978 legislative session included manufacturers, doctors, and other vendors who provide services to public aid patients. The total cost to taxpayers for the beneficial legislation was more than $50 million.

For years doctors, nursing home operators, and other vendors complained that payment levels for services had not kept pace with inflation. In protest, some refused to treat public aid patients. They lobbied for increases during the Walker administration and in Thompson's first year. In 1978, Thompson agreed to recommend major increases. The legislature considered the plan as part of the budget for the Department of Public Aid.

Until the 1978 change, vendors received "usual and customary" fees up to 70 percent of the normal fee schedule. The fee schedule was arrived at by asking for charges from all vendors, averaging them across the state, and taking 70 percent. Under the change of 1978, all vendors were paid a flat 70 percent of the average. This resulted in an increase of $30 million in payments.

Doctors, nursing home operators, pharmacists, and their associations are liberal contributors to political campaigns of legislators and governors. A number of legislators are investors in, and associated with, nursing homes and pharmacies, and they openly lobby the director of public aid and the governor's staff for increases. In 1978, pharmacists were not included in Thompson's proposal because they had received an increase two years previously under Walker. But the legislature passed an increase anyway, and it was signed by Thompson.

Bakalis, opposed to the increase, raised the possibility of a payoff, with vendors likely to contribute heavily to Thompson. The governor replied: "The medical society supported me before. They won't support Bakalis. But that has nothing to do with political matters. Traditionally, doctors support Republicans and not Democrats."

Beginning in March, 1976, and continuing through the 1978 election, the Illinois Medical Political Action Committee had made gifts totaling more than $55,000 to Thompson. The largest gifts were $10,000 in March, 1976; $10,000 in September, 1976; and $8,750 in September, 1978.

With a Republican in the governor's chair, business and industry expected favored treatment, and Thompson responded to that expectation by supporting elimination over six years of the sales tax on purchase of new and used equipment and refurbished machinery. The exemption cost Illinois about $20 million during the first year, and will cost a total of $182 million in annual lost sales tax revenue during the sixth year.

Originally Thompson proposed a tax rebate plan for equipment at new or expanded facilities in Illinois that would have been an incentive to expand. However, the state Chamber of Commerce and legislative Democrats were pressed by labor to support the bill, because of the potential for more jobs, and they broadened the measure. Thompson prevailed on the long-term phase-in, and the bill passed. Thompson and Bakalis, who also favored the plan, admitted the tax reduction would not create new jobs immediately. They agreed the reduction was symbolic and designed mostly to entice business and industry to move to Illinois from other states.

Symbolic or not, Thompson earned a gold star with business interests. The $20 million raid on the budget occurred without a murmur, and business maintained its strong financial support of the Thompson campaign.

Routinely, Chicago Democrats come to a legislative session with an agenda of special interest bills, especially those dealing with money. Much of the session is spent haggling over the bills, and trading votes with downstate interests. In 1978, Chicago interest legislation seemed skimpier than usual. After getting Crosstown Expressway funds the year before, Chicago decided not to be too greedy. As a result, one of the major victories for Chicago turned out to be a $1 million grant for museums in the omnibus appropriations bill, hardly an amount worthy of Chicago interest in other years. The request inspired one downstate legislator to say, "If that's all they got, it's okay with me. Usually, we're dealing for stuff a lot more scurrilous. I take my kids up there to the Field Museum and Museum of Science and Industry all the time."

The subject of greatest interest to Chicago was off-track betting, or OTB, as it was called. The lure was an estimated $21 million in revenue for the city if OTB were legalized and, accordingly, the full force of the Democratic organization was behind an effort to pass legislation in 1978.

As "sweeteners" to collect downstate votes in the legislature, the bill provided for six "core cities" where OTB operations would be permitted, thus providing revenue opportunities. The cities, in addition to Chicago, were Rockford, Peoria, Decatur, Springfield, and East St. Louis. One legislative estimate of the first year's yield looked this way: $18 million to the state, $40 million to cities, $29 million to racing interests.

Legal betting on horse racing away from the tracks is permitted in a few locations across the nation, most notably New York State and Atlantic City, New Jersey. Proponents in Illinois cited OTB's convenience to the thousands of persons who like to wager on horse races but are not able to reach the track. These proponents also promoted the increased revenue potential for cities, many of which are desperate for new sources of money.

Opponents attacked from two sides. One, the Methodist churches of Illinois, called the proposal "immoral" since it encouraged families with minimum income to squander money that otherwise would be spent on necessities. The other opposing viewpoint represented private and public law enforcement agencies. They raised the specter of organized crime moving in on OTB and creating an across-the-board increase in all crime in Illinois cities.

Chicago politicians have tried for decades to legalize betting in the city. The subject has taken several disguises, but the proposal always was clear: Take advantage of the public desire to bet on horse races to raise revenues for the city. Governors and mayors have quarreled over this issue through the years, beginning as early as 1934 when Henry Horner was governor and Edward J. Kelly was mayor of Chicago. Horner, a Democrat and associate of Kelly, vetoed a bill that would have permitted bookies to be licensed in Chicago. Kelly wanted the law for its potential licensing revenue and the opportunity for patronage and payoffs. Emphasizing the high-stakes nature of the subject, the veto cost Governor Horner Mayor Kelly's support in the 1936 elections.

Regardless of its onerous connections with crime and immorality, OTB has always been presented as a painless way to get more revenue for Chicago without a raid on the state treasury. Once approved, the backers said, OTB would be a perpetual money machine.

Quite naturally, then, OTB came up in political negotiations between Thompson and Bilandic in 1977, when they made various arrangements for measures to benefit Chicago and provide Thompson with a balanced budget. Crosstown was the centerpiece in 1977, and OTB was the same for 1978. Thompson acknowledged a couple of telephone conversations with Bilandic on OTB about mid-1977.

As a means of obtaining evidence on which to raise public support, Thompson in 1977 named the "Governor's Revenue Study Commission on Legalized Gambling," with a reporting date coinciding with the 1978 legislative session. He named Thomas A. Reynolds, Jr., as chairman. Reynolds was chairman of Citizens for Thompson and a partner in the law firm of Winston and Strawn. Writing in *Chicago Magazine* in November, 1978, Paul McGrath said Reynolds "had represented the owners of Balmoral Park Race Track and his firm still did."

There were interesting connections in the background of other commission members, too. One member was Dan Webb, a former associate of Thompson during his prosecutor years; in 1977, Thompson named Webb director of the Illinois Department of Law Enforcement. Another was Marshall Korshak, a Democrat, lawyer, and respected Chicagoan. Korshak served in the state senate in the early 1950s where he came to know another commission member, Elbert Smith of Decatur, a Republican who served a term as state auditor. Once a major factor in Chicago Democratic affairs, Korshak had suffered through the years because of his brother Sidney's reported association with underworld characters. Marshall, however, had maintained a "clean" reputation, serving with honor as director of the Chicago Revenue Department and as Kerner's director of revenue from 1965–66.

After attending a first meeting of the Governor's Revenue Study Commission, old friends Korshak and Smith spent some time together over a drink in Korshak's office on the afternoon of October 5, 1977. In a personal memo later dictated and filed, Smith recorded: "We think it is questionable that a commission without legislative members can produce a report that would be very acceptable to the legislature. That remains to be seen."

Smith puzzled further over organization of the commission. In his memo he noted, "I am not informed as to the membership of the commission. . . . There was no prepared agenda, no one appeared to serve as secretary, although Mr. Reynolds made some notes. No items were distributed." Smith inquired about the commission's organization and charge. "Mr. Reynolds said that it was not established by an act of the legislature and presumably was established by executive order. No copy of the order was presented and our duties and responsibilities are somewhat obscure."

Nevertheless, Smith deduced early what mission the commission had been given. "It seemed to appear that our study would be confined to off-track betting. . . ." Reynolds told the commissioners that they were to determine the potential revenue from OTB and, as Smith wrote, "what, if any, would be the consequences to the revenue presently derived from the taxation of racetrack activities."

The press had trouble finding out about commission meetings, and attendance by members was erratic. In December, 1977, Chicago newspapers reported the commission had voted unanimously to recommend that OTB be established. Smith, unaware of any such vote, wrote Reynolds on December 19: "Perhaps this report [in the press] was without foundation. In any case I respectfully decline to join in such advice or recommendation to Governor Thompson." Reynolds wrote Smith that the vote occurred on December 15, and "those members of the commission who were present unanimously voted to include in the commission's report to the governor a recommendation that off-track betting be legalized in Illinois."

McGrath reported that Thomas H. Coulter, chief executive officer of the Chicago Association of Commerce and Industry also missed the vote. McGrath wrote, "He said that he understood the commission's mission was finding a way to implement off-track betting, that it was a fait accompli."

The public finally heard of the commission's full report in April just as the legislature warmed up, and Democrats submitted a bill to legalize off-track betting. Mayor Bilandic endorsed the proposal, and Lieutenant Governor O'Neal argued, "We have legalized gambling already ... and I think basically people in state government are looking for any ways they can to increase revenues without raising taxes...."

Thompson insisted he had not taken a position on OTB. "I don't know what bill, if any bill, is going to get out. I object to people saying I'm making early legislative judgments.... The bill may be radically different when it comes to me." Thompson left all options open, creating a sense of approval. His 1978 "nonposition" was in conflict with statements made during the 1976 gubernatorial campaign, and newspapers reminded him in stories and editorials.

In October, 1976, Thompson had said, "I certainly would be opposed to off-track betting run by municipalities." On another occasion, he had declared "... I would not support any new form of legalized gambling." Thompson said his position in 1978 did not conflict with his 1976 statements.

As a vote neared in the house late in May, Thompson came out of his corner. He appeared before a Republican caucus and asked fellow party members to vote to keep OTB alive and send it to the senate for further study. Despite press speculation that supporters were several votes short of passage, OTB cleared the state house by a single vote on May 26, the deciding ballot cast by a Republican.

Passage sounded alarm bells across the state. Sensing a snowball effect in the legislature—the state senate generally supports the Chicago viewpoint—powerful forces entered the contest. The Chicago Crime Commission began a systematic campaign to arouse editorial opposition, counting as allies the two major Chicago newspapers. In a series of press releases, the commission—on which Thompson once served—criticized the governor for interfering in the party caucus and charged him with supporting OTB. The commission's major argument against OTB rested on an alleged link with organized crime.

The *Chicago Tribune* raised its voice in an unusually strong criticism of Thompson and against OTB, saying: "Whatever his motives, he [Thompson] cannot avoid responsibility for last week's disgraceful action. Such euphemisms as 'keeping the bill alive' and 'resolving problems' mask nothing. Mr. Thompson not only kept the bill alive, he pushed it over a major hurdle. We urge him to return to the good sense of his pre-election stand on the matter."

Thompson refused to budge from his "keep it alive" stance. In a reply to the *Tribune*, he said, "I don't know that OTB would lead to bookmakers and juice loans." Indulging in a bit of breast-beating, he added: "I'm keeping it an open subject and taking a great deal of heat on this."

One individual who applied heat was Fred Inbau, Northwestern

University law professor and Thompson's mentor during the 1960s. Inbau, in a rare display of disappointment at Thompson's action, wrote him of his sadness that his friend appeared to be supporting OTB. "It was the only time Freddy and I had that kind of disagreement," Thompson said later. Thompson indicated he listened to Inbau's complaint, but he did not say whether it influenced his decision.

While the bill languished in the state senate through June, apparently short of the votes needed for passage, other events occurred which affected consideration of OTB. The combination of these issues—pressure against OTB from the *Tribune* and the Chicago Crime Commission, and Thompson's own second thoughts—resulted in adjournment of the legislature without action on the bill. Thompson and legislative leaders vowed to consider it anew during the fall session.

OTB was under consideration by the legislature at the same time Thompson was putting together support forces for his re-election campaign. One of the pressure points was the support of the Illinois AFL-CIO. As Thompson neared an endorsement by this union organization, Bakalis became alarmed and sought help to beat back Thompson. Bakalis turned to Bilandic, who of course was vitally interested in passage of OTB. The governor held the legalized gambling issue hostage, thus making it difficult for Bilandic to come to Bakalis's defense. But the mayor did intervene and saved the AFL-CIO endorsement for the Democratic ticket. The switch by Bilandic miffed Thompson, and he felt betrayed. In mid-August Thompson declared opposition to OTB. "If the people of Illinois want off-track betting they'll have to elect someone else as their governor. I will neither support an OTB bill nor sign one." Thompson said he opposed OTB because "it is wrong to rely on people's weaknesses . . . to support government."

Although technically Thompson did not reverse his field—his final decision confirmed 1976 statements—the moral implications of his comment sounded hollow after months of begging the issue. Thompson's consistency at the beginning and the end was interrupted in the middle by hesitation, and did little more than enhance his reputation as a pragmatic governor.

Thompson's behavior on OTB characterized the first two years of his administration. There were no bold strokes of genius and great successes, nor were there any demonstrations of shocking weakness and failures. Most issues settled down somewhere in between. Consequently, the small pieces of fabric have to be searched for hints of his character.

In that context, the aberrations uncovered by a vigilant press in the first two years are important, although individually they may seem of little consequence. In 1977, Thompson survived the Kentucky Derby fiasco, a brush with staff abuses of the state airplane fleet, and an airing of his views on membership in private clubs. In 1978, media surveillance uncovered another collection of peccadilloes, the sum of which deserves attention.

They prompted this editorial comment in the Lindsay-Schaub newspapers: "...all this raises some legitimate questions about Thompson's judgment across a range of issues that confront governors and presidents. The questions involve his feel for the impact of government on the lives of average people, his sense of priorities, and his personal operating definition of ethics in public life.... The governor should recognize that questioning will be more intense and widespread the more he steps out into the national stage in pursuit of the presidency."

The first addition to the collection in 1978 involved an investigation of expenses incurred by the Thompsons in operation of the executive mansion. Bill Lambrecht, then a reporter for the *Alton Telegraph*, revealed that the mansion budget had increased from $77,800 in 1968 to $312,000 in fiscal 1978. Lambrecht also explained in detail how the Thompsons spent money for entertaining, including purchases of shrimp, lobster tails, crab meat, egg rolls, and large quantities of liquor.

Thompson cried "cheap shot." Revealing a deep sensitivity to criticism of a personal nature, the governor and his wife "concluded that the story was unfair and distorted." Implications of high living in the mansion irritated the governor. "Inflation hits everybody's grocery budget," he pointed out. "There wasn't a word in the story about what kind of entertaining is done at the mansion.... It's silly to conclude that we, by our lifestyle, have caused all these expenses to go up."

Thompson vigorously defended his wife, who managed the mansion accounts. "And I feel badly because my wife can't really practice law because of the demands of her position. She can't even do it part-time because of the demands of her position. All she's got left is to try and run the mansion fairly and efficiently."

Unwilling to leave the subject at that, Thompson ordered an investigation. The resulting report said food and beverage expenses during Thompson's first year in office showed a 44.8 percent decrease from 1976. The report's figures were based on calendar years, while the original story used fiscal years. Thompson's report did not directly attack Lambrecht's study, and most of the reporter's statements stood unchallenged.

Shortly after the mansion episode, the Associated Press began a story from Springfield with this introduction:

"For Rent (sort of): Nice 1 bdrm apt in Chicago, plush near-North Side neighborhood. Close to schools. $185 a month. Absentee landlord, lots of security. Contact owner, James R. Thompson, at Governor's Mansion, Springfield."

The AP revealed that Thompson had taken a 1977 federal income tax deduction of $2,370 for expenses related to the upkeep of an apartment in his house at 544 W. Fullerton Parkway in Chicago. The apartment had not been rented since 1976. The apartment was on the first floor of the residence and the Thompsons lived upstairs when they were in Chicago. Thompson said state troopers lived rent free in the apartment. The story indicated that apartments must be rented for the deductions to be allowed. Thompson's tax consultant claimed the deduction was valid under tax laws. The Internal Revenue Service showed no public interest in the report.

Continuing its vigilance, the AP on June 15 unveiled the results of an extensive investigation of telephone use dating from early 1977 and involving Thompson and his staff. It revealed that state phones were used extensively for personal political business. One Thompson aide, Gayle Franzen, made at least twenty-nine personal calls, the AP said, costing more than $55. Franzen repaid the state. So did most other individuals found to have used the phones for other than state business.

The report said that over more than a year's time Thompson and his aides had placed at least 107 calls to Douglas Bailey, the governor's political strategist in Washington. The amount paid by taxpayers for the calls totaled $282. One aide who felt the need to consult Bailey frequently was Peg Blaser. She called Bailey when "I wanted to know what the governor's position was on something." Bailey said later that he and Thompson talked two or three times a month on an average.

Other political uses surfaced, including dozens of calls from Springfield to Citizens for Thompson offices in Chicago. Each time Thompson traveled outside the state to partisan functions, political calls were made and billed to the state. Several calls to Market Opinion Research in Detroit dealt with research work done for Thompson's campaign.

Thompson responded by admitting that "we slipped up . . . obviously we didn't do our job. I suppose in the rush of excitement of taking over an office as large as the governor's some things that are routinely done in business, for example, as a matter of control, didn't get done."

About his personal calls billed to the state, Thompson said he hadn't kept a list but "if everyone else in the office is going to reimburse their phone calls, then I guess I should, too." A day later Thompson sent a check for $97 to the state to cover the charges and a note which read: "How in the world do you say 'I'm sorry' to a whole state. . . ."

Thompson complained in private of the media's treatment of the mansion expenditures, apartment rental, and telephone abuse matters, but he kept a cool head publicly. His control prevented the incidents from being enlarged by press reports. However, in another personal matter—his salary as governor—he complained openly and never concealed unhappiness. From almost the time of his election in 1976, Thompson complained about his $50,000 annual salary. (He also received living quarters at the mansion, plus other fringe benefits including transportation and an entertainment allowance.) The last ballot hardly had been counted when he called for a pay raise for members of the cabinet and himself.

"No one should have to make a financial sacrifice year after year because he chooses to serve the public," he said. At the time of his inauguration, Thompson's pay ranked fifth in the nation behind the governors of New York, New Jersey, Texas, and Pennsylvania. Six other states paid governors the same as Illinois.

During the first months of his administration, Thompson persisted in his financial lament, which led to a couple of discoveries on his part. The first was that the press and the public saw a contradiction between his salary appeal and his call for a "year of sacrifice" to balance the state budget. He admitted a "surface inconsistency." The second discovery was the public's deep-rooted sensitivity to pay increases for public officials. Open criticism and hostility to the suggested increases silenced the governor.

Thompson reopened the pay raise subject later in the year by appointing former governor Samuel Shapiro, a Democrat, chairman of a commission to study state pay levels—including the legislature—and report to him in 1978. Thompson said the recommendations would form a proposal to the legislature.

The Shapiro Commission recommended a salary of $75,000 for the governor, or an increase of 50 percent, and similar percentage boosts for other elected state officials, judges, and legislators. A public outcry followed, focusing on the large percentage increases. Thompson said it only looked like 50 percent, arguing that the increase worked out to about 5 percent a year from 1973 when the pay was last adjusted. The public did not buy the explanation, and Bakalis joined the criticism of Thompson. He said only the legislators deserved an increase, and not nearly as much as recommended. Thompson said his mail ran "about 90 to 10 against."

As weeks passed, the issue became too hot for Thompson. At a meeting of broadcast journalists he said, "I just think government salaries have been too low, but it's not a message you can get through to people in an election year." On May 19, Thompson announced he would veto any pay raise bill passed by the legislature. To make the most of the announcement, Thompson flew around the state for separate press conferences. Thompson defended the expense "because I think this is a question of great widespread interest to the people of Illinois."

Editorial pages across the state applauded Thompson's decision. The Decatur Herald said "... The coming campaign is better rid of the pay raise issue. The performance of Illinois government and the state of the state are more important questions than the pay levels of public officials."

Shapiro was surprised by Thompson's announcement and burial of the issue. He had an inkling of the veto pledge, Shapiro said, "but I thought compromise would occur. It's a dead issue until next session." That may have been the thinking of editorial writers and Shapiro, but the subject never was far from Thompson's mind, or the thoughts of the legislators. In a July interview, Thompson complained of not being able to fly to

Wisconsin for recreation at his vacation home "because it costs too much to fly." In the same conversation, he announced undertaking a book-writing project "because I need the money." The legislature took no action on the bill to raise salaries, carrying the issue over to the fall legislative session, which was to occur after the elections.

The period after an election and before the seating of a new legislature has been a favorite for consideration of government pay increases. Anticipating action on salaries by a lame duck legislature, Thompson earlier had said he wouldn't sign a bill passed during that period. "I don't like the usual and customary practice of waiting for the last day of a lame duck session to pass a pay raise bill which could then be signed by a governor who was assured of four more years," he said.

The issue was forgotten in the election melee. But on the eve of the November legislative session, Chicago newspapers said Democratic leaders intended to resurrect the pay increase bill, make some alterations, and pass it before the year ended. Within a few days, legislators changed the bill to give themselves a 40 percent increase, or $8,000 annually, and the same dollar increase for the governor, and passed it. Pay raises also were authorized for state officials and judges.

After the election, Thompson had left Illinois for a Republican governors' conference in Williamsburg, Virginia, and a vacation afterward in South Carolina. The pay raise action occurred during his absence but with his knowledge. After legislative approval, Thompson issued a veto message from South Carolina, making good on his earlier pledge. Within hours the house and senate overrode the veto, and the salaries went into effect.

Thompson rejected other alternatives, including holding his action until later in the year, and after adjournment of the legislature. "That's playing games with legislature," he said. "I felt for the sake of my relations with the legislature . . . if there were the votes to override me, I'd give them that chance." Another alternative was to veto his pay, and approve the others. "I didn't ask for it," he said.

The roof blew off the state, but legislators and Thompson expected the explosion and waited for the cry to abate, as it had done other times after legislative action. Public criticism, spurred by editorials in dozens of newspapers and headline stories on television, mounted, but the legislature adjourned its fall session without a thought of reconsideration.

In at least one respect, timing could not have been worse. The Carter administration, through its inflation fighter, Alfred Kahn, had declared war on institutions and companies that ignored the president's voluntary guidelines for price and salary increases. Kahn joined a chorus against the Illinois action and held telephone conferences with Thompson in an effort to reverse the process.

While some criticism focused on the amount of the increases, the culprit was the method, especially after indication earlier in 1978 that the issue was dead until another legislative session. Thompson emphasized the point. "I haven't seen a single editorial or story that said my salary was unreasonable...." He declared that if the public didn't think he had earned his salary over the next four years "then they can throw me out."

The uprising gathered momentum. Individuals organized a "tea bag" protest symbolic of the Boston Tea Party and thousands of tea bags arrived at the governor's mansion and at his office in the statehouse. Thompson responded by conferring with legislative leaders to see if they would reconsider. The answer was "no." After two years of playing ball with Thompson on budgetary matters, the legislature was prepared to stand its ground while the governor perspired.

Over the Christmas and New Year's holidays, the complaints from citizens and in the media grew. Feeling the pinch of criticism, and having received 22,000 tea bags, Thompson called a special session of the legislature for January 5, saying: "I'm convinced that an overwhelming majority of the people of Illinois favor a rollback and phase-in of salary increases...." He proposed a plan raising salaries from $20,000 to $24,000 in the first year, and another $2,000 in each of the next two years, to reach the total of $28,000. His salary would have gone up $5,000 in the first year and $3,000 in the next.

Legislators grumbled but gathered in Springfield to reconsider. After eighteen hours of wrangling, they agreed to implement $5,000 of the $8,000 raise in the first year and the rest in the second. The same plan applied to Thompson. Kahn and the Carter administration applauded the gesture as helpful to inflation control, and all concerned hoped the issue would vanish.

Three days later, Thompson stunned the state by spending about a quarter of his thirteen-minute inaugural speech apologizing to the citizens of Illinois for his errors on the pay raise matter. He said, "I did veto them, but many people concluded that the manner in which I did so, to paraphrase Macbeth, kept the word of promise to your ear and broke it to your hope. And you were right, and I apologize." Thompson said he called the legislature back to deal with the rollback because of a letter he received from a woman who enclosed his campaign button. "She said she couldn't wear it any more. And that is when I knew that the matter had to be set right."

The 1978 Campaign

Jim Thompson's second campaign for governor had a remarkable similarity to the plot of a daytime television soap opera. It had a consistent story line, handsome actors, occasional drama, and a predictable outcome that barely reflected reality. A citizen of Illinois could have left the country for weeks, returned, and never lost the thread of the story.

An appropriate title would have been "Big Jim Starts for Washington." Nothing happened in the campaign to impede Thompson's pursuit of a national audience. He demonstrated a durability that can be admired by presidential talent scouts and a resilience under fire that helped avoid the political death suffered by some of the nation's best-known politicians. And he proved again, as he had in 1976, that it is not necessary to make promises to win 60 percent of the vote.

Nevertheless, as Thompson prepared for the campaign, some supporters fretted. They feared complacency, especially with private polls showing Thompson comfortably ahead of Bakalis. Recent Illinois voting patterns were not good omens, either. Voters had rejected Ogilvie after one term in 1972 and Walker after a single term in 1976. No governor had been re-elected to a second term since Kerner in 1964, and his plurality had been only 179,000 votes. Also, before the campaign started, Thompson's advisers detected the first winds of anti-incumbency that ultimately swept Senator Edward Brooke of Massachusetts, Senator Robert P. Griffin of Michigan, Governor Meldrim Thomson of New Hampshire, and Senator Richard C. Clark of Iowa out of office.

One reason for Thompson's advisers to be alert involved Attorney General Scott, the person who gave Thompson his first state job in 1969.

By late 1977 and into 1978, newspapers reported a continuing investigation by U.S. attorney Thomas P. Sullivan of contributions made to Scott's political campaigns in the late 1960s and early 1970s. The apparent target of the investigators was some $50,000 in contributions allegedly used by Scott for personal purposes. If true, the matter raised obvious questions covered by federal tax laws. Scott fought tenaciously through the press and courts to thwart what he considered harassment by the U.S. attorney. He said the action was politically inspired by Democratic enemies and kept alive by leaks to Chicago newspapers.

The matter became increasingly uncomfortable for Thompson. The possibility of an indictment of Scott—which finally happened in 1979—had major implications for the Republican state ticket, right down to the county level. Also, Thompson's background as prosecutor, and his friendships with employees in the prosecutor's office, made him vulnerable to charges of aiding the U.S. attorney or being the source of media leaks.

Speculation arose, fanned by those suspicious of Thompson within the party, that if Scott had to vacate his position on the ballot—something he vigorously denied would occur under any circumstances—Thompson would promote his friend and former U.S. attorney, Samuel Skinner, for the ballot position. Scott was angered by the talk, and Thompson and Skinner denied any conspiracy. Still, no one doubted Skinner's interest in the attorney general's position if Scott were out of the picture.

Thompson tried to keep quiet, but in a March interview he explained the dilemma. "Many people working on this case are appointees of mine. I am staying away from the U.S. attorney's office. I don't have any influence in that office. I am not plotting overthrow." He called rumors of a Skinner-for-Scott swap "not true" and "damaging to me, Bill Scott, Sam Skinner, and damaging to the Republican party." The rumors persisted, and Scott wanted a demonstration by Thompson that the air was clear between them.

As part of Scott's counterattack on the U.S. attorney through the media, Thompson began appearing at Scott's side at press conferences. Early in June, Thompson attended a fund-raising event for the attorney general at which he gave Scott a rousing vote of confidence. (Skinner received an invitation but was out of town.) The show of unity between Thompson and Scott put the rumors to rest temporarily.

Whatever the concerns, Thompson's re-election never was in doubt. Only twice was his control of the campaign threatened (both times by tax-related questions), and each time he quickly regained a footing. Thompson's large lead confirmed the political wisdom of Democrats who in 1977 refused to challenge the governor because 1978 looked like a Republican year. It was definitely a Thompson year.

To begin with, Thompson had all the benefits of incumbency and few of the liabilities. When the campaign began in earnest in July, he had been in office only eighteen months. On election day, November 7, Thompson had been governor two months less than two years, hardly enough time to turn Illinois in dramatic new directions, even if he were so inclined. So, in his favor he had the psychology of not quite being an incumbent in the public's mind. It was improbable that an electorate would throw Thompson out of office in the absence of a major scandal or calamity.

In reality, of course, Thompson had all the advantages of an incumbent. He commanded instant and continuous media coverage, he had a substantial reservoir of funds left over from 1976 with which to hire a large staff, and he had done enough state business to know where sources of new money could be found. The experience of a previous gubernatorial campaign taught him how to avoid bear traps planted by the opposition and, more importantly, how to plant some of his own.

Thompson was a much wiser person on the threshold of the 1978 campaign than the greenhorn ex-prosecutor who entered the battle with Howlett. He knew the intricacies of campaign strategy. For example, in outline form, the campaign directive for Thompson looked simple: Be the governor, avoid mistakes, defend only when necessary. On the other hand, Thompson hoped to steal the election from Bakalis before midyear with several subtle maneuvers aimed at the Democrat's base of support.

A first consideration, however, was to take the measure of his opponent. A former professor at Northern Illinois University, Bakalis was a handsome, slightly built man with dark features, reflecting his Greek parentage. At thirty-eight he projected some of the youthful good looks and manner of a well-dressed Kennedy, and he worked at being a contrast to the casual, fun-loving Thompson. In taking the serious approach to campaigning, Bakalis lacked sparkle and often appeared humorless. In truth, Bakalis had a quick wit, but he did not bend easily in public and in the presence of the media.

The governor never underestimated Bakalis, although publicly Thompson often appeared to disdain the challenger. Bakalis had earned the reputation as a tireless campaigner, skilled at coming from behind in statewide elections. In 1970 he defeated incumbent Republican Ray Page for superintendent of public instruction, and in 1976 he defeated incumbent Republican George Lindberg for comptroller. He was not a throwaway candidate.

As portrayed by the media, the contest featured contrasting styles and personalities. Bakalis projected an image of statesmanship, decorum, and conservatism but, as he said many times, "with a touch of heart." Thompson put on a dazzling display of personality campaigning, more polished than in 1976. Supremely confident of his charm and voter acceptance, Thompson created a series of improbable situations which left the impression of boldness with a common touch. One episode occurred on an early morning stop in East Peoria. After shaking hands with factory workers at the plant gate, Thompson went across the road to a tavern. The media followed. He sat at the bar and ordered a Lebanese breakfast complete with a shot of whiskey and a beer chaser, which he drank as the cameras rolled. The media soaked it up, and the Thompson cult blossomed.

While the public tried to decide which personality struck its fancy, Thompson whittled away at Bakalis's strengths. These included the Chicago Democratic organization, the labor unions, and the forces of education. Bakalis's experience as state superintendent of schools and a college professor gave him an entrée to the votes of thousands of public employees. With Chicago and the unions firmly committed and supplemented by the resources of elementary, secondary, and higher education, Bakalis needed only a break or two on issues to begin thinking of a third upset victory.

By working closely with the Bilandic administration on Crosstown in 1977 and off-track betting in 1977 and early 1978, Thompson had chiseled at the foundation of Democratic support before the Bakalis campaign got warmed up. Thompson hoped the deals would neutralize the Democratic-controlled legislature, which under normal conditions would give a Republican governor fits in an election year. Bakalis, on the other hand, planned to work closely with Democratic leadership to fashion issues for the campaign. However, Thompson's work was so thorough the legislature did little more than give lip service to Bakalis.

Whether or not Bilandic's arrangements with Thompson were overt steps to keep a friendly Republican in the governor's mansion, they had that effect. The lack of unqualified Chicago support created doubts about the Bakalis candidacy in the minds of party workers. "Is Chicago supporting him?" They wondered in the courthouses across Illinois.

That took care of one phase of Thompson's plan to undermine the challenger's strength. A second target was the potential for support among teachers, faculty, and administrators throughout the state education system, from kindergarten through graduate school. Thompson had made education a priority for state spending in 1977, but the amounts did not satisfy anyone. Only the knowledge that other agencies and departments got less prevented a revolt. If Thompson could not produce more funds in 1978, Bakalis would have an issue—the shortchanging of the children of Illinois—with which to attack Thompson.

Thompson's budget eliminated any doubts about his priorities, whether or not Bakalis had the issue. The budget recommended an amount for higher education that was 84 percent of the amount requested; elementary and secondary education received 55 percent of the requested amount. The state Office of Education and Superintendent Joseph Cronin complained. They took their case to the Democrats, but the shortage was not enough to justify blaming Thompson for abandoning education. The amount budgeted for education in 1978 became Thompson's best investment.

Thus by March, months before the public began to give much thought to the upcoming contest between Thompson and Bakalis, the governor had pulled off two minor coups: he had undermined Bakalis's base of support from both Chicago Democrats and state educators. However, the boldest move by Thompson was yet to come. It involved the support of Bakalis and the Democratic ticket by labor unions. As with education, organized labor can sway thousands of votes as well as contribute money and assistance at the precinct level. There were doubts whether labor could marshal the rank and file to a single bugle call and, without a united front of labor officials, a Democrat looked weak and ineffective. Thompson wanted Democratic workers to ask: "Is labor supporting Bakalis?"

The point man for Thompson in the attempt to break down labor support for Bakalis was Deputy Governor James Fletcher, whose experience as a negotiator had been proven in the Crosstown Expressway business. He met with Teamsters officials from Chicago and downstate in an effort to bring them solidly behind Thompson. Teamsters unions had supported Republicans before, so no new ground was being broken. But if the Teamsters publicly declared for Thompson, and if the United Auto Workers, which had strong downstate locals, came over, a bandwagon effect could be achieved, thus diverting money and support from Bakalis. At the least, defections would indicate a lack of confidence in Bakalis. At the most, they might create enough momentum to sway the AFL-CIO. That would be news.

By May, Fletcher had done his work and the Teamsters in Chicago and downstate supported Thompson, an endorsement covering 165,000 members. A Teamsters official stated the preference in these words: "It's just that we think Thompson's a better man."

Irked by the endorsement and by the general slowness of labor contributions to his campaign, Bakalis said the arrangement would backfire on Thompson. Apparently, he referred to speculation that Thompson had done the Teamsters pension fund a favor by agreeing to buy the old Sherman House property in Chicago's Loop for a state office building site.

This purchase by the state—which was approved by Thompson—meant the owners could repay a $5 million loan from the Teamsters. Otherwise, they were faced with defaulting on the loan. "It has the appearance of a deal," Bakalis said. Thompson replied, "If I were going to cut a deal with the Teamsters, I wouldn't have been part of the deal in public." He denied knowing of Teamster involvement in Sherman House ownership. He assumed "local Democrats" were among the investors.

The involvement of Thompson and the Teamsters with state office plans in downtown Chicago illustrates the complexities of doing business in the city. It is a political environment. There can be no nonpolitical or uninvolved business arrangements as long as Chicago officials depend on results for jobs, campaign contributions, and community growth. Any association on Thompson's part with city hall, Chicago-area contractors and businessmen, or the labor unions of Cook County draws him inexorably onto dangerous turf. In Chicago, where city hall is king, the governor's leverage and control are diminished and the opportunities for political liabilities are plentiful.

Bakalis also claimed that Thompson agreed to favorable wage settlements between the state Department of Transportation—controlled by the governor—and the bargaining Teamsters locals. Denying any prior arrangement on wages, Thompson said he told the Teamsters only that they would be treated fairly in state contract discussions and that he would be "open and accessible" to union officials.

The Teamsters endorsement and the one from the UAW (135,000 members) were not fatal blows to Bakalis, but they did not help his foundering campaign. At the same time Thompson's aides were in contact with officials of the state AFL-CIO. They came within a hair of gaining the endorsement of the union organization, which had a membership of more than a million persons. If Bakalis was unaware of any threat to AFL-CIO support, it was because Republicans were almost never considered for that endorsement, particularly for governor. The AFL-CIO had too much to lose in jobs to jump back and forth politically. Its loyalty to the Democrats seldom wavered.

But this time there was a reason why the union organization negotiated with Thompson: off-track betting. OTB would have pumped about $21 million a year in new money into the city revenue system and would have meant favorable consideration for union wage increases, more money for construction and repairs, and jobs.

Eventually, word leaked out that Thompson and the AFL-CIO were close to agreement. Faced with total collapse of his candidacy in that event, Bakalis sought direct assistance from Bilandic and Cook County Board President George Dunne. Thompson and his aides worked furiously to blunt the last-minute involvement, but failed, and Bakalis got the endorsement.

A final irony occurred in mid-September, after the announcement of union commitments. Thompson addressed the AFL-CIO state convention and told delegates, "I will not be satisfied until every public employee has the right to collective bargaining. If the legislature passes the collective bargaining bill I will sign it." He also pledged to veto any right-to-work bill passed by the legislature. The delegates roared and gave him a standing ovation.

AFL-CIO backing for Bakalis was tepid. One official summed up Bakalis's problem: "Unless the locals get out the vote, get the people out on the streets, the state council's endorsement is meaningless."

Having successfully reduced the power supply to Bakalis, Thompson should have coasted to a comfortable election triumph, except for two items: one was Bakalis's doggedness, and the other was the issue of tax reduction. Despite being thwarted at every thrust by the agile Thompson, Bakalis never quit looking for the Big Issue that would turn the campaign around. Bakalis explored several during the legislative session, but none caught on. He tried and abandoned education, potholes, Medicaid fraud, and more. Until June, Bakalis had not given tax reduction a second look, although there was considerable legislative activity.

Thompson, however, fought a couple of preliminary battles on tax reduction in the 1977 legislative session, and early in 1978. Both involved proposals by State Representative Donald Totten, a conservative Republican from suburban Schaumburg and a nemesis of Thompson. He proposed an automatic increase in the $1,000 per person state income tax deduction with each increase in the rate of inflation. The proposal would have cost Illinois millions of dollars in revenue, and Thompson helped defeat the plan.

Also in 1977, Totten submitted a proposed constitutional amendment to limit state revenues to 7 percent of total personal income in Illinois. Totten modeled the plan after one offered in California by former Governor Ronald Reagan. Totten had managed Reagan's 1976 presidential campaign in Illinois. With state revenue tied to an income formula—an act likely to reduce state income over several years—local governments would have been forced to cut programs and rely more heavily on local property taxes.

In the fall of 1977 the house approved Totten's amendment 115–45, and Totten then sought approval by the senate early in 1978, so the measure could be placed on the November ballot. Chicago interests, concerned about any restrictions on state revenues, worked with Thompson to kill Totten's amendment. Nevertheless, the legislature seemed interested in some sort of tax reduction or ceiling, and there was one still alive in committee but of no particular interest to legislators. The plan called for partial property tax rebates to families with annual incomes up to $25,000 and who paid more than 3.5 percent of their income in property taxes. Supporters said the rebates would have averaged $28 per household in the first year. The plan had strong support from the Illinois Political Action Council—a loosely organized statewide consumer group devoted to reduction of taxes and utility rates—but by early June it had not caught fire with lawmakers.

That picture changed dramatically on June 6, when California residents approved Proposition 13, a major reduction in property taxes that created tax cut hysteria, a so-called "tax revolt," across the nation. Bakalis saw an opportunity to become the Illinois tax cut champion. Thompson was not interested in any plan that would reduce state revenues. With cooperation from the Democratic-controlled legislature, Bakalis took over the IPAC tax rebate plan and called it "The Bakalis Tax Rebate Plan."

Thompson resisted panic in the wake of California's vote. He said Illinois was not California and Proposition 13 proposals had no place in his state. He misjudged the intensity of the feeling. Economist Milton Friedman, a Nobel Prize winner and longtime associate of the University of Chicago, said the attitude "may not cost him another term as governor, but it will certainly hurt his prospects in the presidential sweepstakes."

The bill, which was in doubt until the final hours of the legislature, passed the house 113–40 and the senate 32–22. The Democrats gave Bakalis a major campaign issue. Thompson appeared undisturbed by the proposal, but his aides worked hard to defeat the bill. Thompson sent officials of the Bureau of the Budget to call on newspaper editors with statistics demonstrating the high costs of Bakalis's plan. Bakalis said rebates would cost the state $33 million in lost revenues the first year, Thompson set the figure at about $90 million.

After passage of the bill, Thompson toyed with the issue; he threatened to veto the bill but agonized publicly over the need for tax reform. On July 5, he vowed not to sign the bill. Bakalis and the IPAC lobbied furiously for a reversal and began a petition campaign to pressure the governor. Thompson kept his word, saying "rebates aren't reform," and vetoed the bill on July 27.

In California after passage of Proposition 13, Governor Jerry Brown, involved in what then appeared to be a difficult run for re-election, embraced the proposition, performing one of the most successful acrobatic flips of the year. Before June 6, Brown had opposed the proposition and worked to defeat the measure. Afterward, he became the proposition's champion and almost immediately outran Republican opposition in the preference polls.

After announcing he would veto the property tax rebate bill, Thompson still needed a plan that would satisfy the public's alleged craving for a tax reduction. On the morning of July 18, the governor went to work with an idea for the "Thompson Proposition." Without assistance from Springfield aides or his paid political strategist, Douglas Bailey, Thompson conceived an idea that would grow into the most bizarre episode in the 1978 campaign. Bailey denied published reports that Thompson consulted him before making the announcement. "He did it, then he called me," Bailey said. The proposition stated: "Shall legislation be enacted and the Illinois Constitution be amended to impose ceilings on taxes and spending by the state of Illinois, units of local government, and school districts?" Thompson had proposed an advisory referendum, but he worded it in such a way as to raise expectations of action. To get the Thompson Proposition on the ballot, Thompson needed almost 600,000 signatures. If passed, the proposition bound no one to take action. Thompson aides acknowledged that the Bakalis campaign for property tax rebates had worried them and that several weeks before the announcement they had begun to develop a plan for seizing the tax reduction initiative from Bakalis.

Cautiously, some Thompson supporters said they liked the idea. Percy, also seeking re-election, said the people needed a chance for expression, even if it did not bind anyone to action. Bailey, looking at the proposition in political terms, said it gave Thompson "a vehicle to demonstrate where he is on the tax subject. I think it's a good idea." Furthermore, Bailey said, Thompson intended to follow through after the election with a tax-ceiling proposal. He, and others, noted that Thompson's proposal included no specific ceiling percentages.

Outside that circle of supporters and staff, Thompson took a bruising. Editorial pages across the state ridiculed the proposition as meaningless; a waste of time, energy, and money to put it on the ballot, and too blatantly political. Samuel Witwer, president of the 1970 Constitutional Convention, said amending the constitution "with a high degree of specificity" is "a dangerous policy."

Chicago Sun-Times political editor Basil Talbott, Jr., who called the proposition "empty," listed its political advantages to the governor: "For the first time it gives him the offensive in the tax relief issue.... The referendum is likely to increase voter turnout. Thompson would benefit from a higher turnout.... The catchy Proposition gives the governor something to talk about as he travels the county fair circuit.... Thompson seems to have mended a breach with GOP conservatives."

The major risk was in failing to get enough signatures. Even then Thompson could say there hadn't been enough time to circulate petitions. Having snatched the tax issue to his side of the board, Thompson spent much of the remaining time before August 21—the deadline for filing petitions—scouring the state for signatures. He talked about it at county fairs and sent O'Neal on excursions to promote the proposition. A special booth at the state fair in Springfield was used to promote the proposition, and workers played a recording of Thompson urging visitors to sign the petition. Thompson had put his reputation on the line and committed campaign funds to finance the project.

The petition drive cost more than $200,000 from Thompson's campaign treasury. The bulk of expenses was for television advertising, salaries of state employees who took leaves to work on the drive, printing of petitions, and supplies. One newspaper reported the expenditure of $625 for food and beverages for a party at the governor's mansion to celebrate meeting the deadline.

The list of expenditures included one controversial item: Thompson paid workers to collect signatures. Originally, he offered to pay $100 for every 750 signatures collected and, according to one accounting by Thompson's staff, $6,874 was paid for such work. *Chicago Tribune* columnist Richard Ciccone called the practice "bounty hunting." Ciccone also criticized Thompson for offering patronage jobs to persons who obtained the most petitions.

No matter what the critics called the practice, Thompson needed incentives to get enough petitions. The quest went down to the wire, with a last minute media blitz and airplane trips by Republican officials to collect petitions. The *Chicago Sun-Times* trumpeted: "Thompson tax sign-up over top." The final count showed 43,020 petitions bearing 607,410 signatures or about 18,000 more than the minimum needed. Thompson delivered the petitions to the state Board of Elections, flashed a "thumbs up" sign, and declared the drive "a political miracle."

Attackers waited in the wings, for there had not been much they could do to stop the petition-signing machine. Volunteers for the Illinois Education Association—concerned that momentum would be generated for a tax ceiling that would limit funds available for education—and a Springfield Democrat with a nose for publicity, State Representative David L. Robinson, went over the petitions and in a few days challenged them officially.

Bakalis and other Democrats called the proposal "Proposition Zero." Bakalis branded it a "meaningless absurdity." But, strangely, Bakalis said he would vote for the proposition and would not make it a campaign issue. "I won't say 'Vote against it' if it's on the ballot. If it is on the ballot on November 7, I'll probably say, 'Yes, I'm for putting a ceiling on taxes and spending like everybody is.'" Within a week, Bakalis ate the words in one of the campaign's most peculiar turnarounds. He declared opposition because "so many questions of ethics" had arisen in inspections of the petitions. Thompson badgered Bakalis unmercifully for the flip-flop. Using Bakalis's words against him, Thompson said, "I think his whole treatment of the Thompson Proposition has been absurd."

By the last of August, Thompson stood on the threshold of probably the most hectic two weeks of his administration. The Thompson Proposition, challenged and criticized, hung in the balance, and risks grew each day. Thompson suffered personally, too. Thompson's close friend Sam Skinner said Thompson became sullen and depressed under media bombardment and by the determination of those fighting to keep the proposition off the ballot. Peggy Boyer of the *Illinois Times* reported Thompson became "testy" and that his "mood darkened" as the investigation of petitions unfolded.

By law, the forces challenging Thompson's petitions had five days in which to survey more than 600,000 names. Joining Robinson were the IEA, Independent Voters of Illinois (which endorsed Bakalis), and scores of Democrats who searched voting records in counties where alleged fraudulent signatures were obtained.

The search and revelations created a media event. As each day passed, newspapers and electronic media reported scores of isolated cases of alleged fraud, leaving the mistaken impression of widespread illegal activity. Robinson, always available to the press in Springfield, gleefully told of the signatures of dead persons showing up on petitions. His only motive was to get attention, and he succeeded. After the five days passed, Robinson formally challenged 26,000 signatures.

Recovering from his daze, Thompson snapped back at the challengers. In a Chicago press conference he refused to take any responsibility until accusations and allegations were backed by fact. At another time, he said, "I took those signatures in good faith and until it's proven to me that they're not in good faith, I'm going to assume they are in good faith. I don't believe you can file 607,000 signatures gathered from around the state of Illinois without finding some problems with them."

The Board of Elections, under pressure from Robinson and Thompson's attorneys, decided to take testimony September 1 on the challenged petitions. Board members, representing both political parties, subpoenaed witnesses. Unexpectedly, one of the persons subpoenaed, Vicki Sands, executive secretary to O'Neal, announced through her attorney that she would plead the Fifth Amendment if called to testify. She had notarized 7,000 challenged signatures. Thompson called her announcement a "hit in the belly."

Thompson avoided a showdown over Sands' testimony by calling elections board chairman John Countryman and offering to withdraw the 7,000 contested signatures. Although that procedure was not permissible once petitions were on file, attorneys for Robinson and Thompson agreed to the withdrawal. Sands retreated, erasing a potential embarrassment for Thompson. With the media keeping vigil at the capitol, the elections board announced a decision at 2 a.m. September 8 to permit placement of the proposition on the ballot. Thompson and supporters partied until dawn at the mansion.

Throughout the ordeal Thompson received little public support from fellow Republicans. Among officials of both parties, opinion was almost unanimous against the proposition. In one instance, however, criticism boiled to the surface and nearly spilled some Republican blood.

The critic was Ogilvie, who by then had established a record of occasionally calling a press conference to criticize a gubernatorial action. He called the proposition "too simplistic" and suggested empaneling a blue ribbon committee to recommend changes in the tax structure. The suggestion served no useful purpose from Thompson's standpoint, as it gave editorial pages and Bakalis one more reason to sound off. Bakalis used a reference to Ogilvie's criticism in television advertisements.

Waiting several days until he cooled down, and not wanting to appear overly eager to lick the wound, Thompson sat down with Ogilvie in Chicago to discuss questions raised by the criticism. Neither man reported publicly on the "secret" meeting, but a Republican official said: "There have been news reports that look as though Ogilvie and Thompson were at war. One purpose of this meeting was getting everybody back together again."

The proposition petition controversy died slowly. Robinson and allies appealed, but lost. Grand juries in northern Illinois counties investigated alleged petition fraud, and in one case turned up a potential embarrassment for Thompson. The first person indicted for forgery was Michael P. Dunn, Thompson's former patronage chief. But as headlines in Illinois subsided, national correspondents and columnists began to dissect the squabble and its effects on Thompson.

Rowland Evans and Robert Novak concluded a long recitation of Thompson Proposition ailments with this exaggeration: "Fairly or not, it [the court challenge] tarnishes Thompson's reputation as the U.S. attorney who put crooked politicians in jail.... Big Jim Thompson has demonstrated how to self-inflict political damage in confronting the tax revolt."

Time magazine, normally a promoter of Thompson's image, commented that "Thompson has not been personally implicated in the improprieties, but he certainly was embarrassed by them.... At the very least, Thompson's chances for the 1980 GOP presidential nomination have been damaged."

James Dickenson, writing for the *Washington Star* after visiting Illinois and observing Thompson on the campaign trail, reported: "No one accuses the governor of wrongdoing, but the question is whether his gamble on the tax and spending proposition will succeed and offset charges of political miscalculations, which are serious enough to stifle a possible presidential campaign before he can even get it going."

On November 7, the Thompson Proposition passed with 83 percent voting yes. Hardly a mention was made in the same newspapers that two months earlier had played the story as if it were a major scandal. Thompson meanwhile continued to pledge a ceiling on taxes and spending.

The campaign had other serious moments and discussions of issues, many of which came during four debates shown on a statewide public television network. They were the first gubernatorial debates in the state's history, and they matched two skilled, articulate men who had unlimited confidence in themselves. Bakalis saw the debates as an excellent opportunity to prove his worth in head-to-head combat, and Thompson was determined not to give an inch to the Democrat.

Several factors detracted from the debates as a center of attention. First, they were shown on public broadcasting channels in competition with commercial programming. Thompson said after the first debate, "I looked at the ratings and we didn't even come in a respectable last." That worked to Thompson's advantage, because it limited exposure for Bakalis to about 500,000 estimated viewers.

Also, the first debate occurred in June, during the summer vacation season and well before any public interest had been generated in the campaign. That debate, on taxes and state financing, may have been the most important in terms of subject matter, considering the eventual shape of campaign issues, and the fact that the legislature was considering a property tax rebate plan.

Bakalis opened with a broad attack on Thompson, accusing the administration of "broken promises and broken hearts." Thompson defended himself by labeling Bakalis and his Democratic friends as spendthrifts. Neither of the candidates scored major points, and most observers rated the debate a draw. The Thompson strategy of insisting on a first debate in June succeeded.

At the outset of the second debate, which was held in Carbondale on September 6, Thompson took the initiative by vowing to implement a tax ceiling. Bakalis struggled all evening to gain momentum. With the issue of the Thompson Proposition petition in the air, Bakalis accused the governor of signing the names of "people from the dead," but Thompson ignored him. Finally, with Thompson refusing to be riled, Bakalis proposed a moratorium on utility rate increases and stole the next morning's headlines. But again Thompson escaped serious setbacks.

By the time of the third debate, held on September 19 in Peoria, Bakalis had gained no ground on Thompson, and commentators said the challenger needed a clear victory, especially as Thompson had escaped the petition fraud matter unscathed. Bakalis and Thompson swung from the heels, barely stopping short of using the word *liar*. Robert Hillman of the *Chicago Sun-Times* recorded some bombardments from portions of the debate, the subject of which was transportation and business development:

BAKALIS: If Mr. Thompson would tell us the truth, he would say that the problem [with getting federal funds for highways] is that we don't have available the required matching state money.

THOMPSON: There is emerging a familiar pattern: The truth not being told about what is happening in Illinois.

BAKALIS: The truth is hidden by a barrage of rhetoric.

THOMPSON: It's not the rhetoric. It's simply untruths. He's not telling the truth.

Thompson's strategy of defending but not opening any serious new ground for exploration had prevailed through the first three debates. Bakalis blamed the format, which featured a panel of journalists asking questions. He did not like having press representatives set the subject agenda with their questions. Bakalis wanted each debate to be a head-to-head match with only a moderator to keep the peace. The fourth debate on October 12 in Oak Brook, a Chicago suburb, placed the two combatants against each other with no panel and only a moderator.

On the weekend before the debate, Bakalis pulled a last ace out of his sleeve by pledging to reduce property taxes by 20 percent over four years, if elected. He also promised not to seek re-election if he failed. In the days preceding the debate, Thompson chose to criticize the cost of Bakalis's plan to the state, thus diverting attention from a discussion of merits. Then, during the debate, while Bakalis tried to sell the audience on his tax cut, Thompson bore in, characterizing the idea as "a $2 billion fraud masquerading as a tax cut." Baffled by the Thompson attack, Bakalis stuck to a figure of $360 million, but defended it poorly on camera. In the days after the debate, Thompson kept up the barrage. Finally Bakalis admitted he had misjudged the cost and revised the figure to $1 billion. His credibility was damaged, however, and Bakalis virtually dropped discussion of the plan from his campaign appearances. Thompson had stolen Bakalis's last thunder.

Bakalis wanted a fifth chance at Thompson in a debate on the subject of abortion and taxes. Thompson toyed with the idea, appearing to favor a meeting, but searching for a reason to say no. Bakalis gave Thompson a reason when he accused the governor of double-talk on the subject of the Jewish Holocaust. Thompson accused Bakalis of "injecting religious and ethnic bigotry into this campaign." Thompson declared: "A man must exhibit grace under pressure. Bakalis has shown no grace at all under pressure, and as far as I'm concerned there will be no debate."

While the candidates waged war in the media, there was another battle being waged of a more personal nature. This occurred as the candidates dashed across the state to a myriad of meetings where they spoke, shook hands with the voters, and displayed themselves away from the pancake makeup and the press releases. There was no draw in the contest on the streets; Thompson won hands down.

Whether he drank beer with young persons in Alton, or blew up balloons for children at the state fair, Thompson—sometimes traveling in a recreational vehicle—took his campaign to the level where he had confidence in his ability to relate directly to people. His political senses—with assistance from research findings—told him that the voters wanted to talk to the candidate, and not necessarily about issues. "Most people are not into politics and they want reassurance that the politicians have a human quality about them," he told an interviewer.

To make a point that people were not preoccupied with affairs of state, as newspapers wanted to believe, Thompson told the story of a campaign trip to Blue Island south of Chicago in July. He walked the streets, he said, talking to citizens and conducting his own survey. The issues of importance he discovered were in the words of the people: "How are your dogs?" (Thompson had to take his dogs for "dog psychology and training" to the University of Illinois after they bit him during a playful romp); "Don't you know better than to get in the middle of a dog fight?"; "Will you keep supporting ERA?" (he said he replied yes); and "Keep putting those crooks in jail." Thompson smiled, while saying that not a single citizen had asked him about tax relief.

They asked about his dogs in July, but after August 3 they asked about Samantha Jayne Thompson, daughter of Jim and Jayne. She was born at Memorial Medical Center in Springfield and weighed seven pounds, four ounces. Jayne's doctor said the mother had developed a low-grade form of high blood pressure late in the pregnancy, and after fifteen hours of labor he decided to deliver the child by cesarean section.

All other issues—taxes, Congress, the Middle East—faded. At the top of TV broadcasts and on front pages across the state, Jim Thompson stood in a light green surgical gown, fighting back tears as he described Samantha to the world. "She's beautiful, that's all I can say. She's just gorgeous. She's just perfect."

There had not been a child born to a sitting governor in seventy-two years (Charles Deneen was the last governor-father), and the outpouring of presents was just a small sample of the public's interest. Dozens of gifts arrived for Samantha, whose yellow nursery in the mansion was brightened with stuffed animals the governor had retrieved while campaigning at county fairs. Most of the generous people were strangers, but the new parents sent a thank-you note to each person who had sent a gift. One woman who received a note said, "I had never before sent anything to a famous person. I really did not expect to hear anything from the Thompsons, but Jayne sent the nicest letter I've ever got. She invited me to the mansion. I'm going to have the letter framed." Samantha Jayne, only days old, had become of inestimable political value to her father.

Cynics who had grumbled the previous Christmas about Thompson's timing of the birth of his first child kept quiet in August. Nothing could be done except hope that Samantha would drop from the headlines as fast as she captured them in the first place. But the Thompsons had no intention of putting Samantha in her 100-year-old antique cradle and leaving her with a baby-sitter. As soon as mother and child were healthy, they campaigned by dad's side. Raw weather or fair, Jayne and Jim bounced and cuddled Samantha across Illinois.

About the time it seemed that Samantha would become a fixture on the campaign trail (October 2, to be exact), she was admitted to the hospital with bacterial pneumonia. The ailment persisted, with the media dutifully reporting, and Thompson stayed close to home. As the hospitalization continued, Thompson began campaigning again. Samantha was still the attraction, although she was not on hand. Everywhere Thompson went the people asked, "How's Samantha?" In one speech he said, "The mothers and the grandmothers are going to ask me 47,000 times, but I'm going to answer your question before you ask me. Samantha's getting better."

Thompson described graphically the difficulty in giving Samantha intravenous medication. "She's got a tube in her foot," he said. "They [intravenous needles] don't stay in the veins of the little ones, they keep pulling out." He carried a set of color baby pictures and without provocation displayed them, saying: "The truth is she's got her father's looks and her mother's temper."

Samantha recovered and returned to the campaign. She accompanied her parents to vote on election day (cameras recorded the event). At the victory celebration that night, Samantha made an appearance that earned her a picture and story in the next day's Chicago papers. Regardless of whether the Thompsons planned the birth of their child to coincide with the campaign, that is when the birth occurred, and the Thompson's took advantage of an adoring public's natural interest in a governor's child.

Bakalis suffered in silence, for he knew that an attack on Samantha was suicide. Besides, he had memories of other frustrations in the personality campaign, such as the time in May when he held a press conference on the second floor of the statehouse to announce his plan for tax relief. At the same time, on the third floor, Thompson was astride a horse that had been taken up on an elevator as a promotional stunt for a horse show. Bakalis sniffed, "Those are his priorities—horses, slides, T-shirts. Oh, yes, and dogs, too."

One of Bakalis's best media moments occurred late in October, long after the campaign had been decided but not before Bakalis was ready to retire. Full of seeing Thompson in a variety of costumes, Bakalis decided to fight T-shirts with T-shirts. He called a press conference in Chicago to announce a gift for the governor. "To underscore the kind of buffoonery that we've seen in this state in the last year . . . I want to present this T-shirt to Governor Thompson." He displayed a shirt imprinted with "You cannot fool all the people all the time."

Reporters following Thompson's campaign made lists of his antics, and many were published. One list that received special attention in newspapers was made by T. Lee Hughes, Springfield correspondent of the Associated Press. He listed some of the notable items from Thompson's "personality scrapbook:"

> A fondness for T-shirts, collected by the hundreds, with every conceivable message or slogan. . . . Regular dashes into nearby stores to pick up packets of health food, a stuffed toy, or some other trinket for the family. . . . Pin-on buttons, like the red one on his black tuxedo that reads 'kids are real people.' . . . Munching hot dogs and German bread and stuffed pizza.

Thompson's appeal touched persons of all ages. The young knew him, even if they did not know why. An *Alton Telegraph* reporter called him a "sex symbol" to women over fifty, because they seemed attracted to him. The elderly thought of him as a son because he spoke sympathetically of their problems. Thompson spread warmth, whether holding hands with Jayne or holding Samantha in his arms.

As reporter Hughes observed, many voters "have grown familiar with the well-publicized details of Thompson's personal life and lifestyle. By now, those details are congealing into what amounts to almost a cult—with its own rituals and objects of adoration."

As the Thompson juggernaut rolled on toward November 7, everything fell into place, as if ordered specially by the candidate. Public awareness of his lead over Bakalis caused the money to flow, making it possible to wage a strong media advertising campaign, which in turn added to the lead.

One could describe Thompson's fund-raising prowess only as awesome; in the period from July 1, 1977, to just a month before election day, Thompson's campaign received almost $2,300,000. That did not include a final burst of dollars that carried through the election. However, the force of his fund-raising is seen in receipts from the period July 1 to October 8,

1978, just a little more than three months. In that time, contributions totaled just short of a million dollars.

Money came from all corners, reminiscent of broad-based giving to the statewide campaigns of Senator Charles Percy and William J. Scott. Real estate brokers, Teamsters, utility executives, businessmen, contractors, bankers, insurance brokers—the list read like a "Who's Who" of Illinois influence-peddlers and kingmakers. If big money interests got a "piece" of Thompson in 1976, they got a "slice" in 1978.

But the list lacked one important name: Ray Kroc, board chairman and founder of the McDonald's fast-food empire. In 1976, Kroc, then living in the Chicago area, donated $46,500 to Thompson against Michael Howlett. Kroc did not contribute a dime in 1978.

"My thoughts about Jim are the same now as they were two years ago," Kroc told reporter Carol Alexander. "I think he's a great guy.... But there's a difference in trying to become governor and then being governor. I felt Jim was the kind of fellow Illinois wanted. Once he got elected, it became his situation to show what he could do."

Kroc acknowledged he had telephone conversations during the campaign with Thompson during which the subject of money arose. "He said television advertising is expensive," Kroc reported. But Kroc did not tumble to Thompson's hints.

Meanwhile, Bakalis had to borrow money, cut expenses, and make special appeals that took him away from campaigning in order to get enough funds to pay for last-minute television commercials. Even with all the adversities, media speculators considered Bakalis within striking distance of Thompson with about a month to go in the campaign. National columnists, rubbing their hands together over Thompson's alleged troubles with petition fraud, claimed private polls showed Bakalis within five percentage points of the incumbent.

None of the private polls, taken for the candidates in the contests for governor and U.S. Senate, showed Bakalis ever any closer than ten points. Gary South, campaign manager for Alex Seith, who nearly defeated Percy, said the reports of a close gubernatorial contest reflected a wishful media looking for an election contest on which to focus.

Public polls did not confirm the findings of a scientific poll taken in mid-August by Richard Day Research of Urbana for the Lindsay-Schaub newspapers which showed 55 percent of voter support going to Thompson, 28 percent to Bakalis, and 17 percent undecided. Dr. Day based his findings on a random, statewide sample of 800 persons. In late October, Day polled a random selection of 500 persons from the original 800; the results showed Thompson with 59 percentage points to Bakalis's 32, with 9 percent undecided. That final poll hit Thompson's election percentage almost on the head. Bakalis peaked before the campaign began, columnists and wishful thinkers notwithstanding.

The official count on November 7 gave Thompson 1,859,684 votes or 59.5 percent. Bakalis received 1,263,134 votes or 40.5 percent. By all standards, Thompson's margin of victory deserved rave notices. He was the first governor since Kerner in 1964 to win a second term, and the pluralities of the 1976 and 1978 elections were larger than in any contests for governor of the state. Detractors noted the margin fell short of the 1.4 million plurality over Howlett, but they forgot to rate the two opponents. Bakalis was a bona fide candidate, not put up to run only in a primary, and he was clearly the classier of the two challengers.

Thompson left amazingly little political debris on the landscape. The only promise to linger after the campaign was the proposal of a tax ceiling, and Thompson moved in that direction immediately after the election. No scandals remained, and the minor flaws uncovered by the press and Bakalis were quickly discarded by the public, as shown by the final vote.

For a second time in two years Thompson had swept the electorate off its feet, this time blending steady performances during the four debates, a nonbinding proposition on tax ceilings, and a well-developed personal style of campaigning. Nevertheless, as familiar as the public was with how he succeeded, it was no closer than in 1976 to identifying Thompson's purpose or mission. He had not told the citizens of Illinois where he was taking them, or where they might be when he left.

The Media

The first page of a present-day politician's handbook carries the title "Handling the Media," and in Illinois Jim Thompson has polished the text and added footnotes. He is far and away the state's most successful user of media.

The nation is full of politicians who rode a temporary crest of media attention to dizzying heights. Their downfall comes when interest is not sustained, either by achievement or guile, and the pursued—the media—becomes the pursuer. The media has no match for cruelty when love turns cold. So far, Thompson has sidestepped the traps, and kept the media hustling after him.

There are many theories about the cycle of news coverage as it relates to a president or governor; one of the most widely quoted theories says a chief executive goes through three stages with the media. In stage one, the media supports the candidate; in stage two, the media is neutral toward the officeholder; and in the last stage, the media is outright hostile. Jimmy Carter moved into stage three in less than two years. Thompson's predecessor, Dan Walker, who enjoyed early success as a media user, ran through the neutrality stage in less than a year.

Incredibly, Thompson has survived more than seven years (four as U.S. attorney) in the media limelight—much of it under scrutiny of the fickle Chicago media—without moving out of stage two. He has handled the media without alienating reporters, news directors, editors, and publishers. There are a few exceptions, of course, but several of the state's most powerful and influential media moguls are known to be his boosters.

He has maintained this cordial relationship by seldom attacking the media or its representatives. Some reporters see this strategy as directly related to national ambitions. "He knows if he emerges on the national scene, the Illinois press will be the first ones the national writers look to for assessments beyond the normal six-foot, six-inch crime-busting federal prosecutor bullshit," says Bill Lambrecht, Illinois correspondent for the St. Louis Post-Dispatch.

If he can maintain this strategy, Thompson could surface as a national figure with the bulk of the Illinois media in support. Carter came out of Georgia with only occasional sniping by Atlanta Constitution editor Reg Murphy, and even that died away when Murphy left Georgia for San

Francisco early in Carter's presidency. Otherwise the president counted on Georgia's media not to spoil his candidacy.

Some newspapers in Illinois already have stipulated how Thompson can earn their support. One is the *Bloomington Pantagraph*, which after the 1978 elections observed that Thompson said he would devote his attention "for the next six months" to solving the problems of Illinois. That inspired an editor to write, with only a hint of sarcasm: "But what about after he has Illinois problems solved in six months? Won't Springfield pale on him? With problems solved, he can be free to play the role of Jimmy Voterseed, striding tall among the hummocks and grass roots of national politics. But, what the heck, if Jim Thompson can solve, or make sure someone solves, Illinois problems by next July 4, we'll help send up his presidential rocket."

Thompson's media success looks simple in a narrow political sense, but it is much more complex. In detail, the relationship reveals something about Thompson that the public record does not.

To understand media strategy in Illinois, one must first understand the system of distribution and coverage. The principal market for both print and electronic media is Chicago. More than six million people live within range of Chicago's media.

There are nine television stations in the market, four of which are considered important for news coverage and advertising. They are Channel 2, WBBM (CBS); Channel 5, WMAQ (NBC); Channel 7, WLS (ABC); and Channel 9, WGN, a station without network affiliation but owned by Tribune Company, which also owns the *Chicago Tribune*.

Unlike stations in most television markets, Channels 2, 5, and 7 are "owned and operated" by the networks. Each of the networks maintains a bureau in Chicago and feeds stories directly to the network news shows, making the stations of special importance to a person seeking a national audience.

The state's two largest newspapers are published in Chicago. The *Chicago Tribune* has the larger circulation (more than 780,000 daily and over 1,150,000 Sunday) but shares the market with the *Chicago Sun-Times* (over 670,000 daily and 720,000 Sunday). Both are financially healthy. The *Tribune* once claimed to be the statewide newspaper, much as the *Des Moines Register and Tribune* is in Iowa, but in the last decade it has withdrawn to the city and suburbs for its news coverage and financial sustenance. The *Tribune* also publishes the *Suburban Trib*, a separate newspaper for suburban areas. Until 1978, Field Enterprises published the *Chicago Sun-Times* and the *Chicago Daily News*, morning and evening newspapers, respectively. But the financially ill *Daily News* was dropped in 1977, leaving just the *Sun-Times* to compete with the larger *Tribune*. The *Sun-Times* and the *Tribune* are carrier-delivered downstate, but editions reaching those locations carry day-old news.

Also serving the Chicago market are nearly forty AM and FM radio stations. In the suburbs, a variety of weekly and small daily newspapers are published, which report mainly local and regional news.

A candidate or officeholder who makes the evening television news and the front pages in Chicago, therefore, is guaranteed an audience in the millions. Reaching the urban and rural population outside the metropolitan cluster of counties is more difficult but important, since this area frequently provides the balance of power between Chicago and its suburbs.

The major television markets downstate are Rockford, Peoria, Springfield, Decatur, Champaign-Urbana, Rock Island–Moline (part of the Quad Cities), Metro-East (served by the St. Louis TV stations), and stations in the southern tip of the state. Politicians in the late 1960s and early 1970s discovered only one surefire way of appearing on all the downstate TV news programs on the same day. That is done with a "fly-around," in which the candidate, usually in a private plane, makes a series of airport stops for brief news conferences in places like Marion, Springfield, Decatur, Peoria, Champaign, and Rockford.

Downstate areas are served by dozens of daily newspapers, many of which are part of publishing chains. The Gannett Company, which owns the largest number of newspapers in the nation, publishes papers in Rockford and Danville; Copley newspapers are published in Joliet, Springfield, Aurora, Wheaton, and Elgin; Lindsay-Schaub newspapers (now part of Lee Enterprises of Davenport, Iowa), with a daily circulation of 160,000, are published in Decatur, Carbondale, and Edwardsville. Small newspapers are published in Kankakee and Moline. The *Peoria-Journal-Star*, the state's third largest newspaper, is not aligned with a chain.

The quality of news coverage outside Chicago varies greatly, depending on the standards applied. In recent years, most of the newspapers have sent correspondents to Springfield for at least periodic reports on local legislators and some expanded coverage of gubernatorial activities. Those known for aggressive news coverage and occasional investigative work (the Chicago newspapers do almost no investigative reporting out of Springfield) are the Rockford newspapers, the *Quad-City Times* in Davenport, Iowa, the *Alton Telegraph*, *Peoria Journal-Star*, and Lindsay-Schaub newspapers.

The St. Louis market is a peculiar one for politicians seeking extensive media coverage in southwestern Illinois, where there are large concentrations of population. Illinois audiences are a small percentage of the media's total reach, and Illinois politicians must compete for time on television and radio with Missouri politicians. Generally, politicians aim for news shows on the network stations—KMOX, KSD (owned by the Pulitzer Publishing Company, which publishes the *St. Louis Post-Dispatch*), and KTVI (owned by Newhouse Publishing Company, which publishes the *St. Louis Globe-Democrat*). A popular public-affairs radio station is KMOX, which aims much of its programming at Illinois audiences.

The *Globe-Democrat* and *Post-Dispatch* have readership in the two Illinois counties next to the Mississippi River, but circulation beyond that area is sparse. Points more distant receive early editions with day-old news. Both newspapers have daily circulations of about 250,000, but the Sunday *Post-Dispatch* sells over 425,000, while the weekend *Globe-Democrat* has the same circulation as its daily edition.

A center of media activity is the state capitol pressroom in Springfield. TV camera crews from Chicago frequently are present; a full-time newsman is there for stations in Peoria and Champaign-Urbana. Chicago newspapers maintain bureaus; in recent years, however, the importance of state news has been downgraded in the main editions of Chicago newspapers, and coverage has been less intensive. Included among resident Springfield correspondents are employees of the Associated Press and United Press International. Most newspapers outside Chicago receive the bulk of their state news from one or both of the wire services. Each service maintains a large office in Chicago.

Thompson's initial encounters with the media occurred while he served as first assistant U.S. attorney to William Bauer in 1970–71. Before that, Thompson demonstrated a flare for publicity and hijinks but rarely had a chance to use it. After Thompson became U.S. attorney in 1971, he became a full-blown "media darling."

Thompson's rise professionally and his "discovery" by the media coincided with major changes in emphasis of newspaper and television news content, and with shifting attitudes of the public. These factors made Thompson an appealing and refreshing public character.

By the early 1970s, Americans had wearied of the 1960s and the multitude of seemingly insoluble domestic problems. As U.S. involvement in the Vietnam War withered, citizens became less interested in issues and more concerned about self, as much to avoid the leftover problems as to taste the good life. Many Americans discovered leisure time, and the demands for recreational equipment increased dramatically. Apathy replaced commitment among students on university campuses, and those who retained ideals sought pragmatic ways of pressing their causes within the system.

Research companies and rating services discovered and reported a national malaise and prescribed short stories and jokes for TV newscasts. With huge revenues at stake, "happy talk" formats flourished and caused audience ratings to soar. News shows featuring exploration of serious subjects plummeted in ratings and dropped from sight.

On the newspaper side, circulation declines accelerated in metropolitan areas and eventually occurred in the smaller monopoly markets, too. A young breed of editors, encouraged by worried and profit-motivated publishers and owners—especially those associated with large public-owned chains—redesigned news pages to "brighten" the appearance, and leaned more on features and less on "heavy" news on the assumption that more people would buy papers for the frosting than for the cake. A casualty of this trend was serious treatment of local, state, and national news. A corrective process started later in the 1970s, re-emphasizing news coverage, but that came after Jim Thompson reached the peak of popularity in Chicago. The vehicles for his rise were feature stories and the blazing headlines of his accomplishments. A constant search for handsome, dashing, young personalities led the newspapers increasingly to the U.S. attorney.

It was no wonder Thompson made such a hit in Chicago. He rode the white horse of law-and-order and had charm, too. Unlike the heroes of a decade before, who tackled problems of racism, civil disorder, and war—with many dying in the process—Thompson tackled crime foes closer to home and won the hearts of a fearful population in the city. Thompson's efforts did not persuade people to stay in Chicago, but they cheered him lustily as they fled to the suburbs.

Separating the Thompson personality and appeal from his work became impossible, especially as he used his media appearances to send messages to corrupt elements. Those former colleagues and friends who defend his media appearances to announce indictments and comment on convictions believe Thompson's actions deterred persons who otherwise might have indulged in unlawful practices. Of course, there is no evidence to confirm their contention.

In 1974 *The Nation* said, "The crusading prosecuting attorney who bags top officials and lower functionaries of both parties alike is more familiar to Chicagoans as a fictional hero than in real life.... Television reporters consider him the top personality on local screens, and feature articles deal as much with his passion for antique collecting and his role as Chicago's more eligible bachelor as with his performance in office."

It did not take the Chicago newspapers and TV stations long to recognize that Thompson had a flare for living, as well as for prosecuting. His interests became instant public knowledge—from romping with children of friends and associates at a Wisconsin hideaway, to collecting antiques. The *Chicago Sun-Times* recorded in 1972, about a year after he became U.S. attorney: "Thompson is a bachelor who lives in a 42nd-floor apartment overlooking Lincoln Park. He collects antiques avidly and knowledgably, drives a Mercedes-Benz [often referred to as a "brown Mercedes" in later stories] and dines, as bachelors will, several evenings a week with the families of his staff...."

His recreational habits filled space, too, for to an affluent population in the city and suburbs who sought open spaces for weekends and vacations, Thompson's frolics had appeal. As the *Chicago Sun-Times* said, "On weekends when he can, he retreats to a 21-acre lakefront property he owns in Wisconsin, where he water-skis in summer and snowmobiles in winter...."

At age thirty-five, when he became prosecutor, Thompson related well to the active social life of young singles and couples. Newspapers, directed by the results of research studies, saw potential circulation growth in delivering information that would draw this audience back to newspaper readership. Thompson became a circulation builder for the newspapers.

After a while, articles about Thompson had an "ooze" to them. They did not pretend to probe his mind or seek the essence of the man. On the main news page in one edition of the *Chicago Daily News* a feature article appeared under the headline "World of Big Jim Thompson." It was characteristic of most stories about him, featuring his size, where he bought his clothes, what his house looked like, and concluding with this description of his clothing: "Flamboyant, but with style. . . ."

Other than to pass on stories of dubious importance and whet appetites for gossip, many of the articles were vacuous. The following selection appeared in a story about Thompson's home in Chicago: "The apartment has four rooms full of handsome antiques, a large collection of Victorian glass, an unerotic sculpture called 'Orgy,' a cozy outdoor brick patio, crystal chandeliers, parquet floors, two marble wood-burning fireplaces, and three handsome chess sets." Then the author passed along a major discovery to readers. "I don't play chess," Thompson was quoted as saying. "It requires thinking ahead, and since I spend twelve hours a day thinking ahead, I don't like to do that when I'm off work."

Thompson's bachelorhood, and supposed pursuit of a marriage partner, received more than one turned phrase. Once he told a women's group that its members could help in the search for a wife. When the *Chicago Tribune* published an offhand remark made by Thompson to a TV reporter to the effect that 1974 was the year he was looking for a wife to take care of him, stacks of letters arrived from would-be candidates.

The press listed his moves in detail: when he changed residences, when he went to Wisconsin for sustenance, when he ate at a particular restaurant (Arnie's was a special haunt), when he sprained his back playing touch football (it healed in time for him to host an Israel Bond dinner in the city).

Thompson worked at establishing friendly relationships with the reporters for Chicago newspapers and radio and TV stations by meeting and talking with them on their own ground and outside of press conferences. "Whenever you have a pressroom in a building, it is a gathering place," Thompson explains. And when the reporters are young and the U.S. attorney is young, it's natural. "I was likely to wander to the pressroom and sit down and put my feet up and have a beer," he said. "I had a crew of young lawyers working for me that the press admired very much, so it was a natural thing of camaraderie—we were the good guys and they identified with that." Thompson recalled that in the five years he served as prosecutor "not a single critical editorial word was written about me." He called that "remarkable," and it was no exaggeration.

While he rubbed elbows with reporters, Thompson kept his distance from editorial directors of the city's newspapers. He saw them at meetings, and he knew editors such as Clayton Kirkpatrick of the *Chicago Tribune*, but not socially. A friendship grew between Thompson and Michael Kilian, an editorial writer for the *Tribune*, and they often had lunch together. But after Thompson became governor, the two parted company over personal differences.

Part of Thompson's success with the media was a technique of establishing a person-to-person relationship. Rather than challenge reporters, or give them the cold shoulder over an irritating story, he openly courted them. *Seduction* might be too strong a word to describe the process, but some reporters and editors admitted being embarrassed rather than angered by the approach. They found it hard to get mad at someone who wanted to be a friend, or who wanted to share a common experience. Looking back at those situations, reporters' integrity and credibility were at stake. Thompson's theory about friendship with reporters took public form at a meeting of Illinois editors in October, 1977. His comments were drawn from six years in the media trenches:

> ... I don't know what is meant by an adversary relationship between a public official and someone in the press. I think that's really a wrong term. An adversary relationship might develop on the editorial page and, if so, that would be a proper function over issues, policy, and philosophy, but if an adversarial relationship develops on the front page, then something's wrong with the relationship on the press side.
>
> ... I developed a number of relationships with members of the press, especially younger members of the press, that were friendly and warm. I guess both of us used to be embarrassed sometimes if I came to a small town and there'd be a reporter that I'd never met before, and then he spent a day with me, and he'd come up afterwards and say, "How am I going to write this story, I like you?"
>
> Campaigns do that to people. ... I don't think any of that really colored the coverage of the campaign in 1976, but it did provide the basis for friendships between myself and members of the news media. ...

There is no greater newspaper champion of the Republican party in Illinois, or the nation, than the *Chicago Tribune*, and a Republican candidate for governor would have to be a tragic figure indeed not to receive the paper's endorsement. The *Tribune* liked Thompson from the beginning of his prosecutor days and gave its endorsement enthusiastically in 1976. The *Tribune said*, "We expect him [Thompson] to open a new era in Illinois politics. We reach that judgment partly because of Mr. Thompson's own style and character, which have impressed us strongly, and partly because of the unusual political situation of this state. Mr. Thompson is the candidate of a minority party...."

The *Tribune* described Thompson as "a tough prosecutor, a powerful enemy of political corruption in either party, and a man of blunt personal honesty."

In a somewhat less effusive declaration, the *Chicago Sun-Times* commented, "Illinois needs a vigorous, thoughtful, ethical leader to guide the state through the fiscal, education, and social storms threatening in the next two years. Republican James R. Thompson best fits that profile."

The *Chicago Daily News* voiced the same endorsement as the *Sun-Times* because of common ownership, saying that Thompson had "demonstrated a capacity for leadership and understanding of the problems facing Illinois that would bring the fresh approach needed in Springfield."

The apparent sigh of relief, and anticipation of a calmer time in Springfield, reflected the Chicago newspapers' negative reaction to four years with Walker.

Across the state, smaller newspapers and newspaper groups said essentially the same words about Thompson, while taking kindly swipes at Howlett. The papers shared the *Chicago Tribune's* conclusion that Howlett should have been seeking re-election as secretary of state. A few papers expressed concern over Thompson's ability to survive in Springfield, including the *Bloomington Pantagraph*.

While enthusiastically endorsing Thompson for governor, the *Pantagraph* said: "Our only reluctance in supporting Mr. Thompson lies in the nagging fear that he, as much of a tyro as Walker, will not function successfully in the deep recesses of state capitol politics. Yet he has avoided the principal Walker error, that of promising Illinoisans that the General Assembly had better shape up, by golly, or he will govern without it by frequent consultation with the 'people.'"

Thompson's lead over Howlett and the near-unanimity of editorial support created an atmosphere which the national press observed with delight. By mid-October, *Newsweek* christened Thompson "one of the bright young GOP lochinvars out of the Midwest." The *Wall Street Journal's* Albert R. Hunt quoted Democrats and Republicans as identifying Thompson as a probable national candidate. *Time* looked ahead two years exclaiming, "If he ... is resoundly re-elected ... he will clearly be in contention for a spot on the 1980 Republican national ticket. Thompson will then be only 44, and Guv just a little over 4." The prelude completed, Thompson began a new odyssey with the Illinois press.

The media's need for someone in the governor's chair who makes news is exceeded only by the governor's desire for the media to be present when he needs them. They have built a mutual defense pact. In 1977 both institutions got what they wanted. Thompson obliged and the media responded.

In many ways, the year progressed as an extension of the love affair begun during the campaign. That was not surprising as many of the reporters stationed permanently in Springfield had accompanied the governor in the campaign. Thompson received occasional editorial criticism from downstate papers, but he continued to be a favorite with Chicago television stations and newspapers, adding strength to the belief that Chicago newspapers were going to give the governor plenty of rope.

When the governor did stumble and it was reported in the newspapers, a strange geographic chauvinism among the media minimized the impact. It was as if Chicago papers would not give space to stories they did not originate, and downstate papers would not use stories originated by Chicago papers. This jealousy, built up over decades of media sectionalism, kept much of the state's population from learning of such problems as abuse of state airplanes by Thompson staff members.

The airplane stories first appeared in downstate newspapers and were not carried in Chicago. When a Thompson aide was fired, the Chicago papers published wire service stories. A review of Chicago coverage reveals that readers knew only a small part of the airplane abuse problem in Thompson's administration. The converse occurred when Chicago papers reported Thompson's membership in private clubs that barred women members. Some comment appeared on downstate editorial pages, but papers outside Chicago used wire service accounts on inside pages and in abbreviated form. Such erratic play of statewide stories that presented a negative picture of Thompson spared the governor some political headaches.

But those episodes had occurred late in 1977. In the first days of the administration, Springfield press corps reporters bathed in the euphoria created by Thompson's open relationship with the press. Richard Icen, a writer for the Lindsay-Schaub newspapers whose tenure reached back to the Kerner days, wrote: "Walker's relationship with the Springfield press was chilly almost from the day of his inauguration. . . . Richard Ogilvie had different sets of reporters over to the mansion for breakfast during his first year in office. This practice was dropped when some reporters complained about being scooped by their colleagues."

A new day dawned with Thompson. He went to the pressroom instead of sending his press secretary. During the early part of the legislative session, when he presided over the deadlocked senate presidential contest, Thompson often drifted to the press area during recess to have a beer and participate in informal banter.

Reporter Bill Lambrecht, then with the *Alton Telegraph*, wrote for his readers: "What struck everybody as most peculiar was his sudden appearance in the pressroom around 5 or 5:30 of an evening where he would sit reporters down for an informal chat in the press kitchen-lounge. Reporters here are used to being herded, cursed, put off and lied to." Mostly the conversations wandered to inconsequential matters, such as when Thompson updated reporters on the progress of his dog Guv at obedience school.

Response from the press to Thompson's style varied. One reporter said, "Thompson's so accessible I don't know what to ask him anymore." Others saw his appearance in the pressroom as a chance to observe the governor in an informal atmosphere and later wrote about it or used some TV film of it to show the governor in residence. The wire services, for example, dispatched pictures around the country showing the governor sprawled over furniture in the press lounge.

While Thompson enjoyed generally warm relations with reporters, he had problems with some editorial writers, and it moved him on one occasion to be critical in a magazine interview. The interviewer asked how Thompson felt about editorial criticism in the Rockford and Lindsay-Schaub newspapers of his trip to the Kentucky Derby. Thompson said:

> Oh, I got mad, like any other human being. I thought the Rockford editorials were unfair. I thought the first made a valid point. It said I shouldn't have gone to the Kentucky Derby. Well, I don't think that was any great cosmic issue. But after I got the word from some friends who thought the same thing, I stood up at my dinner and apologized. That should have been the end of it. The rest of that editorial was filler. The next time, they came out and blasted me twice as hard, but this time, I thought, unfairly, because they just dredged up all the old stuff again. I don't know why. Who knows what compels people to write editorials?

Thompson's question stimulated this author to research editorials that appeared in the *Chicago Sun-Times* and the *Chicago Tribune* during 1977, Thompson's first year in office. Commentary in these two papers daily reached more households than all other Illinois newspapers combined, and influential people outside the state watched these papers for signs of support or condemnation as a means of rating Thompson as a national political figure. More than one theory held that both papers planned to treat Thompson kindly unless he embarrassed the state.

Did the *Chicago Tribune* go easy on Thompson during his first year as governor?

My analysis of twenty-nine *Tribune* editorials during 1977 focused on those that clearly leaned toward or away from Thompson and his positions and actions. The findings showed that the paper unhesitatingly supported the governor on virtually all issues. On those rare occasions when the *Tribune* criticized Thompson, the paper couched it in the context of broader support so the negative comments had less impact.

The *Tribune* wanted to be helpful to the new Republican governor in his first months, and editorials during that time were especially complimentary. Editor Clayton Kirkpatrick of the *Tribune* told a fellow editor when asked about Thompson: "We are taking it easy on him, but watching, too. After all he's a Republican and there aren't many of those around."

The compliments poured from the *Tribune* editorial page on such topics as Thompson's plans for reorganizing state government and relaxing pollution controls to provide better business conditions. After he appointed two advisory bodies to study the state's fiscal and economic situation, the *Tribune* said, "This action shows that he prefers to base his decisions on facts rather than preconceived theories. We like that in a governor." The *Tribune* liked his proposal to provide more prison cells and improve conditions in prisons, in contrast to former Governor Walker, who ignored penal reform.

Criticism in the early months was soft and gently prodding. The *Tribune* did not like Thompson's program to allow corporate executives to assume state jobs while on leaves of absence from their corporations, and it said Thompson had insufficient justification for the program. Then, choosing words carefully, the editorial concluded: "So if Mr. Thompson can justify higher pay for specific jobs, he should make his case to the legislature and the public. It won't be easy, but then being governor is not an easy job."

The paper maintained a constant, if not hard-nosed, pressure on the governor. It urged him to shorten the length of the Illinois primary election period, and complimented him on a tightly planned budget for fiscal year 1978. When Thompson signed a bill authorizing self-service gasoline stations, the paper applauded.

During the first part of 1977, the issue of greatest interest to the *Tribune* was also the major political issue of the year for Chicago: The Crosstown Expressway agreement. The *Tribune* had supported a Crosstown plan for years, and cheered loudly when Thompson showed an interest. On February 28, in an editorial entitled "Crosstown: Thompson Is Willing," the paper encouraged Bilandic and Thompson to negotiate, adding there was no sensible reason to postpone the benefits of a new highway any longer.

When Crosstown came to pass in May, the *Tribune* was euphoric and praised Thompson and Bilandic for putting civic needs ahead of political ones in their agreements on a modified expressway. "The agreement is a political coup for both [Thompson] and Mr. Bilandic," the editorial said. In an editorial on June 29, the paper said Crosstown gave the two politicians a quick record of accomplishment. The paper obviously agreed with the arrangement.

Early in the administration, Thompson began making good on campaign promises to take initiatives in the criminal justice field. Praising the governor as a "doer" rather than just a "talker," the paper cheered his crime-fighting proposals in April. "The governor has not simply made a speech or issued a press release. He is proposing legislation and a couple of new agencies...." Polishing the governor's image, the paper added: "The main point is that Governor Thompson is fulfilling his campaign promises to do something about crime."

Controversies over crime legislation, especially Thompson's Class X proposals, continued through most of the year, and the *Tribune* kept close watch. When crime bills failed to pass the legislature by July 1, the *Tribune* blamed Thompson for not compromising. The paper said he was "grandstanding on this issue.... He has time before the special fall session to work out some compromise.... But we urge him not to oppose an excellent bill just because it isn't his."

When Thompson finally compromised on the provisions of Class X, the *Tribune* welcomed the turn of events. "We are grateful to Mr. Thompson for getting this effort back on the tracks." As the legislature and governor continued to wrangle over the bill into September, the *Tribune* kept the pressure on by praising the governor for going "a considerable way toward ending the deadlock...."

Thompson insisted on the Class X designation during the fall legislative session, and the *Tribune* lost its patience for one of the few times during the year. Commenting on the name, the *Tribune* said: "The name given the eventual product should be irrelevant. The goal is effective legislation, not slogans." When the bill finally passed both houses in November, the *Tribune* said in satisfaction, "The bill is an impressive showing for the year in crime legislation." All was forgiven regarding the governor's stubbornness over Class X.

There were a few occasions when the *Chicago Tribune* supported an unpopular decision by Thompson, such as on September 17 in an editorial entitled "State Money and Abortions." The editorial agreed with the praise and support Thompson received for vetoing a bill forbidding use of state funds to finance welfare abortions. On another controversial measure—a bill to control pornography—the paper counseled Thompson that his veto "...in our view adds nothing...and amounts to a waste of time.... There are more constructive uses of the veto."

Tribune editorials on Thompson seldom outlined a course of action for the governor to follow. Almost all the commentary occurred in reaction to Thompson's proposals, statements, or decisions. Rather than attempting to lead the governor or the state in a particular direction, the paper seemed content to remind him of its presence.

At the *Chicago Sun-Times*, Thompson took more criticism during 1977. The paper offered broad support but frequently added reservations. Twenty-one *Sun-Times* editorials were carefully analyzed for content and comment.

Early in the Thompson administration, the *Sun-Times* set the tone for an occasional twitting of the governor on some minor indiscretion. On January 7, the paper slapped Thompson's wrist for driving a car with auto dealer plates (the car and plates were loaned to him by an automobile dealer/friend). The editorial pointed out that this was a violation of state law and finished by saying "ignorance of the law excuses no man. . . ."

On two other occasions, *Sun-Times* editorials snapped at Thompson's personal behavior. One came after Thompson revealed he accepted gifts and favors from individuals and organizations and listed them in a special book. While not saying that Thompson was influenced by the gifts, the paper suggested that he should not take any more. Later in the year, after stories appeared about Thompson's membership in private clubs that barred women members, the *Sun-Times* suggested the governor resign from the two clubs. "That may be going the extra mile. But that's not too far for leaders in 1977."

The *Sun-Times* was more interested than the *Tribune* in issues affecting Chicago and Cook County. When Thompson dragged his feet on reorganization of state government, the *Sun-Times* urged him to move more quickly. It cajoled and nudged Thompson to help choose and support a Republican candidate for mayor of Chicago, saying "Governor Thompson isn't being much of a leader of his party when he suggests the Grand Old Party support an independent or a Democrat." The Republicans did nominate someone to seek the mayor's job, and Thompson offered support.

The *Sun-Times* and *Tribune* seldom differed on major questions relating to the city. On Crosstown and crime legislation, the *Sun-Times* pushed every bit as hard as the *Tribune*. In January, the paper said Crosstown's fate rested in Thompson's hands; then in May, after the agreement was announced, it offered unrestrained praise of Thompson for putting the interests of the metropolitan area ahead of politics.

Interestingly, both Chicago newspapers implied that The Thompson-Bilandic agreement on Crosstown transcended political considerations when, in truth, Crosstown was the major political action taken by either the mayor or the governor during Thompson's entire two-year governorship. Also, while the *Sun-Times* preferred to emphasize the interests of the metropolitan area, it pointed out that the Crosstown agreement also included substantial funds for projects elsewhere in the state.

Again, the *Sun-Times* took a position similar to the *Tribune's* on Thompson's veto of the anti-abortion bill and the pornography measure. On two other social issues, the *Sun-Times* congratulated Thompson for signing bills that could work toward elimination of redlining (racial discrimination) in housing, and for appointing the first woman chief of the state racing board.

The *Sun-Times* also showed intense interest in the package of crime bills, and Thompson's Class X designation. However, the paper maintained a more critical tone than the *Tribune* about the measure's shortcomings. In April, the *Sun-Times* disputed Thompson's "get-tough" policy on crime, suggesting instead that Thompson was getting tough on criminals. The general aim of his plan could help the cause of justice, the paper said, but "it's annoying, however, that Thompson announced his plan in red-hot terms."

The *Sun-Times* also pressured Thompson to compromise with Democrats in the fall. An editorial on September 26 snapped: "Thompson's elusiveness isn't helping anybody—least of all those who want Illinois to have a modern, effective system of criminal justice." Then on October 10, the paper delivered its most critical commentary on Thompson's performance under the headline, "Sleazy Tactics on Class X." The editorial said: "In his attempt to stamp 'Class X' on Illinois's criminal-sentencing law books, Governor Thompson rates a Class A for zeal and a Class Z for class." But in November, when a bill passed and was signed, the *Sun-Times* applauded.

With only fifty editorials of a critical nature in both papers during 1977, the Chicago press, on the basis of volume, cannot be accused of pinning Thompson to the wall during his first year as governor. A regular reader of both papers would have ended the year convinced that the papers supported Thompson.

Editorial support of Thompson by the Chicago newspapers was a distinct disadvantage for Bakalis as the 1978 campaign began, but it was only one indication of the hammerlock Thompson had on the media. The challenger ran uphill all year trying to keep the media from paying too much attention to the governor and more attention to himself.

While Thompson kept his opinions on the media to himself, Bakalis's personal view was that the media either overstepped their authority or shirked their responsibility much of the time. During his campaign for comptroller in 1976, Bakalis proposed a media review board to field complaints against the press; this suggestion earned him the wrath of media editors. He seldom felt fully at ease around reporters or editors.

Bakalis complained of slanted reporting in the *Chicago Sun-Times* and on some Chicago TV stations, undoubtedly agreeing with a cynical comment made by David Axelrod, a reporter for the *Chicago Tribune*, during the last days of the campaign: "My greatest fear is that the press plane will crash with Bakalis aboard. If that happens, it will be reported on page 5. If the plane goes down without Bakalis, it will make page one."

Thompson breezed through the contest with an abundance of media coverage, much of it casting him in a favorable light. Some reporters chafed at not being able to get answers to their questions and a few felt manipulated by the governor's polished public relations techniques, but nobody laid a hand on him. When the last weeks of the campaign rolled around, the endorsements rang out:

Mr. Thompson is not a superman. . . . But as a governor who had to compress the work of four years into two . . . he has scored impressively high.—*Chicago Tribune*

His vetoes of bills to legalize laetrile and deny government funding of abortions for the poor were courageous; both bucked powerful currents, as demonstrated by the easy veto overrides. He resisted pressure, too, in opposing off-track betting and refusing to subsidize a Chicago sports stadium. . . . He had laid a good foundation for a more energetic, innovative four-year term. . . . —*Chicago Sun-Times*

Thompson has not recommended much in the way of new programs in his administration, but we believe that is to his credit. The people do not want new programs that will add more to the tax burdens; they want better administration of existing programs. . . . —*Springfield Journal-Register*

Thompson for...

Does Jim Thompson want to be President of the United States? Yes. "I want to be President, sure," he said in September, 1977.

Is he a candidate? Maybe. "I'm not going to be in a frantic rush. I want to look at what's going on before I make any decision to plunge in," he told the *Washington Post* in October, 1978.

Regardless of his hedging on the actual candidacy, most persons familiar with the semantics of presidential politics believe Thompson is a candidate.

So, those are the easy questions and answers. The tough ones—which cannot be dealt with until he is actually a candidate—remain. Does he have the support? Can he raise the money? Is he ready for a national campaign? Can he win? What year?

Without final answers, a psychological profile is helpful. In that framework, there are two mental conditions necessary for a presidential campaign:

1. The candidate must want the job, to the exclusion of all others.
2. The candidate must believe he can do the job better than anyone past, present, or future.

The first condition spurs the kind of desire and drive that makes men mad enough to risk their health, marriages, financial stability, and career to openly seek the job. The second condition can also be described as supreme confidence. Without it, no person in his right mind would want the most worrisome job in the world.

Thompson appears psychologically ready for the presidential pursuit. He apparently has no other personal goal. His self-confidence is unshakable, although at times he parades his soul-searching in a manner reminiscent of the verbal musing of Adlai E. Stevenson II who fretted openly about the presidency in 1951 and 1952.

Another asset necessary for a successful run at the presidency is luck. Columnists and Thompson himself have acknowledged its importance to his career so far.

Norman C. Miller, writing in the *Wall Street Journal* in October, 1977, said, "So far Jim Thompson has had one vital thing going for him—luck. His big win in 1976 was a tribute not only to his own campaigning but also to the fact that the Democrats had a clinker as a candidate." In August,

1977, Jack Germond and Jules Witcover observed "luck has been a lady" for Thompson. David Broder concluded an article on Thompson in October, 1978, with these words: "He could hardly hope to find opposition for the presidency as inept as that he has faced in Illinois. But then again, given his luck maybe he will."

Thompson addressed the subject in an interview with *Illinois Issues* magazine. "The more I study presidential politics," he said, "the more I'm convinced that in addition to planning intelligently and perceiving public moods and notions, where the issues are and where the present administration is right and wrong—there's an awful lot of luck involved."

Those persons also agreed the current resident of the White House, Jimmy Carter, had his share of luck, too. As Thompson puts it, Carter "worked hard. . . . And he's a damn smart politician, one of the best around. Carter is shrewd, cunning, tough. . . . He had a lot of luck, too. . . ."

Still one man's luck is another man's skill. Thompson's easygoing manner belies his success in creating luck. For example, while he may have been lucky in drawing Howlett for an opponent in 1976, part of the reason Bakalis became the nominee in 1978 was Thompson's ability to scare off stronger opposition among the Democrats.

Lucky or not, full of desire or not, self-confident or not, there is more to becoming a candidate for president than mind-over-matter and fate. First, there has to be an opportunity for candidacy. No political medicine man can look to the skies and call on the wisdom of the ages for a vision of the primaries of 1980. There must be signs of an earthly nature.

Few political observers believe a single Republican candidate can preempt the field by the end of 1979 and breeze unmolested through the primaries. Republican professionals acknowledge the strength of Ronald Reagan and the constant presence of former president Gerald Ford; but until one candidate has strength enough to squeeze out the rest of the field, speculators see a glimmer of hope for a contest well into 1980.

Jack Germond, a national columnist and political reporter based in Washington, believes the nomination will be won in the primaries. "I know I'm in the minority," he told this author, "but I think enough support will be withheld from Reagan and Ford to permit a fresh face to openly contest the primaries." Others who speculate on presidential nominations, including David Broder of the *Washington Post*, foresee Reagan leading a pack of contenders into the primaries. Douglas Bailey, whose strategy firm of Bailey and Deardourff worked for Ford in 1976, agrees. "Reagan appears to be in it to stay, and he will be difficult to defeat. I'm not even sure how someone could do it." Those comments were made prior to a strong showing by John Connally.

The political pundits and professionals sketch a scenario that could include Thompson, or some candidate viewed as being in the "moderate" wing of the party.

The scenario begins with the assumption that contenders will fall into two clearly defined philosophical camps, conservatives and moderates. Leading the conservative field is Reagan, with Illinois congressman Philip Crane and former Texas governor John Connally close behind. Also a possibility is New York congressman Jack Kemp, the sponsor of conservative economic legislation in Congress. Crane, a declared candidate since 1978, has vowed not to retreat in favor of Reagan, although his candidacy by mid-1979 has faded badly.

Connally's candidacy is viewed by many in 1979 as of great danger to Reagan and likely to draw some moderate support. His eloquence before audiences of contributors and his strength in Texas and other southern states make him attractive to Republicans seeking an alternative to Reagan. Connally is able to raise large sums of money and is expected to remain in the contest at least through the early primaries of 1980.

Those considered to be in the moderate-to-conservative camp are Senator Robert Dole, the Republican vice-presidential candidate in 1976; Congressman John Anderson of Illinois; George Bush, former director of the Central Intelligence Agency and former head of the U.S. liaison office in Peking; Senator Howard Baker of Tennessee; Ford; and several of less recognition, including Thompson.

The scenario has the two camps jockeying for position to gather enough support and money for the primaries. Recognizing that not all of the moderates can make it, and acknowledging Reagan's lead, the moderates rally behind a single candidate to contest the conservatives in an open, and probably bloody, primary arena. The scenario ends there. No one is willing to say what might happen if one moderate and two conservative Republicans start down the primary road in New Hampshire in February, 1980. However, the implication in the story is that a moderate, once past New Hampshire, has an advantage in a popular contest and would go to the convention with enough delegate votes to deny nomination to a conservative on the first ballot.

For Thompson to be dealt into that picture, he would have to be viewed by other moderates as the single person who could prevent a conservative from being nominated. With that kind of support—not unlike the backing given to Dwight Eisenhower in 1952 against Senator Robert Taft—Thompson could take the moderate cause to the people. No moderate is going to beat Reagan or Crane or Connally in the state caucuses or backrooms of grass-roots Republicanism, where conservatives virtually control party machinery.

Meanwhile, Thompson can be expected to bide his time while trotting out his well-worn statement about the presidency: "The best thing I can do is be a goddamned good governor of Illinois...." Or, as he said on election night, 1978: "Before anybody runs for president, he'd better have the makings of a president. He must demonstrate the qualities and abilities to be president."

It is interesting to note that early in 1979, in an attempt to quiet talk of his every move being aimed toward a national candidacy, Thompson said he was not a candidate for the office. Although some persons interpreted that as a withdrawal statement, it did little more to clarify Thompson's position than previous statements in which he said he would take the presidential subject in stride. As an act designed to quiet critics, Thompson also ended his business relationship with the Washington firm of Bailey and Deardourff.

Assuming there is a beginning for everything, how does a governor of Illinois earn recognition as a presidential possibility? First, it is not unusual for the governor—or a senator—of Illinois to be mentioned for the presidency because of the state's 26 electoral votes. (Only California, New York, Ohio, and Pennsylvania have more.) Coming off that statistic there are some interesting, if not conclusive, parallels between Thompson, a Republican, and Adlai E. Stevenson II, a Democrat, who served as Illinois governor from 1949–1953 and sought the presidency in 1952 and 1956. Stevenson's candidacy is the last true presidential "draft" on record.

Stevenson and Thompson both graduated from Northwestern law school. Stevenson was elected governor in 1948 without previous elective experience; Thompson was elected in 1976 without having run in a political campaign. Stevenson served three years as governor before running for president; Thompson would be in office three years if he runs in 1980. Stevenson, in 1952, was unmistakably a "fresh face," when that counted for something; Thompson, too, has been declared in that category, when compared with Reagan and Ford. Both Stevenson and Thompson developed loyal followings in a short period of time. Further, Stevenson came into demand within the party when officials realized it was in their own best interest to rally behind a single candidate for the nomination. Thompson's appeal might be to those partisans who feel a conservative nominee would be disastrous for the party in 1980 and would therefore align themselves with a single moderate candidate.

There may also be a piece of advice for Thompson in the Stevenson case, because some of the governor's advisors have urged him to pass up the 1980 contest and wait until 1984. Stevenson faced a similar situation in 1952, when aides asked him to wait and seek the nomination in 1956. Carl McGowan, a lifelong associate of Stevenson, is quoted in John Bartlow Martin's biography of the governor as viewing the choice this way: "When the mysterious tide that carries you to the presidency sets in, you had better go if you want it."

It takes more than historical perspective and an Illinois residence, however. Another element is a record of achievement, either in politics or public life.

Thompson's reputation as a prosecutor cannot be discounted as important to his early mention as a 1980 candidate. His work in Chicago launched a successful gubernatorial career and opened eyes and doors on the national level. Hardly a background article on Thompson is written without reference to the Kerner case, for instance.

Thompson is not the first prosecutor to ride the crest of popularity into elective politics. Thomas E. Dewey, who sought the presidency in 1944 and 1948, made headlines as a prosecutor in New York City, and served twelve years as governor. Vice-President Walter F. Mondale first achieved statewide attention in Minnesota as attorney general, when he prosecuted a charity fraud case and later was appointed to fill a vacant Senate seat.

Thompson also has successfully responded to public opinion, beginning with his prosecutor days and continuing through the first years as governor. His sense of timing, of what the public wants, and how the public will react gained him a measure of national attention. That sense of timing has served a number of public officials from the grass-roots political level to the presidency. Notable among those who rose to national acclaim by accurately sensing public moods was Richard M. Nixon.

As a congressman, Nixon jumped on the anti-communist topic well before it became a national bandwagon. Feeding the public raw meat as if it were a voracious tiger, Nixon advanced to the U.S. Senate in 1948 and the vice-presidency in 1952. With memories of Nixon's final days as president still fresh, the public forgets that he once charmed the public with a glib tongue and a sharp sense of the public mood. At the time, no one questioned Nixon's use of anti-communism as a means to an end. That occurred when biographers began exploring the Nixon political phenomenon years later.

Even if a person lusts openly for the presidency, it will not come to pass without the "Great Mention." A potential nominee must be elevated to contention and given legitimacy by media attention. In this media-conscious world, the power of television and the press to declare a person "legitimate" is unchallenged. Although President Carter came out of Georgia, a small state, into the nominating process, he became a factor in the presidential contest when the media offered full recognition of his early caucus victory in Iowa. His initial primary victories followed to increasing press acclaim.

Michael J. Robinson, writer and observer of politics and the media, declared in a 1978 edition of *Public Opinion* magazine, "Thompson has already received the Great Mention—indeed, over a period of two weeks early this year, he received four 'Great Mentions' in the national press. Print is talking about Thompson. . . ." There were some earlier mentions, too, that broke the ice. "Fat cats and the hired guns of Republican politics have tabbed him a comer," David Broder of the *Washington Post* wrote in October, 1976, before Thompson had served a day as governor. In the same month, James M. Perry, then of the *National Observer*, wrote, with pen in cheek: "He will become the most exciting Republican 'moderate' since . . . well, since George Romney was elected governor of Michigan in 1962."

Always looking for new stories to tell, the media jumped at Thompson in 1977. Thompson is an "antique buff with a salty sense of humor and a well-rounded sense of time," *Newsweek* said. Thompson is "at home in flannel shirts and boots," Ken Bode wrote in the *New Republic*. There were more, but the first comments focused on Thompson's personality and surface qualities.

In 1978, Thompson's name appeared frequently in the national press, mostly in a favorable light, and he proved to be a durable media object. Evans and Novak, national columnists, called him a "non-imperial governor."

Even if anointed by the likes of *Time* and *Newsweek*, Thompson needed recognition by political insiders, such as John Sears, who managed Reagan's campaign in 1976 and since has become a guru of the "New Right." In mid-1978, Sears gave Thompson a Great Mention worth remembering. Writing in the May-June issue of *Public Opinion*, Sears said: "I see six truly potential candidates: Ronald Reagan, Gerald Ford, Robert Dole, Howard Baker, John Connally, and Governor Jim Thompson of Illinois."

Broder picked up the Sears comment and expanded it into his syndicated column. George Will, a conservative columnist, wrote about Sears' comment: "Gov. Thompson, Sears says, can have the 'Rockefeller Republican' support without doing much to get it, which is the only prudent way to get it." Sears' ranking of the candidates was one of the most widely quoted statements of 1978 regarding prospective Republican nominees.

As statements helpful to Thompson were made, occasionally someone said: "I'm not sure he's done anything."

The reply is that Thompson has done what is necessary: maintain a public image. As long as he is the new kid on the Republican block that may be enough, for the gallery of tired and familiar faces recalls a long string of failures with a national audience. Reagan has been mentioned as a presidential nominee since 1964; Ford, who was the nominee in 1976, has been around party affairs for three decades; Dole and Baker, while younger, are familiar faces in Congress and their popularity may depend on how the public feels about the Senate more than how it feels about the men; and Connally has been in the wings since turning Republican in the late 1960s.

Well into 1979, Thompson's Great Mentions continued, although the questions had toughened and criticism began to appear. Jack Germond remained a doubter, and Evans and Novak, their conservative biases showing, suspected Thompson as a Rockefeller stand-in.

From 1976 through 1979, Thompson's name has appeared in polls conducted by Gallup and Harris, the two most widely used national opinion samplers.

In an October, 1977, Gallup poll on name awareness of Republican possibilities, the list included twenty-four names. Respondents were asked to say if they had heard anything about them. Thompson showed up near the bottom of the list. Only Senator Harrison Schmitt of New Mexico, Senator Richard Lugar of Indiana, and Mayor Peter Wilson of San Diego scored lower. In the same poll, Gallup sought a rating on "highly favorable" from respondents. In the poll, Thompson showed up No. 10 behind Ford, Reagan, Baker, Senator Robert Griffin of Michigan, Governor Robert Ray of Iowa, Elliot Richardson of Massachusetts, Dole, Schmitt, and Senator Mark Hatfield of Oregon.

In August, 1978, Gallup asked respondents: "Here is a list of people who have been mentioned as possible presidential candidates for the Republican party in 1980. Which would you like to see nominated as the Republican candidate for president?" The list included eight names, with Thompson among them. Ford led with 37 percent, followed by Reagan with 31 percent. Thompson was in seventh place with 2 percent, just ahead of Bush. Gallup said polling had been done before Crane announced his candidacy. When Thompson's overt presidential activity ended early in 1977, he was dropped from mention in most presidential preference polling.

Polls taken a year or two before the presidential primaries have not always been reliable and are usually good for indicating public sentiment only at a given moment. In the 1972 presidential nomination process, for example, George McGovern trailed badly in polls as late as January, 1972. A Gallup poll then showed Senator Edmund Muskie in front, with Senator Edward Kennedy and Senator Hubert Humphrey following in that order. Muskie led with a rating of 32 percent while McGovern had 3 percent. In a March, 1975, Gallup poll, just a year before the primary in Illinois, the first choice of Democrats was George Wallace, with Humphrey second. Carter did not begin to show well in the polls until late 1975.

The Republican lineup of persons with designs on getting to the 1980 presidential primaries is long on age, party seniority, and loyalty to a cause, none of which is Thompson's long suit. From that list, Reagan is recognized as the leader. Evans and Novak called him "the party's presumptive 1980 presidential nominee." Others would disagree, especially Ford, who in 1978 maintained slight leads over Reagan and Connally in national public opinion polls. However, those familiar with the nomination process do not believe Ford could overtake Reagan, if Ford were to decide to run against him.

Just as party professionals and observers agree on Reagan's lead, they acknowledge his liabilities. He will be sixty-nine years old in 1980, and Germond believes that fact will ultimately deny him the nomination.

Others claim Reagan would not win the presidency if nominated. Lou Harris concluded in a 1978 poll that "a [conservative] candidacy would probably be doomed to failure." After dissecting Reagan's appeal, Harris said: "It is reasonable to predict that the conservative vote, which now makes up 35 percent of the electorate, will go Republican. But the newer groups in politics, who tend to feel most comfortable without a firm party label, and who are increasingly important to the outcome of elections, are likely to reject an all-out conservative candidate."

If a moderate is to win in 1980, the voters will have to be convinced that Reagan or Crane or Connally cannot win. Moderates have talked about running since 1964—William Scranton and Nelson Rockefeller, for example—but have not directly challenged a more conservative candidate in the primaries. Since 1936, the pre-nomination leaders have prevailed at the convention. The names are familiar: Landon, Dewey, Eisenhower, Nixon, and Ford.

With Reagan the acknowledged front-runner for the 1980 Republican nomination, the other candidates have committed themselves to extensive speaking tours to keep close in the polls. By June, 1978, the *Atlanta Constitution* reported that Dole had visited thirty states and gone to New Hampshire four times. Crane was in second place, having journeyed to twenty-eight states. Thompson brought up the tail end of the list with six states visited. In a separate report, David Broder said Bush had visited New Hampshire six times by late summer, 1978.

Thompson realized from the outset that he needed to be seen and heard in forums outside Illinois. Although he traveled several times after the 1976 election, it was not until early in 1977 that national media began to notice. The most important trips for him that year were the six he made to Washington between late February and early July. The Washington trips brought Thompson in contact with government officials, congressmen, and reporters—especially reporters. On one trip, February 27 through March 2, Thompson met at a breakfast with news bureau chiefs hosted by Godfrey Serling of the *Christian Science Monitor*. The exposure paid off in several newspaper articles.

The Washington trips resulted in a lengthy article on the first page of the *Washington Post* on June 6, 1977. Political writer Lou Cannon introduced Thompson to *Post* readers, the most sophisticated political groupies in the nation, with a comparison of Thompson's style with that of Carter. Cannon observed both men wore "blue jeans and plaid shirts in the executive mansion." He said both preached "government reorganization and a balanced budget." Yes, Cannon said, even their critics say they are "long on style and short on substance."

Cannon concluded the story with a quote from Thompson: "As governor, you find that a lot of problems just are not soluble, or if they are, they're not soluble very quickly. It's a difficult job." The self-deprecating style worked for John F. Kennedy and others who took their political appeal to the people.

Some of the stories written about Thompson during his journeys skimmed the surface while a few, such as Cannon's, probed a bit more deeply. A typical first-time-around story on Thompson appeared on April 20, 1977, in the *Christian Science Monitor*. It concluded: "This man who relaxes by going antiquing with his wife, who reads spy thrillers (Howard Hunt and John D. MacDonald are favorite authors) also loves the theater, collects inkwells, and is still trying to shake his prosecutor's image."

In that first year in office—1977—Thompson visited Louisiana; New York City, for a meeting with Nelson Rockefeller and fund-raiser Maxwell M. Rabb; Arizona; Mississippi; Ohio; Wisconsin; and New Hampshire, home of the first presidential primary in 1980.

The Republican Governors' Conference at Bretton Woods, New Hampshire, did not turn out to be one of Thompson's better performances. At a seminar on election campaigns, he offered his gospel on wearing cowboy boots at county fairs, which irked his colleagues. Much of the time, reporters noted later, Thompson worked the media for interviews, especially the *New York Times*. A reporter for the *Chicago Tribune* recorded an occasion when Thompson insulted two New Hampshire Republicans and incurred the wrath of right-wing newspaper publisher William Loeb. One of the Republicans who claimed he had been insulted told John Margolis of the *Tribune*'s Washington staff, "I've seen a lot of politicians come and go but I've never seen anyone as rude as [Thompson] come down the pike." In an editorial, Loeb called Thompson the "Percy-Rockefeller candidate of 1980."

That performance might be chalked up as the failure of a rookie governor who tried to take his colleagues and professional politicians by storm, and failed. However, Thompson's problems with fellow governors arose again later in the year at a midwestern governor's conference in Oklahoma. The episodes began to form a pattern.

James Flansberg, writing in the *Des Moines Register* after the Oklahoma conference, compared Thompson to Carter, but in an unflattering sense. Flansberg said: "When Carter was governor of Georgia, he used the regional and national governors' conferences as a launching pad to call public attention to himself. . . . Thompson is trying the same thing."

Flansberg gave Thompson poor marks in upstaging other governors. His report card continued: "Thompson made part of the agriculture-water session, but missed everything else, except the hour or so when the governors debated the details of a strongly worded resolution on energy. Then the 6-foot-6 210-pound Thompson cruised into the room, his pink or orange open-neck shirt and blue jeans in splendid contrast with the business attire of the other governors." Thompson, Flansberg said, tried to take over the meeting. "But it's not something to laugh at when you consider where that sort of thing led Jimmy Carter and that's clearly where Thompson has his sights set. . . . Right now Thompson's at the image-making stage where it is worth the risk of insulting the other governors [for favorable newspaper stories]."

Undaunted, Thompson moved into 1978 and another round of conferences and political sessions around the country, including a blitz on Washington in the early part of the year. The Washington meetings included sessions at the White House on the coal and farm strikes and the national governors conference.

Thompson's behavior at the late February meeting of the National Governors Association, his fourth time in Washington in 1978, was in sharp contrast to his appearances in 1977. He moved quietly about the meetings, avoided flashy clothing, and deferred to California governor Jerry Brown, who by all accounts hogged the media. Reporters suggested Thompson had the stomach flu—or was it just a desire to improve his image? Still, Thompson made headlines. The *Washington Post* updated its work on him under the title "Buttoned-up Politics/James Thompson Has an Eye on 1980." Richard Icen, covering Thompson for the Lindsay-Schaub newspapers, wrote: "There was an interview with Roger Mudd of CBS during which Thompson again denied any current plans to run for president in 1980."

Unable to upstage Brown nationally, Thompson earned headlines in Illinois newspapers by having breakfast with Illinois congressmen and asking politely for them to remember the nation's financially ailing state governments at appropriations time.

Thompson curtailed his visits to Washington and other out-of-state places for the remainder of the 1978 gubernatorial contest with Bakalis. But after re-election, he again left Illinois for the Republican governors' meeting in Williamsburg, where he grabbed national TV as well as national press attention, beginning with an appearance on ABC's "Issues and Answers."

He cruised openly, dodging questions about the presidency and proudly displaying his wife Jayne and daughter Samantha Jayne. Samantha's appearances inspired Michael Kilian of the *Chicago Tribune* to suggest a national trend might develop. "There are more than 500,000 elective offices in this country. . . . Can the country cope with a half million new babies every election year?"

Kilian's snide comment echoed others from the conference, as Thompson again pushed in front of colleagues and elbowed his way to the TV cameras. Thompson's coyness over his presidential intentions irritated reporters, causing the *New York Times'* Adam Clymer to write: "Reporters swarm over governors asking them about 1980. They hear in return the customary bland denials of interest, even from such governors as James R. Thompson, whose associates here say they think he is likely to run."

Nationally syndicated columnist Jules Witcover declared Thompson foremost among Republican governors in terms of national recognition, then took a swipe at the Illinoisan that was similar to Flansberg's criticism from 1977: "In terms of visibility and ambition, if not of the esteem of his colleagues, recently elected James Thompson of Illinois seems to come closest [to challenging Reagan]. But no other governor is breaking his neck lining up behind him." Witcover nailed a fact that could haunt Thompson through 1979, if it became necessary to solicit the support of governors: His fellow governors think he's too pushy.

Witcover's writing companion, Jack Germond, compared Thompson's reputation with governors to Carter and Reagan. "They [the governors] used to dislike Reagan. Lots of Democrats disliked Carter when he attended these meetings. They were publicity hounds. It's not that [Thompson's] disliked, but he's been out front about the presidential business and the others think he's rushing matters." Germond acknowledged that neither Reagan nor Carter were deterred by the opinions of associates.

Thompson's cool relationship with governors notwithstanding, some liabilities relating to his performance in Illinois could affect a national candidacy. Thompson's vetoes in 1977 and 1978 of bills designed to curtail use of government funds for abortions, and to prohibit the legal sale of the so-called cancer drug laetrile, irritated persons emotionally involved with the issues. Right-wing, single-issue lobbys have not openly opposed his gubernatorial campaigns, but on a national level they might become more active. He also has incurred the wrath of opponents of the Equal Rights Amendment, and their activities often overlap with anti-abortionists.

Conservative Republicans in the Illinois legislature are openly hostile, and some columnists have used that as evidence of Thompson's political weakness. Evans and Novak, on a foray into Illinois during 1978, tried to chill Thompson with conservatives. They wrote: "Thompson's fiscal conservatism and anti-crime program do not convince conservative Republicans in the legislature." The statement was true as far as it went, but it failed to note that right-wing Republicans in the legislature, however vocal, total only a handful.

The columnists pinpointed another matter of much greater concern to Thompson, however. They revealed Thompson's poor standing with Republican county chairmen. The combination of pesky conservatives and disgruntled chairmen could disturb Thompson's plan of having a delegation to the 1980 national convention united behind him either as a bona fide candidate or as a favorite son.

The Illinois delegation will be selected during the primary election in March of the presidential election year. Each congressional district elects two delegates and the state party apparatus chooses ten delegates at large. The skirmishing for delegates began in 1978. Thompson intervened in a downstate state committeeman election because he feared the outcome would affect delegate strength in 1980. The target of Thompson's involvement was George Washington Woodcock, a downstate ally of State Representative Donald Totten of suburban Chicago. Totten, a supporter of Reagan, hoped to run Woodcock for state chairman and influence the selection of the ten at-large delegates, but Thompson helped dump Woodcock in the election, and assured selection of a chairman favorable to the governor. More such fires will need to be extinguished before March, 1980.

Other political analysts believe Thompson's greatest liability has nothing to do with his appeal, or intra-party squabbles. They suggest his position and location—governor of Illinois—are major hurdles that could restrict Thompson as a national candidate. Among those voicing such concerns are two of Thompson's allies, Charles Percy, and political strategist, Douglas Bailey.

Percy believes Carter's performance as president has soured voters on the ability of governors to administer the federal government. Without exposure to national issues, Percy sees Thompson having difficulty convincing voters he can move from Illinois to Washington and do the job. "For Jim to have a real presidential shot," Percy explains, "he somehow has got to have a position and familiarity on national issues, he's got to deal with national problems, not just the state legislature, which is quite different." Percy sees Reagan untouched by this liability because he has been away from California issues so long. "It's too bad for Jim that he's got that handicap which is a big load to carry to start with, and remember he's also got the job of running a great, complex state."

Bailey agrees in part, calling "the image of on-the-job training" a governor's greatest liability in seeking the presidency. He, too, believes Carter's early problems in dealing with Congress, organizing his staff, and providing leadership are credited by the public to his lack of experience in Washington.

Being a governor is not all liability, however. Those governors who have become politically prominent since 1936 have been from large, industrial states such as Illinois. (Stevenson in 1952 was the last big state governor to be nominated by either party.) In the electoral college these states carry weight out of proportion to others. In the presidential primaries, they get the most media coverage and have the most influence on delegates in other parts of the nation.

Running for president while holding a governorship can be restricting. It requires the candidate to campaign at night and on weekends, and still leave the impression he is running the state no matter where he may be. In Illinois, the possibility of Thompson's candidacy has raised questions about who would be in charge. Thompson addressed that matter in March, 1977, during a meeting with reporters in Washington. If he decided to seek the presidency, he could "run hard" in the primaries and still serve as governor, he said. "A governor doesn't run the state day to day, from his desk. That's what the cabinet and bureaucracy are for." Later, Thompson admitted "running for president would be difficult, but not incompatible" with being governor. During the 1978 campaign he told columnist Broder, "I've been in my Springfield office only five minutes in the last two weeks and I've not neglected my job. A lot of it is paperwork, and that you can do on the plane."

In some instances, being away from Washington and the constant view of the eastern media has advantages. Thompson can bury himself in state issues while those in Congress and candidates out of office are hounded by reporters to comment on stategic arms limitations talks, ceilings on federal spending, and the full range of controversial questions. Thompson can pick and choose when to speak on national questions. He carries no baggage into the discussions, and with care he should be able to avoid pitfalls until he is prepared to speak on matters of state.

On other counts, Thompson appears able to mount a national campaign. He has demonstrated an ability to raise large amounts of campaign donations by accumulating approximately $6 million in a period from 1975 through 1978. His contributors cut across the political spectrum and include such traditional Republican sources as businessmen and lawyers, and also independent sources such as the United Auto Workers.

His staff is criticized for being too green, and Thompson probably would have to seek help of a more high-powered nature if he planned to actively campaign. Until that decision is made, his Illinois "whiz kids"—as they are disparagingly called at times—are adequate. They have embarrassed Thompson with a naivete around national reporters and party pros.

Thompson has worked to cultivate an image of being involved in organizations that affect public policy outside Illinois. In 1977, he joined the Trilateral Commission, an influential international club of scholars, public officials, and business and labor leaders who meet to discuss world issues. The commission's founder is David Rockefeller, chairman of the Chase Manhattan Bank. President Carter, former Secretary of State Henry Kissinger, and about seventy other persons were members when Thompson joined.

Thompson's campaign strategists, Bailey and Deardourff, have substantial experience and sound credentials in the political world. The firm developed Ford's advertising campaign for 1976 and has worked for Republican governors in Ohio, Missouri, Michigan, and Illinois. Senator Percy also used their services.

Also in Thompson's favor is his apparent willingness to spend most of his waking hours either running Illinois or campaigning in remote Republican strongholds.

Broder wrote during the 1978 campaign, "The passion for the presidency burns as brightly in him as in any politician in the land." That will lead him, Broder says, to work all day at a desk in Springfield, jump aboard a jet in the evening, appear at a fund-raising dinner in another state, shake hands until midnight, and return to Illinois in the early hours, to be back on the job by 8 or 9 a.m.

The columnist also sees Jayne Thompson as a partner in the pursuit of national acclaim, and that will make absences easier on domestic life. Others share Broder's assessment of Thompson's energy to campaign, and his political instincts. Strategist Bailey called him "an instinctive politician—and in some instances that gets him in trouble." Bailey says Thompson's willingness to jump before thinking has hurt. "He's not a calculating guy and I mean that in the sense of wanting to be sure he knows all the implications of the words he expresses. That means to me he's his own guy, and it's his political strength."

Bailey is hardly an objective voice on Thompson's abilities, but he has worked with some good candidates and some bad ones. "Thompson's single most appealing thing is that he is the same all the time. It was a great strength of Gerald Ford—people sensed that was the real guy, and no bull."

Others agree with varying enthusiasm. John Topping, president of the Ripon Society, said in 1978, Thompson has "considerable potential. He is a strong campaigner." Adam Clymer of the *New York Times* noted Thompson can campaign "as effectively in German delicatessens as in country clubs." Broder injected realism in the discussion: "Thompson is at least the equal of Jimmy Carter when it comes to spouting political pieties, and therefore a worthy contender. . . ."

The process of which Broder speaks—mounting a national primary election campaign while serving as governor—is insane. Witcover, in *Marathon*, his book about the 1976 election, labeled the primary system a "debilitating primary obstacle course." Most persons who have seen primaries up close know what they can do to contestants. Still, primaries are where a moderate Republican must seek victory. In 1976, there were thirty Republican primaries, and they accounted for 71 percent of convention delegate votes. The percentage has increased steadily each four years and will be larger in 1980.

Melodramatically, Theodore H. White, author of four books on presidential races, has called a primary a "deed" and an "underdog's classic route to power in America." While White acknowledged the drawbacks of primaries, he found that they give us a special glimpse of the candidate. White said they test the person under stress; test the person's staff; and through the primaries we find out what issues interest people. "They tell a story," White said. Furthermore, White wrote, primaries serve a purpose. In 1960, the primaries buried anti-Catholicism as a campaign issue. In 1964, the primaries exposed Barry Goldwater and his brand of conservatism. In 1968, the primaries forced the American people to see the Vietnam War in a different light.

Insane, impractical, draining, expensive—all apply to primaries. But they will happen in 1980. New Hampshire is first, and while many candidates would just as soon forget that snow-driven landscape, few can afford to dodge the primary. There, as in all primaries, getting media attention is a first goal.

Franklyn Nofziger, press secretary to Reagan and formerly a member of the Nixon administration, has made the point that "you go into a place like New Hampshire and you've got two things in mind. Primarily is winning New Hampshire. Secondly is getting out the stories about your candidate and where he stands and all that to the rest of the country. The more we have Ronald Reagan's name with the proper things in the papers, the better off we are, because it looks like he's moving around and it looks like he's active."

That, Broder, says, is why Thompson must be considered a potential threat. "He's a good media candidate, and in the early primaries you win or come in second only by taking the candidacy into the living rooms."

While New Hampshire has been the burial ground of some early favorites in past elections, the opportunity is enormous. In *Marathon*, Witcover observed that "in such a low-budget state a candidate with little notoriety or money can gain a toe-hold with a good showing and then survive for the more costly later primary tests." With a large GOP field entered, Thompson could make a good showing even with a small percentage of the vote.

A Thompson weakness would be the state party caucuses where Reagan, Baker, Connally, Ford, and Dole—familiar party names—would be expected to score heavily. Nevertheless, in two states adjoining Illinois where caucuses are used to selected delegates—Iowa and Missouri—Thompson has a distinct advantage. By never leaving Illinois he could appear on television in the Quad Cities (Moline and Rock Island are across the Mississippi from Davenport and Bettendorf, Iowa) and reach millions of Iowans. By appearing on St. Louis television, he could reach millions of Missourians in the same manner.

A similar advantage exists in two other adjoining states where key primary elections are held. Chicago television reaches into Wisconsin and Indiana, and Thompson's appearances in Chicago would reduce the time he would have to spend actually campaigning in the neighboring states. The Wisconsin presidential primary is early in April and Indiana's comes a month later.

One of the early primaries in 1980—after New Hampshire, Massachusetts, Connecticut, Vermont and Florida—occurs in Illinois. The date will be March 18, unless changed by the legislature. The Illinois election is really two tests. One is a preferential popular vote in which the candidates for president vie for the largest number of votes. The most important vote, however, is for delegates in each of twenty-four congressional districts.

Candidates for delegate can run either declared for a particular presidential nominee or "uncommitted." Thompson will need a solid Republican organization, county by county, to sew up delegates loyal to him. Throughout 1979, agents of Crane and Reagan worked the precincts of Illinois raising money for delegate candidates, insuring a struggle for Thompson if he wants a united delegation. In 1976 Ford captured 60 percent of the popular vote and 85 percent of the Illinois delegates, thanks mainly to groundwork laid by Ogilvie and Percy over about nine months time. They got commitments from candidates with local name recognition, a deciding factor at the congressional district level. The governor's relationship with Ogilvie has been unpredictable. Late in 1978, for example, Ogilvie announced he would not work for Ford's campaign in 1980, but might consider working for Reagan. Then in 1979, Ogilvie said he was working for the presidential campaign of Illinois congressman John Anderson.

Thompson has some favors to collect from Percy, dating back to the 1978 election when the senator faced possible defeat with only two weeks left in the campaign. Thompson, comfortably ahead in his own race, diverted time and energy to campaign for Percy. However, that may be a dubious advantage for Thompson. When it comes to Percy and Ogilvie, the former governor has much more influence among county chairmen than Percy.

Regardless, Thompson in seeking Illinois delegate candidates could lay ground for a major embarrassment in the March primary. If Thompson were unable to score a convincing victory in his own state, his candidacy would be ended.

Whatever the winds of 1980 bring for Republicans, Thompson will not be far from the center of activity. With his proclivity for timing and "luck," the results could fool all the experts and most of the candidates. Anything can happen. It could even turn out as predicted by a bumper sticker that appeared in Chicago in 1978. It read: "Ford and Thompson."

Index

PRINTED IN U.S.A.